WE THE PEOPLE

WE THE PEOPLE

FORMING A MORE PERFECT UNION

CLIFFORD L. SANDERS, JR.

ARPress

ILLUMINATING IDEAS.
EMPOWERING VOICES

ARPress
45 Dan Road Suite 5
Canton MA 02021

Hotline: 1(888) 821-0229
Fax: 1(508) 545-7580

Ordering Information:

Quantity sales. Special discounts are available on quantity purchases by corporations, associations, and others. For details, contact the publisher at the address above.

Printed in the United States of America.

ISBN-13:   Softcover   979-8-89330-447-3
             eBook   979-8-89330-448-0

Library of Congress Control Number: 2024900782

TABLE OF CONTENTS

CHAPTER 2: LEAVING THE PAST BEHIND

CHAPTER 3: WE THE PEOPLE

CHAPTER 4: CLOSING REMARKS

DEDICATION

This finished work is dedicated to my Mother, Annie Will Sanders. You were my best friend, my cheerleader, my confidant, my motivator, my counselor, my disciplinarian, my encourager, my teacher, my educator, and the molder of my character. I wish that life would have afforded me the opportunity to begin and to end this journey with you, but God had other plans for us. It is Friday, May 12, 2023, Mother's Day weekend, and as I reflect back on my life past, present, and future there are some things that I know for sure; everything that I am and everything that I hope to be, I owe to you. There is not a day that passes that I do not miss you, and long to talk to you, and it is during those quiet times when I find a tear rolling down my face, I realize that the greatest miracle of all is that you will never die because your spirit dwells within me. This is where I obtain my strength to move forward daily without you. Thank you for giving me life, thank you for your love, thank you for your guidance, thank you for the firm foundation that you placed me on, thank you for teaching me who God was, but most of all, thank you for making me the Man that I am today. I will always love you and I will see you in heaven.

Your Son, Clifford L. Sanders, Jr.

WHY AM I WRITING THIS BOOK

By now, unless you have been living on the planet Mars, you have seen the headline story in the media for the past three and one half years. "Reverend Wright" is a hateful, un-American, unpatriotic, racial divider, and by the way, because President Barack Obama attends his church, he is guilty by association. He must be the same type of person. This type of devilish ploy sounds a little presumptuous, arrogant, ignorant, hateful, divisive, and insidious to me. Why do I say that? Because first of all, you mean to tell me that out of the over 8,000 parishioners in the congregation of Rev. Wright's church, then Senator Obama is the only person who is guilty. You mean to tell me that without knowing then Senator Obama on a personal level, you can listen to a 30 second sound clip of a 60 minute sermon and come up with a psycho-social history of then Senator Obama? You mean to tell me that without even attending the church that is in question, and without knowing anything about Rev. Wright personally, you can label him in this manner? Wow! That takes a great deal of intellectual prowess for anyone to accomplish a feat like analyzing the character of a man without knowing anything about a man. I spoke to several psychologists to ask them if this is at all possible, and each one of them told me that it is a medical and professional impossibility, and expounded by further stating that with all of their education, residency, and practice, that they could never accomplish such a feat without speculating and missing the mark. Therefore, since this is a medical impossibility, then there must be something sinister that is at work here. Could it be that a black man with a multi-racial heritage who is well educated, accomplished, has character, integrity, loves God, loves people, and has a good heart is now the President of the United States? Could it be that he is a man who sought to run against all odds, against an established system of capitalists, oligarchs, and plutocrats, because he loves people and continues to see so much poverty, degradation, oppression, death, lies, cheating, depression, selfishness and could no longer stand by idly and remain silent without it affecting him spiritually and ethically? This is key and will be the reasons why President Obama and many great men and women will come after him seeking to serve their country. The problem with that is, this country wants you to remain ignorant and divided along racial lines, so that control can continue to be maintained by the capitalists, Pharisees, and hypocrites. Let me enlighten you and set you free and you can choose to accept this reality or not accept it. This Presidential race, Congressional race, Senatorial race, Gubernatorial race, Mayoral race, and many other races beyond this election cycle is not about race at all. It is not about white, black, yellow, or red, it is about GREEN! Yes green, as in the COLOR OF MONEY. That is why Senator Clinton during her eight years of experience as the first lady, did not overly concern herself with helping address any of the issues of poverty, degradation, death, and lies during her husband's years in the White house. More specifically, more people of color were incarcerated under her husband's crime bills in the White House, more people lost jobs under her husband's N.A.F.T.A. bill that outsourced all of the high paying jobs in America but the media does not want to talk about that. She continued to talk about debating then Senator Obama one on one, but remained silent about New York police officers who murdered Sean Bell and seriously injured his friends by firing fifty shots at them! Isn't New York in her district as a Senator? Is she not running for President of All the People as well? But the media gave her a free pass, yet Rev. Wright was the subject of the race. How about Senator McCain? Who displays a veneer of integrity, while he drops little subliminal messages like Obama is elitist, out of touch, does not care about the people and is corrupt!

This is a man who rides on his wife's private jet, not knowing how many houses that he has, votes against a holiday honoring Dr. Martin Luther King Jr., votes to bail out corporations, send money to Iraq, but not lower the gas prices, or bail out Americans who he states that he wants to represent, but sits idly by while families continue to be thrown out of their homes. But the media does not analyze that! Again, Rev. Wright was the issue of this election, not high gas prices, not a bankrupt nation, not high food prices, not foreclosed family homes, not a collapsed economic infrastructure, not unemployment, Rev. Wright! Moreover, to add insult to injury, Senator McCain told the truth once during this period when he stated that the economy is doing just fine. To those who are experiencing the opposite, let me help you because this is one of those elite, republican code words that has often been used by President Bush, media tabloid pundits, and Vice President Cheney that defies logic. Translated, Senator McCain and most of his Republican colleagues from this Congress who has a 10% national rating means their "economy" is fine. Therefore, that is all that is important, too bad about the rest of you who are struggling. "I've got mine, you better get yours, you just keep sitting in your foreclosed homes, wringing your hands, walking the floors at night consumed with worry, feeling like a failure, and I will call on you again when I need your vote again. But the media will never analyze these statements and code words, because of who owns these media outlets; The Capitalist elite.

My disappointment with the manner in which this country has been deceived, has prompted me to write this book, as I have observed how this election has unfolded where one candidate was and still is, being shamelessly attacked even to date and placed under a cloud of suspicion based upon conjecture and innuendo, while the other two candidates and the Republican lawmakers received and are still receiving free passes by the media 24 hours per day, seven days per week. For example, was there a discussion about which Senator(s) Clinton and McCain's pastors were? How about a female Republican candidate who's Pastor engages in witchcraft? How about their voting records on the outsourcing of jobs? How about their civil rights records? How about their ties to other persons like the Koch brothers, special interest, separatist, terrorist groups, and other organizations? How about stonewalling Republicans and spineless blue dog Democrats who are seemingly interested in killing President Obama's American jobs package for the working class? (Crickets are now chirping). Continue to read and understand that knowledge is power, and if you can get your mind free, then there will be a shifting of your perspective before voting in any election. Remember the power only resides when "We" the people come together on one accord, and unite towards one goal, Equality and Justice for ALL. That is why "We the People" must be written, because it not only represents a book but a movement and a spiritual, psychological, and physical awakening.

Contrary to popular opinion that rings true in most instances that in this Capitalist society that we call the United States, I am not writing this book to achieve a "profit margin." No! As a matter of fact, while I was writing this book, my family was experiencing a "personal recession," but I was busy saving money little by little each week in order to afford the publication of this book; I experienced the shame of being labeled as naïve, even idealistic for not seeking the "financial safety net" that a publishing company could afford me. But that is not why I wrote this book, and no I am not naïve but passionate and purposeful; Passionate about the truth that continues to get lost in translation, and purposeful about restoring the unity of this country behind those leaders who demonstrate their care for us by the actions that they take on legislation that directly impacts the voter. My hope is to give the people or electorate a candid view of how deceptive and vicious the capitalist power base is in keeping us divided along racial lines, while they continue to fleece the citizens through secret deals made in smoke filled rooms. The truth of the matter is that the very candidates that they choose to represent their interests do not care anything about them until it is time for them to run for their seats again. They give you "hocus pocus" like Paul Ryan, John Boehner, tea baggers and Mitt Romney to "make you lose focus." In short, the only ones that we can depend on are ourselves because no one is coming to save us or bail us out. But that is okay because the true power is in the hands of the people, and if we decide to read and research with understanding and develop an insight concerning political matters, place our petty differences aside, transcend above the subliminally imposed racial hatred and mistrust for others, and realize that politics and America has nothing to do with color and everything to do with money, power, oppression and class; then we will realize that up to this point, we have had no place at the economic table. No! Many of your representatives do not care anything about the people; they are just a means to an end! Grasp this reality before it is too late!

INTRODUCTION

W e the People of the United States, in Order to form a more perfect Union, establish Justice, insure domestic Tranquility, provide for the common defense, promote the general Welfare, and secure the Blessings of Liberty to ourselves and our Posterity, do ordain and establish this Constitution for the United States of America. (Preamble to the U.S. Constitution)

Interpretations and Analysis:
"People of the United States"

People of the United States" has sometimes been understood to mean "citizens." This approach reasons that, if the political community speaking for itself in the Preamble ("We the People") includes only citizens, by a realistic implication it specifically excludes some groups who have historically been viewed and considered as non-citizens in some fashion. It has been argued in some intellectual circles, that the term citizen did not apply to the Negro. In my opinion, this logic is said to be flawed due to the belief that it has also been construed to mean something like "all under the sovereign jurisdiction and authority of the United States.

This phrase has been construed as affirming that the national government created by the Constitution derives its sovereignty from the people, as well as confirming that the government under the Constitution was intended to govern and protect "the people" directly, as one society, instead of governing only the states as political units. The Court has also understood this language to mean that the sovereignty of the government under the U.S. Constitution is superior to that of the States. Stated in the phrase in negative terms, the Preamble has been interpreted to mean that the Constitution was not the act of sovereign and independent States. In short, although in some ways the meaning and implications of the Preamble are contested, at the least it can be said that the Preamble demonstrates that the federal government of the United States was not created as an agreement between or coalition of the States. Instead, it was the product of "the People" with the power to govern the People directly, unlike the government under the Articles of Confederation, which only governed the People indirectly through rules imposed on the States.

But does the term "We the People" really mean All the People? After conducting research concerning this question, consideration of the Plessy vs. Ferguson court decision of the late 1890s, challenged the very premise of the preamble. Let us consider this case and its implications. According to historical documents, the case grew from the passage of an 1887 Florida law, whereas states began to require that railroads furnish separate accommodations for each race. These measures were unpopular with the railway companies that bore the expense of adding Jim Crow cars. Segregation of the railroads was even more objectionable to black citizens, who saw it as a further step toward the total repudiation of three constitutional amendments. When such a bill was proposed before the Louisiana legislature in 1890, the articulate black community of New Orleans protested vigorously. Nonetheless, despite the presence of 16 black legislators in the state assembly, the law was passed. It required either separate passenger coaches or partitioned coaches to provide segregated accommodations for each race. Passengers were required to sit in the appropriate areas or face a $25 fine or a 20-day jail sentence. Black nurses attending white children were permitted to ride in white compartments. In other words, there were citizens of this country who did not desire to comingle with people of color. No one would think that their wish would be granted; as I never want to be anywhere I am not wanted. However, in 1891, a group of concerned young black men of New Orleans formed the Citizens Committee to Test the Constitutionality of the Separate Car Law. They raised money and engaged Albion W. Tourge, a prominent Radical Republican author and politician, as their lawyer. On May

15, 1892, the Louisiana State Supreme Court decided in favor of the Pullman Companies claim that the law was unconstitutional as it applied to interstate travel. Encouraged, the committee decided to press a test case on intrastate travel. With the cooperation of the East Louisiana Railroad, on June 7, 1892, Homer Plessy, a mulatto (7/8 white), seated himself in a white compartment, was challenged by the conductor, and was arrested and charged with violating the state law. In the Criminal District Court for the Parish of Orleans, Tourge argued that the law requiring separate but equal accommodations was unconstitutional. When Judge John H. Ferguson ruled against him, Plessy applied to the State Supreme Court for a writ of prohibition and certiorari. Although the court upheld the state law, it granted Plessy's petition for a writ of error that would enable him to appeal the case to the Supreme Court. In 1896, the Supreme Court issued its decision in Plessy v. Ferguson.

Justice Henry Brown of Michigan delivered a very telling majority opinion, which sustained the constitutionality of Louisiana's Jim Crow law. In part, he said:

We consider the underlying fallacy of the plaintiff's argument to consist in the assumption that the enforced separation of the two races stamps the colored race with a badge of inferiority. If this be so, it is not by reason of anything found in the act, but solely because the colored race chooses to put that construction upon it. This argument also assumes that social prejudice may be overcome by legislation, and that equal rights cannot be secured except by an enforced commingling of the two races. If the civil and political rights of both races are to be equal, then one cannot be inferior to the other civilly or politically. If one race be inferior to the other socially, the other cannot put them upon the same plane.

In other words, this decision was one of the catalysts that gave the White majority in the United States the power to marginalize and discriminate against Black Americans, because in essence, this 7 to 1 ruling by the U.S. Supreme Court was the legal linchpin that gave credence to state imposed racial segregation in public facilities. This was made possible to date, because the Supreme Court 7 to 1 argued that stated imposed racial segregation was not "unreasonable" and therefore did not violate the Equal Protection Clause of the 14th Amendment. Though the law has been overturned, it lingers in the consciousness of Black America like a stain that may never be lifted, thus leaving a badge of inferiority on the black race collectively to date.

In a powerful dissent, conservation Kentuckian John Marshall Harlan wrote:

I am of the opinion that the statute of Louisiana is inconsistent with the personal liberties of citizens, white and black, in that State, and hostile to both the spirit and the letter of the Constitution of the United States. If laws of like character should be enacted in the several States of the Union, (voter id laws, telecommunications immunity laws, three strike laws, Eisenhower drug laws, state sponsored terrorism entitled police brutality, etc) the effect would be in the highest degree mischievous. Slavery as an institution tolerated by law would, it is true, have disappeared from our country, but there would remain a power in the States, by sinister legislation, to interfere with the blessings of freedom; to regulate civil rights common to all citizens upon the basis of race; and to place in a condition of legal inferiority a large body of American citizens now constituting a part of the political community, called the people of the United States, for whom and by whom, through representatives, our government is administrated. Such a system is inconsistent with the guarantee given by the Constitution to each State of a republican form of government, and may be stricken down by congressional action, or by the courts in the discharge of their solemn duty to maintain the supreme law of the land, anything in the Constitution or laws of any State to the contrary notwithstanding.

Now I am not a legal scholar, nor do I profess to be, but as I consider this landmark court decision, its ramifications, and its far reaching effects in our present society, there appears to be a fundamental misinterpretation of what the framers of the preamble meant when they wrote, "We the People." This misinterpretation rings true every time a Sean Bell is murdered by policemen who are acquitted by activist judges; every time there is a Jena 6 where the District Attorney can also serve as the Jena High School's attorney; every time a "paid" prostitute can become a rape victim simultaneously; every time a vigilante like Joe Horn can mete out his form of Texas justice and hide behind a grand jury that rubber stamps murder; every time a Michael Vick who by all intents and purposes is a millionaire but is treated like a common thug in the criminal justice system and before you say he broke the law, so did Scooter Libby who is say a white convicted felon, but will never see the inside of a correctional facility because his friend, George Dubya the former President overruled the verdict of a "constitutional jury of his peers which is equivalent to the will of the people," ignored the "constitutional right of sentencing Mr. Libby after a verdict had been reached," and commuted his sentence. Why? Because the President said that he did not want his friend to go to jail! Where were the Attorneys General on this circumvention of the U.S. Constitution? When the U.S. Supreme Court relegated the U.S. Constitution to glorified "Charmin tissue" when they ordered the votes in Bush v. Gore, "to stop being counted" which violates the American voters "right to vote and equal protection under the law," yet when our Black President and the Democrats pass a landmark "healthcare law" that will essentially "care for the poor and the middle class," there is suddenly a "constitutional violation!" Let me be perfectly clear, unless we redefine the meaning of "We the People," and reframe its interpretation to represent inclusion and reciprocation of fundamental fairness under the law of all people, then this great experiment that we define as Democracy will never become as good as its promise.

"To form a more perfect Union"

The phrase "to form a more perfect Union" has been construed as referring to the shift to the Constitution from the Articles of Confederation. In this transition, the "Union" was made "more perfect" by the creation of a federal government with enough power to act directly upon citizens, rather than a government with narrowly limited power that could act on citizens (e.g., by imposing taxes) only indirectly through the states. Although the Preamble speaks of perfecting the "Union," and the country is called the "United States of America," the Supreme Court has interpreted the institution created as a government over the people, not an agreement between the States. Here lies the problem, when the interpretation of our Constitution is trusted to be completed by mere mortals possessing ulterior motives, and then the true meaning of the document will be lost in translation with the power that it wields being abused. Historically, this phrase has been interpreted to confirm that nullification of federal laws in dissenting States, dissolution of the Union, or secession from it, are not contemplated by the Constitution. However, if we are to ever form a more perfect union, all races must be treated as one! For a "Union" is defined as a group of states and nations united into one political body. For under this union that is described as perfect or flawless, there should be no difference between the Jew and the Greek, the Negro and the Caucasian, the Hispanic or the Latino, the Asian or the Chinese, for together where there are no "respecter of persons" we are described as a perfect union. However to become a "More" perfect union, there is much more work to do. Because you see, this country left the tyranny of King George to form their own nation, only to create an atmosphere in the new nation of similar despotic, dynamic, and tyrannical proportions.

"To Establish Justice"

Concerning this concept, and in order to gain some understanding about establishing justice, there must be a dialogue concerning Injustice in America. Injustice? Yes injustice! You know, when the police murders unarmed young men in New York by shooting them 50 times in the back, only to have the Judge absolve them from any responsibility. You know, when a black senior U.S. Senator is "spit on" and called a "nigger" by a Republican supported teabag demonstrator when the healthcare law passes and Fox News labels it as a "party that went bad!" When a President and his republican administration sits idly and watches the elderly and children drown in flood waters in the Katrina aftermath, although the federal government (F.E.M.A.) was created for the purpose of responding in emergency management situations. To further bolster my claims of the utter disregard for human life by the Bush administration, the media ignored their plight and named the victims "refugees," and to add insult to injury, President Bush proclaimed his sense of pride towards FEMA Director Brown for a "heck of a job" that he did. Even in Florida, at a boot camp and on national TV, as America watched a black teenager getting "lynched" by a group of thugs who abused their authority and choked this child to death, only to have an all-white jury acquit the boot camp officials of any responsibility. In spite of these glaring disregards for the law, we are naively taught in this country that "Justice is supposed to be blind!" But on the contrary, Justice is not blind; it is deliberately inaccessible for working class citizens and the poor! Have you ever wondered why we as American citizens do not automatically have access to certain genres of professional schools? Namely, law school! Think about it. There are so many impediments cloaked under the label of "admissions requirements" that are placed upon a potential candidate to even be considered for admission! First of all, it does not matter if one attended graduate school or not, only the grades from your undergraduate institution are considered and given weight! If you are fortunate enough to move beyond this impediment, then you are subjected to having to pass a standardized test called the Law School Admissions test (L.S.A.T.) which on its face is biased. Biased from the perspective of the prospective Law Schools who are not taking into consideration the fact that a potential student may excel in a classroom setting but may not be able to successfully master standardized tests. Yes they purchase study manuals, and make companies who provide study courses for the test wealthy, but oftentimes with no guarantee for passage with a competitive score. In addition, consideration is not given to the racial composition of the writers of the L.S.A.T. not being equally retained by the Law School Admissions Council for the test's creation. Yet most schools utilize this test as a primary determinant for a student's fitness to graduate from a law program, instead of academic records from all schools and practical experience in your field being given equal consideration and weight. If that is not enough, consider the law schools' appointment of an "admissions committee" that is comprised of flawed humans who are tasked with the responsibility of determining "who the school admits!" Are all graduate and professional school programs this encumbered with such "oppressive admissions standards?" Have you ever asked why there are so many impediments in gaining admissions into the programs where you will study the law, and will subsequently become an "Officer of the Court," and will be empowered to fight against racist and draconian legal systems who systematically incarcerate, exploit, intimidate, and impose revenge upon the poor and working class citizens who oppose the status quo of the power base of our country? Just consider the "Citizens

United" decision. If you have or have not wondered why, consider the statistical racial composition of those persons who are ensnared and negatively impacted in a criminal justice system who leads the world in incarceration rates through brutality, death, prosecutorial misconduct, parole, probation, pretrial services, diversion, death row, or longterm incarceration. Now look at the ratio of minority attorneys in our Nation. It begs the question as to why this country is not committed to training more minority attorneys instead of attempting to disqualify them from admission's consideration. How does one justify not having a seat at the table for non-traditional students with a plethora of experience working in the criminal justice system? Who knows how the system works, how unfair it is at times, and who would exhibit more empathy towards their clientele and would work tirelessly to represent them, and who does not place an emphasis on the financial aspect of legal representation. The Oppressive power of this nation's laws that are utilized by President Obama's adversaries has crippled this country, and has threatened to destroy it with police brutality and the unfettered murdering of private citizens, the incarceration of our children at the hand of draconian drug laws, the incarceration of our children through "Jack and Jill" laws, the incarceration of parents who make a stand against these laws in support of their children, revenge prosecutions for black men who "escaped incarceration the first time," and the failure to address prosecutorial misconduct that sends minorities to death row without consequences and challenge, all comes from the law, it's application, it's interpretation, and the strategic appointments that are made to the offices of Attorney General, Assistant U.S. Attorneys, District Attorneys, and Judgeships respectively! The power of the law is so overwhelming, that our President faced a battle and power struggle over an appointment to the U.S. Supreme Court. The Republicans, in their attempt to maintain the legal status quo, has appointed Jeff Beauregard Sessions, R-AL to head the Judiciary Committee who is in charge of approving the President's appointment to the Supreme Court. This is significant for two reasons, first, Senator Sessions is a staunch supremacist who is adamantly opposed to "equal protection under the law" for all citizens, and he represents the conservative viewpoint that loathes the President's progressive philosophy that stresses fundamental fairness for all Americans, and will guide his choice for the appointment to the bench of the Supreme legal authority in our land.

Does this represent Justice? Fundamental fairness? Respect for the U.S. Constitution? Judicial Equality? Or does it represent Cowardice, Partisanship and selfishness? Is this the best that America has to offer? Not likely, but America will never progress beyond its petty differences, racism, and divisions without "We the People" standing up, understanding the game, and demanding accountability. To that end, the question must be raised, what kind of world do you want? Do you want a world of justice, of love, respect and equality? Then you must make a decision as you read the remainder of this book to become an educated, enlightened, agent of change that demands Liberty and Justice for all. For it is later than you think!

CHAPTER ONE

CAUSING DIVISIONS

The God that America claims to know has stated that:

Jesus knew their thoughts, and said unto them every kingdom divided against its self is brought to desolation (sadness); and every city or house divided against its self shall not stand. (Matthew 12:25)

The Amplified translation of this passage is:

"And knowing their thoughts, He said to them, any kingdom that is divided against itself is being brought to desolation and laid waste, and no city or house divided against itself will not last or continue to stand."

In spite of both translations, what every citizen needs to understand about this election, about the tactics that have been engaged in by many of the candidates, the media, and some members of our political parties (and you know who you are) is:

1. God knew your thoughts and your intents before these attacks began and you and this nation will be judged when it is time.

2. God is speaking to the United States in this context as he declares that the divisions that you have caused in this kingdom or country will be to your detriment.

3. How? By causing this country to be laid to waste, making it vulnerable, and eventually causing it to fall. Can you say "Pan American Union" or "North American Union?" Because that is what our country is moving towards, which will be networked by the NAFTA superhighway? This was started under the Clinton administration with the signing of the NAFTA bill,

which could end the existence of the United States as we know it. But it is not completed, with each economic crisis that arises, building upon the next crisis under the Bush administration and continuing with the present stonewalling and filibustering by the Republican Party that caused our credit rating to be downgraded. How un-American and unpatriotic for the G.O.P. to stall the stimulus package and now the American jobs act that may save some working class families from starvation and certain death. Do they not care that the U.S. is in danger of falling? No they do not! Because they have the financial means for survival and could care less about anyone else. That is what they think about you, what will you do America? Where is the media and their discussions of this crisis? Specific media outlets, namely Fox News, are utilizing its airwaves and influence to cause divisions among the American people.

Webster dictionary defines Division as an **"Act or a Process of dividing."** What you are witnessing in this country is an act, and a process that is being engaged upon by design to cause "Division" in this country. What is being done and what we are observing is cerebral and "On purpose and with a deliberate intent". In addition, it has been made into a spiritual matter involving then Senator Obama and God's pastor. Consequently, I must temporarily digress from our discourse while maintaining a spiritual tone, as I remain relevant to my subject matter. W. Carl Ketcherside, in his contributing chapter in the book, "Our Heritage of Unity and Fellowship" describes the Christian Right that have extrapolated race, fear, mistrust, and the alleged against President Obama into this political race, as they hid behind a veneer of self- righteousness!

Mr. Ketcherside argues that:

"No scripture is safe in the hands of a religious partisan. The reason is obvious. The party spirit is a work of the flesh. It is opposed to the Spirit. It will debar one from inheritance of the kingdom. (Gal. 5:17 -21) The factious spirit is indicative of immaturity. Those guilty of it can hardly be addressed as spiritual men, but as babes in Christ. (1 Cor. 3:1) However, the partisan jealously seeks to defend his party.

To do so, he must warp and bend the scriptures. He must make them apply in a sense which God never intended. The revelation of heaven was not given to be the private or exclusive possession of any sect or party. It is not a factional handbook. No uninspired man is an official interpreter of revelation. No group of men can advance themselves as the authorized expositors of sacred writ. God's word is authoritative. The interpretations placed upon it, or the opinions of men about it, are not. It is here the party spirit reveals its true nature. It interprets God's word in justification of the partisan position, substitutes the interpretation for revelation, then demands acquiescence in the arbitrary interpretation as the word of God, and dis-fellowships all who refuse to do obeisance to such tyranny of mind and thought."

This is who President Obama and all Americans who are trying to free their minds are fighting against. However, what we all need to realize is that the insinuations are going to continue, the attacks are not going to cease, the insulting of our intelligence will not end, the guilt by association ploy will only get worse, the attempts to discredit will only increase in intensity, and there is nothing that can be done to stop it. But you can realize who these messengers of misinformation are, and you can control how you react to it! That is right; you do not have to listen to what is being said! I mean, that is if you want to change your current life, feed your family, keep a roof over your head, drive your car, obtain gainful employment, and bring your children back home from a war that they did not send their kids to. Certainly you will perish if you allow this country to remain divided along racial issues. Do you not understand that the people who are behind these attacks care nothing about your issues? Do you not understand that the people who are leading these attacks against President Obama and other targeted candidates are multi-millionaires, have an excellent quality of life, and could care less if you can feed your families or not? If they cared about you, ask yourself this question; why are they not discussing the issues that continue to plague your families? Because these messengers of division and hate are selfish, and are willing to maintain their standard of living at all costs, and at your expense! It is a satanic level of selfishness that has lasted for centuries and has gotten progressively worse, and it is shocking to my conscience that a nation who is suffering cannot open their eyes, use common sense, and realize that the fraud that is being perpetuated against them. However, this time it may cost them their very lives. When I first addressed this issue I came up with the following analogy.

When I look at this loveless and adulterous marriage between the haves and the have nots, I am reminded of the credit reporting system. Now companies rely on this system of reporting because it is a True Measure of a person's propensity or likelihood to be reliable in the future. Well Americans, before you make a decision concerning whether you are going to place your future and the future of your families into the hands of these messengers of mischief, you must look back on their "credit history." You must look back on the history of the media, the politicians' empty promises that have been made to you, the manner in which their own citizens/candidates are attacked, and the current state of our country and your lives are in. If their credit history is found to be trustworthy, then listen to them. But if not, then you must guard your minds and your ears, and turn away from their fables. But I must admit that I can understand why you are susceptible to these attacks, because you have not seen a man of character, integrity, who is also a politician in a long time. "B.O.", before Obama, you have seen lying, stealing, empty promises, pedophilia, special interests, drug abuse, soliciting male prostitutes in bathroom stalls, adultery, embezzlement, election rigging, fraud, constitutional misinterpretation, freeing criminals, and trickery in Washington, D.C. year in and year out before President Obama chose to run. But you should not allow the unfamiliar to invoke fear in you to the point that it will make you susceptible to believe lies, and not change the way things are because that is called Insanity. You know, when you do things the same way over and over again, expecting different results. Your family is expecting that the decision that you make will improve their lives, so now the question is, Has It?

Labeling, Social Stigma, Social Conflict Theory, and Code Words

It's a dirty and vicious game. By now, many of you are wondering why in the world would the subject matter of Rev. Wright last so long in the media, when people are homeless through foreclosures; when people cannot feed their families due to high food prices; when peoples' kids are dying in an unjust war while our representatives are not sending their own kids; when peoples' relatives and family members are literally dying due to their inability to afford healthcare; when people cannot find employment because all of the career track jobs have been outsourced to other countries; when "price gouged" fuel costs have crippled the transportation industry and the private consumer, and while our former President vetoed any attempts to attach windfall taxes on his corporate buddies. We need to ask why? Well allow me to explain to you that it is being done by design! Yes there is a Method to this Madness and we are going to discuss it. First and foremost, I suspect that the culprits who are behind this deliberate attempt to divide our nation and control the conversation based upon trivialities know one thing, that America has an unreported sickness. And it is their knowledge of America's long-term prognosis that has empowered them to move forward with their agenda.

America's Unreported illness

When one reads the leading medical or psychiatric journals, this illness will not make its publication, nor will this condition be covered through healthcare legislation. For it is not born out of normal life functioning, rather it is a disease of the spirit, heart, and mind of a man. This disease is called racism, and from the Jena, Louisiana D.A.'s office to the floor of the Senate it has plagued America for generations past and present. Consider some of these laws, which have historically supported America's illness:

1619-Passage of the Maryland Segregation policy which recommended that blacks be social excluded from society, 1686-The Carolina Trade law barred blacks from all trades, 1691 Virginia Marriage law prescribed banishment for any white woman who married a black man, 1705-Virginia Public Office law which prohibited blacks from holding or assuming any public office, 1723-Virginia Anti-Assembly law which impeded blacks from meeting or having a sense of community, 1790-First Naturalization law where Congress declares the United States a white nation, 1813-Virginia Poll tax that enacted a $1.50 tax on blacks who were forbidden to vote, 1819-Missouri Literacy law forbade assembling or teaching black slaves to read or write, 1829-Georgia

Literacy law provided a fine and imprisonment for teaching a black person to read, 1833-that literacy law was updated in Georgia to provide fines but also to provide whippings for anyone teaching blacks, 1841-South Carolina Observing law forbade blacks and whites from looking out the same windows, 1842-Maryland Information law which felonied blacks demanding or receiving abolition newspapers, 1846-Kentucky Incitement law provided imprisonment for inciting slaves to rebel, 1857-Dred Scott decision where the Supreme Court dehumanized and disenfranchised blacks, and 1868-Southern Black codes which deprived blacks of the right to vote and hold public office. Unfortunately, the initiators of these codes had offspring, so in the year 2009 these Jim Crow babies have decided to challenge a provision of the 1965 Voting Rights Act, which would again deprive blacks the right to vote over 100 years later. You see, currently before the US Supreme Court, and it will continuously be an issue is whether the role of race in American politics has so changed that remedies that were once constitutional are now impingements (restrictive) on state sovereignty. It is called by parties involved, simply "Section 5" and it covers those Southern states (AL, Alaska, AZ, GA, LA, MS, SC, TX, VA) and counties where racial discrimination has been and remains the most flagrant. For those of you who refuse to understand or do not want to understand, let us imagine that David Dukes and Bull Connor are in a smoke-filled room after a tea party rally contemplating this historic win by President Barack Hussein Obama with Rush Limbaugh moderating, I believe that the conversation would go like this:

Dukes: My God Bull what is this world coming to? Electing that spook for President!

Bull: Yeah you right Dukes; things aren't like they used to be when the good ole boys used to determine the outcome of the election.

Dukes: That's alright Bull because I know people in the legal profession and I'll be damn if another darkie will get back in our White house again, it's just plain un-American. (as he adjusts his American flag pin)

Bull: What do you have in mind Dukes?

Dukes: Well, think about this; with Hussein being elected President, and because he is black, then we can make the argument that everything is fair now. We would ignore the obvious discrepancies of an all-white Senate as the republicans are trying to throw the only black Senator out of their exclusive good ole boys club, we will disregard the Southeastern football conference's refusing to hire black coaches in spite of their credentials, we will ignore the refusal of networks to have a black media presence on television, we will look the other way while attempts are made by southern states to continue to pass restrictive voting laws that would disenfranchise minorities and other enlightened Americans, we will not discuss the refusal to grant a new trial to an innocent man in Georgia (Troy Davis) who the criminal justice system is trying to legally ~~murder~~ execute, we will even look past the murder of Sean Bell by New York Police officers who a judge acquitted, the murder of a handcuffed unarmed black man in Compton who was executed by a B.A.R.T. police officer, the discontinuing of liberal talk radio shows on 102.5 WAMJ-fm in Georgia in attempts to keep upward thinking people from remaining informed while they silence dissent, the passage of Arizona's "bigot bill" giving a right to law enforcement to racially profile Hispanics and Blacks alike, and we will render irrelevant the abuse of authority by a racist Jena Louisiana District Attorney who sought to incarcerate six black youth for years to come. Instead we will argue that everything is fair and equal with the election of a black President. Therefore Section five should be lifted on these good ole states where we fear God but hate blacks and Hispanics and believe that they should stay in their place.

Bull: Now I get it Dukes, if we can get the federal government to agree with our logic, let our quintessential divisive mouthpiece Rush convince the people that this legal challenge is the right thing to do in order to decrease any backlash, then we can bring back our fair system of ruler-ship and the South can rise again. <end>

Now if one would consider the historical significance of these laws, this discourse between friends, and would be honest and admit it, we would agree that America has an issue concerning Race! I will not make a blanket statement and foolishly say that everyone in this country is suffering from this illness, but I will say that many persons at least have an inclination to be mean-spirited, and disingenuous towards those who look different than they do or are not similarly situated economically like they are. Now I know that "some of your friends are black, white, etc," but if that is the case, then why is it so difficult for Americans to discuss race, or even celebrate our differences? Because I believe that everyone has the ability to bring different experiences and cultures to the table of brotherhood that will make America richer. Now if we examine the practical application of the term racism, I would argue that in order for a racist to further the agenda of racism, he would have to be in a "position of power" over the subject of harm. Now you can make the irrational choice of being a racist if you please and leave racial signs in others mailboxes, you may even choose to call others terrorists, monkeys, Arab, and threaten to take another person's life, Realistically you are a non-issue! For it is only until you gain access to a "seat of power" that racism begins to flourish and transforms itself into a very real issue. Because now you can deny me equal employment opportunities; now you can deny me the right to vote; now you can destroy my credit rating by evicting me from my apartment; now you can red-line me and deny me from obtaining property by denying me a mortgage or sign me to a "teaser rate" and balloon my payment later and foreclose on my home; you can redraw congressional districts and dilute my vote; you can arbitrarily stop my car, arrest, prosecute or murder me; you can now label me as intellectually inferior and deny me the basic right to attend college; you can now harass me at work; you can now defame, debase, and impugn my character in the media, and you can do it without consequence because you are a member of the power-base. That being said, there is a billionaire power broker, Rupert Murdoch who has dual citizenship in the U.S. and Australia, whose goal as a capitalist is to exploit America's infirmity and shame, while he maximizes his profits and makes his employees rich, which is a primary goal of most capitalists, although the exploitation process may vary. He had a goal and dreams to exploit the masses suffering from the illness of racism, keep them divided along racial lines, control thought, manipulate public opinion, oppress the voices of dissent, and maintain the status quo and power structure in this country. As a result, he founded The Fox Network, and he is indicative of a "secret" society in this country symbolic of la "cosa nostra" that consists of wealthy citizens, racists, Klansmen, bigots, network media sponsors, media personalities, politicians, professed Christians of the Right, and supremacist groups who prefer to keep their identities anonymous while they wear their flag pins proudly. So now let's examine just how he has successfully furthered this secret societies' agenda, while he moves towards realizing his dream of a "Divided and Exploited America."

Labeling and Social Stigma

It all starts with labeling, commonly known as Social Reaction theory; it is interchangeable with the term labeling which occurs in our society. One of the purposes of this criminological theory is to render an explanation as to how criminal careers form based on destructive social interactions (labeling) and encounters. According to the book "Criminology" 9th edition, its roots are found in the "symbolic interaction theory" of sociologists Charles Horton Cooley, George Herbert Mead, and Herbert Blumer. This theory argues that people communicate via symbols, gestures, signs, words, or images that stand for or represent something else. In other words, some groups of people communicate via codes, and the purposes of these forms of communication are for many times, insidious purposes with an undercurrent of ulterior motives. Important to note is that people interpret symbolic gestures from others and incorporate them in their self-image. Symbols are used by others to let people know how well they are doing and whether they are liked or appreciated. People oftentimes are conditioned to view reality based upon the content of these messages and situations they encounter, the subjective interpretation of these interactions, and how they make decisions, and shape future behavior. There is no objective reality. People interpret the reactions of others, and this interpretation assigns meaning.

Social Reaction is said to pick up on these concepts of interaction and interpretation.

Throughout our lives, we as a people, are given a variety of symbolic labels as "unpatriotic", "un-American", "Elitist", "angry", "lacking judgment as a leader", "soft", "inexperienced", "Marxist", "socialist" and these labels are given to represent and define not just one trait but the whole person. Labels can improve self-image and social standing. Research shows that people, who are labeled with positive traits such as physical attractiveness, are assumed to maintain other traits, such as being intelligent and competent. On the other hand, negative labels including troublemaker, radical, mentally ill, eccentric, and angry help stigmatize the recipients of these labels and reduce the public's image of these recipients. However, these labels are most effective when these subjective interpretations are conveyed by trusted sources or even seemingly trusted sources, such as the Mainstream media. Beyond these immediate results, depending on the visibility of the label and the manner and severity with which it is applied, a person or a group may find itself "socially stigmatized" with damaging consequences that are forthcoming. Defined, a Social stigma is "a severe social disapproval of personal characteristics or beliefs that are against cultural norms." Social stigma often leads to marginalization.

Examples of existing or historical social stigmas can be physical or mental disabilities and disorders, as well as illegitimacy, homosexuality or affiliation with a specific Nationality, Pastor, Religion, or being deemed to be or proclaiming oneself to be of a certain ethnicity, in any of a myriad of geopolitical and corresponding sociopolitical contexts in various parts of the world.

Bruce Link and Jo Phelan, in their work entitled, "Conceptualizing Stigma", in the Annual Review of Sociology, 2001, p.363 argued that stigma exists when four specific components converge. (1) Individuals differentiate and label human variations. (2) Prevailing cultural beliefs tie those labeled to adverse attributes. (3) Labeled individuals are placed in distinguished groups that serve to establish a sense of disconnection between "us" and "them" (4) Labeled individuals experience "status loss and discrimination" that leads to unequal circumstances. In this model, stigmatization is also contingent on "access to social, economic, and political power that allows the identification of differences, construction of stereotypes, the separation of labeled persons into distinct groups, and the full execution of disapproval, rejection, exclusion, and discrimination." Subsequently, in this model the term stigma is applied when labeling, stereotyping, disconnection, status loss, and discrimination all exist within a power situation that facilitates stigma to occur. No truer example of this model can be explained as in this current election year with the media's shameless and continuous coverage of then Senator Barack Obama's former pastor, Dr. Jeremiah Wright. By now, many of you have heard the comments or sound bytes of former sermons by Dr. Wright. Sermons that Fox News paid over $3,000.00 to purchase that consisted of 20 year old messages that were edited. The purpose of this coverage was to label former Senator Obama as radical, angry, divisive, and cultish in an attempt to "Socially Stigmatize" him in the eyes of the American voters in an attempt to derail his momentum for the Oval Office. But were these comments any more inflammatory than alleged former Klansman David Dukes' comments on newly elected black President of the Republican National committee Michael Steele? Let us go deeper.

Social Conflict Theory and Code Words

The several social theories that emphasize social conflict have roots in the ideas of Karl Marx (1818-1883), the great German theorist and political activist. You may have heard of this person's name as of lately with the media pundits. For they have decided to label President Barack Obama as a Marxist which I believe is ludicrous, and a term being used to distract We the People from more pressing matters, but I will let you decide. According to my research and my understanding, the Marxist, conflict approach emphasizes a materialist interpretation of history, a dialectical method of analysis, a critical stance toward existing social arrangements, and a political program of revolution or, at least, reform.

The materialist view of history starts from the premise that the most important determinant of social life is the work people are doing, especially work that results in provision of the basic necessities of life: food, clothing and shelter. He thought that the way the work is socially organized and the technology used in production will have a strong impact on every other aspect of society. He maintained that everything of value in society results from human labor. Thus, he saw working men and women as engaged in making society, and creating the conditions for their own existence.

In the social production of their existence, men inevitably enter into definite relations, which are independent of their will, namely relations of production appropriate to a given stage in the development of their material forces of production. The totality of these relations of production constitutes the economic structure of society, the real foundation, on which arises a legal and political superstructure and to which correspond definite forms of social consciousness. The mode of production of material life conditions the general process of social, political and intellectual life. It is not the consciousness of men that determines their existence, but their social existence that determines their consciousness.

Owners are seen as making profits by paying workers less than their work is worth and, thus, exploiting them. In Marxist terminology, material forces of production or means of production include capital, land, and labor, whereas social relations of production refers to the division of labor and implied class relationships. Most prevalent in the 21st century is the exploitation of our workers in America by our United States lawmakers, when consideration is given to their refusal to raise the minimum wage to a living wage, while they voted themselves thousands of dollars in cost of living increases while already making six figures. Not to mention the current bailout of the very same capitalists who exploited the middle class through sub-prime mortgages. This is just two examples of this theory at work. Economic exploitation leads directly to political oppression, as owners make use of their economic power to gain control of the state and turn it into a servant of bourgeois economic interests. Police power, for instance, is used to enforce property rights and guarantee unfair contracts between capitalist and worker say in cases of mortgage foreclosures. Oppression also takes more subtle forms: religion serves capitalist interests by pacifying the population with the promise of heaven if they stayed in their places, with intellectuals and media pundits paid directly or indirectly by capitalists, who spend their careers justifying and rationalizing the existing social and economic arrangements. In sum, the economic structure of society molds the superstructure, including ideas (e.g., morality, ideologies, art, and literature) and the social institutions that support the class structure of society. (e.g., the state, the educational system, the family, the criminal justice system, and religious institutions) Because the dominant or ruling class (the bourgeoisie) controls the social relations of production, and because they usually have the retained services of their Senators, many Pastors, and intellects, the dominant ideology in a capitalist society is that of the ruling class. Ideology and social institutions, in turn, serve to reproduce and perpetuate the economic class structure by any means necessary, oftentimes including the exploitation of the working class. Thus, viewed the exploitative economic arrangements of capitalism as the real foundation upon which the superstructure of social, political, and intellectual consciousness is built.

Marx's view of history might seem angry and completely cynical or pessimistic, were it not for the possibilities of change revealed by his method of dialectical analysis. The Marxist dialectical method, based on Hegel's earlier idealistic dialectic, focuses attention on how an existing social arrangement, or thesis, generates its social opposite, or antithesis, and on how a qualitatively different social form, or synthesis, emerges from the resulting struggle. Marx optimistically believed that any stage of history based on exploitative economic arrangements generated within it the seeds of its own destruction. For instance, feudalism, in which land owners exploited the peasantry, gave rise to a class of town-dwelling merchants, whose dedication to making profits eventually led to the bourgeois revolution and the modern capitalist era. In the criminal justice system and our society, Criminologists do not accept the notion that criminals are bad and wish to trample the rights of others, with the utilization of the criminal law designed to control them and maintain a tranquil, fair society. If that were so, then acts like racism, state-side created militias, sexism, imperialism, unsafe working conditions, salmonella producing peanut factories, inadequate childcare, substandard housing, pollution of the environment, police brutality leading to murder, manipulating a free trade market and war-making as a tool of foreign policy would be True Prosecuted Crimes. Similarly, Marx argues that the class relations of capitalism will lead inevitably to the next stage, socialism. The class relations of capitalism embody a contradiction: capitalists need workers, and vice versa, but the economic interests of the two groups are fundamentally at odds. Such contradictions mean inherent conflict and instability, the class struggle that defines this entire election cycle, a conflict between the ruling class and the working class where a vote will determine the direction of this country. Adding to the instability of the capitalist system are the inescapable needs for ever-wider markets and ever-greater investments in capital to maintain the profits of capitalists (bail-outs). Marx expected that the resulting economic cycles of expansion and contraction, together with tensions that will build as the working class gains greater understanding of its exploited position and thus attains class-consciousness, would eventually culminate in a socialist revolution. Ladies and Gentlemen we have arrived at this age of enlightenment. Despite these applications, Marxism of any variety is still a minority position among American sociologists as it calls for a socialist system.

Despite this sense of the unalterable logic of history, Marxists see the need for social criticism and for political activity to speed the arrival of socialism, which, is not going to be based on private property and is not expected to involve as many contradictions and conflicts as capitalism. Marxists believe that social theory and political practice are dialectically intertwined, with theory enhanced by political involvement and with political practice necessarily guided by theory. Intellectuals ought, therefore, to engage in praxis, to combine political criticism and political activity. Theory itself is seen as necessarily critical and valueladen, since the prevailing social relations are based upon alienating and dehumanizing exploitation of the labor of the working classes.

Since the 1980's, Critical Criminologists have been deeply concerned with the Conservative trend in American politics, and the creation of what they considered to be an American empire. They focused on the conservative agenda that was poised to cripple the economic infrastructure of the United States, devalue the dollar, and create a debt that would become totally unmanageable. This conservative agenda that I call the G.O.P. playbook was initiated by the late Ronald Reagan that called for the following:

1. Lowering labor costs through Union Busting.
2. Setting limits on Welfare programs.
3. Initiating tax cuts that favored the wealthy.
4. Putting an end to Affirmative action programs.
5. Reducing environmental control and eliminating financial regulation.
6. Most importantly, to selfishly utilize the taxpayers' money while they are in office to leverage that money to create wealth for themselves, their party, their corporate friends, and the "Sam hill" with everyone else, with their anger being kindled whenever any policy is proposed by any leader or politician which will obstruct this avenue of wealth generated exclusion.

The agenda of these current political necrophiliacs, who continue to worship a dead politician, also called for the cutting of spending on Social programs while expanding spending for the Military. There was also a rapid build-up of the Prison system, the passage of Draconian criminal laws that threaten civil rights and liberties respectively. All done while there is absolutely no acceptance of responsibility for the results of these "Failed Policies." When the public began questioning the power structure, fear tactics were often imposed upon them. Tactics such as televised Homeland security terror alerts, the strategic periodic surfacing of Bin Laden video tapes that were conveniently translated by the government for the people to hear yet more alleged threats to their safety (of course we don't speak Arabic), and media coverage of terrorist acts that occur around the world. As our society has become more progressive minded and began to ask more questions, there was a concerted effort made by the power structure to neutralize these ever increasing inquiries that exhibited the potential to disrupt their socioeconomic status quo. This has most recently proven to be accurate and blatant with the announced candidacy of then Senator Barack Obama for President of the United States of America. Important to note is that Senator Obama's candidacy, success, and potential nomination for President was made possible by the conservative agenda that was imposed upon America by President George W. Bush Jr. and the G.O.P. who completely decimated the economic, educational, health care, and housing infrastructures of the United States. Now, one would think that, by now, with so many Americans suffering as a result of these inferior managerial decision-making, that steps would have been taken to correct this perpetual pain, but to no avail. Nevertheless, the process of change has begun! Because this candidacy threatened the power structure of the United States, an all out attack was waged upon the inclusive-minded Senator from Illinois. I viewed this attack and made the mistake of compartmentalizing the culprits as operating out of the conservative playbook, which is partially true. However, the primary reasoning behind these attacks is categorically "Socioeconomic" in scope and in nature! What do you mean? I am glad that you asked. The issue here is about MONEY, POWER, CONTROL, and an UNPRECEDENTED TYPE OF SATANIC SELFISHNESS that empowers and makes wealthy, a small group of citizens, while it oppresses, disregards, strips, and renders invisible and impotent the majority of its citizenry. This begs the question as to how this systematic disregard for humanity can occur year in, year out, and throughout each election cycle. Because of a perpetual media machine that continues to run campaign after campaign, utilizing diversionary and divisive issues that have nothing to do with the real issues. Consequently, the American people continue to be a non-priority, while the authentic issues continue to be lost in translation. Issues like our children dying in Iraq, people not being able to find employment and feed their families, citizens who are laboring to drive their cars due to high gas prices, the elderly not being able to purchase their medication due to high Medicaid premiums, millions of citizens being uninsured due to high medical insurance premiums, helpless children who are not even afforded basic healthcare, veterans who cannot attend college because the conservatives cut their G.I. Bill, law enforcement officers who murder unarmed citizens, officers of the court who continue to abuse their judicial authority, and voting rights that are under siege. However, in spite of these issues negatively impacting all races of Americans and there are more, the media's tactics have managed to keep our country divided along racial and moral lines while the powerbase continues to control the economic infrastructure, while we argue over trivialities. That is why there is a call by GOP leader Rush Limbaugh and the tea-baggers for conservatives to "take back their country." But how? The manner in which this is done is through Code Words? Now listen up, ding-ding-ding, that's the school bell ringing as class is in session.

Defined, a code word is a "euphemistic or politically acceptable catchword or phrase used instead of a blunter or less acceptable term." In common terms, code words are used to describe a "euphemism" or word substitution of an agreeable or inoffensive expression and phrase that may offend or suggest something that is unpleasant.

Now it is imperative that you grasp this concept, because it is meant to prepare you to interpret the "divisive language" that the mainstream media is and will continue to use during each election season. You will become a "code cracker" of sorts while watching and listening to these biased media programs. For example, consider this media statement:

Perception: The Official report said the diplomats had a "frank and serious discussion." **Reality:** Frank and serious discussion is code word for an Angry Argument. Let us continue by reviewing the common media code words that you will hear throughout the election cycle.

1) Drastic Slide: Fox News reported on their website entitled, "Far from over!" And the article stated that, **Perception:** Karl Rove would crunch the numbers on Obama's "drastic slide" in the polls. **Reality:** Senator Barack Obama is a formidable Presidential candidate who must be neutralized by the Republican Party. Therefore "drastic slide" is code word for phenomenal success.

2) Card Carrying Liberal: There was a discussion on the Bill O'Reilly show and when he was interviewing actor Matthew Modine, the word "Card carrying liberal" came up to describe non-republicans. **Perception:** This word often refers to those persons that conservatives despise. **Reality:** This contempt is levied towards any group of legislators who pass any legislation that will improve the lifestyles of the poor and dispossessed people of our society that have been rendered invisible, and those persons who vote for them. After all, the Government and its funds are to be used solely to make conservatives rich, at the expense of the poor.

Consider this dialogue between Bill O'Reilly, the bastion of conservatism and Mr. Modine: O'REILLY: OK. Do you believe in income redistribution? Do you believe that the government should come in and take a huge chunk of your assets and give it to people less fortunate, which is what the Democratic Party and the liberal philosophy pretty much stands for now?

Do you believe it?

MODINE: I believe in public education and public health. And I think that people that don't have the opportunity to have a good education, good health care deserve for me to help them, to give them a hand up.

O'REILLY: OK.

MODINE: If you were thirsty, and I had water...

O'REILLY: I give a lot of money to charity. And I assume you do, too.

MODINE: It would be my responsibility to see you do, too.

O'REILLY: I assume you give a lot of money. I do. But I don't want the government forcing me and taking the lion's share of my earnings because I don't really trust the government.

MODINE: Well, this doesn't have anything to do with the government. This is about humanity. and if you really think about what it is to be a liberal, you understand that liberal is being a humanitarian.

Here lies in this discourse, the very foundation of the Republican and Conservative belief system. Most people, not all, formed, adjoined, and espoused a conservative party or club to legislate and incorporate their belief system. To create laws that will maximize their profits, give them a lion's share of income, while ensuring that anyone else who is not rich or is not a Republican's friend will remain insolvent. The state of affairs that this economy is currently experiencing is a prime example. There is not one member of the Conservative party that is struggling financially, yet we have the remainder of Americans suffering foreclosures, lay-offs, indigence, starvation, and hopelessness, while Conservatives like Phil Gramm can tell us to "Stop Whining because things are not so bad." In other words, we in the Republican Party are enjoying a luxurious and exclusive life where our economy is flourishing, so I am not sure why you feel things are so bad, it is all in your minds. I got mine, and if you don't have yours, shame on you. Let us continue this journey of truth.

3) Mentor and Angry: Interesting enough, when I conducted a word search of "angry" at the Fox News site, an article written by Father Jonathan Morris on Black Liberation theology and Rev. Wright came up. **Perception:** Now on the surface when one sees the word anger especially in the context of "angry black man," we shudder with fear and discontent. We are fearful as we see the images and sound-bytes of Reverend Jeremiah Wright that has saturated the mainstream media's airwaves, which continues to depict him as an (code words) angry, raving, divisive, and racist black man who is shamelessly attacking the pure and chaste United States of America; then when one adds the code word "mentor" into this one-sided conversation, then the "guilt by association" postulation that ties Senator Obama to Reverend Wright's labels, somehow becomes legitimized. But not so fast, remember there is a deeper meaning at work here that sometimes transcends our perception.

Reality: Conveniently, Fox decided to have a Republican clad in a clerical collar address this issue. At first I gave him the benefit of the doubt, believing that he was a true man of God. You know one who understands the intimate relationship between a Pastor who is the steward of God's church, and one of Christ's disciples, yet he decided to embrace ignorance and squander this opportunity to do as God called him to do and "uplift" and not "tear down the Man of God." Be that as it may, he disregarded the fact that Rev. Wright was no longer the Pastor of then Senator Obama's church, and framed his rant based upon the past 20 years, coupled with a 7 year old sound-byte to pronounce judgment on both Senator Obama and Rev Wright. This practice is not usually one engaged in by clergy, but it is one that is engaged in by a conservative organization with an agenda. So to that end, let us discuss these code words of mentor and angry.

Father Morris stated that "honest critics would admit that Senator Obama is no Rev. Wright." Let us first examine his statements in this passage before we continue with our discourse:

"Liberation theology finds its historical roots in a school of Latin American theological thought made famous in the 1960s and 1970s. In these turbulent years of dictators and militants, some Catholic priests and bishops, Protestant pastors, and laity sought to revolutionize the church's understanding of its own salvific mission. Instead of giving priority to the spiritual redemption of the soul, they turned their sites almost exclusively to social justice. Their materialistic view of humanity blurred the vertical and horizontal dimensions of the church. They stopped looking up at the Prince of Peace. Their Jesus was now a warrior. Wrong! Liberation theology according to its founder Dr. James Cone argues, this Black liberation theologian says the overriding message of Old Testament prophets — and Jesus Christ — is "a condemnation of the nation and of the religious [establishment] ... for oppressing the poor." (Courtesy Union Theological Seminary)

Cone explains that at the core of black liberation theology is an effort — in a white dominated society, in which black has been defined as evil, and white as superior, is to make the gospel relevant to the life and struggles of American blacks, and to help black people learn to love themselves. It's an attempt; he says "to teach people how to be both unapologetically black and Christian at the same time." Father Morris somehow wants to compartmentalize Jesus as a passive, weak man who was concerned with only peace. But my bible tells me that this same Jesus was wrought with anger as he turned over the tables in the Jewish temple. So at times anger is not only justified but it is biblical. Jesus is indeed shown as displaying anger in the Matthew 21:12-13. However, consider the context of each. In the case of the temple, Jesus threw out usurers and others who were taking advantage of the poor. He was angry at the wrong they were doing and also at the blatant disrespect for God they showed by doing wrong even in God's temple. In the next passage, Jesus was angry with the Pharisees, who wanted to catch Jesus breaking one of their laws, yet were unwilling to consider the morality of the law or to believe in Jesus despite seeing the miracles he did. In both cases, Jesus was angry with people who were doing wrong and refused to listen to God.

And is such anger wrong? To say "God is never angry" or "God should never be angry" is to say that God shouldn't be angry when innocent people are hurt or killed, or that he shouldn't be angry that the Holocaust took place, or when Katrina neglect occurred, or when innocent lives were lost over the years due to U.S. Foreign policy. There are different kinds of anger, as described in the Merriam-Webster dictionary: ANGER, IRE, RAGE, FURY, INDIGNATION, and WRATH mean an intense emotional state induced by displeasure. ANGER, the most general term, names the reaction but in itself conveys nothing about intensity or justification or manifestation of the emotional state, tried to hide his anger. IRE, more frequent in literary contexts, may suggest greater intensity than anger, often with an evident display of feeling cheeks flushed dark with ire. RAGE suggests loss of self-control from violence of emotion i.e. screaming with rage. FURY is overmastering destructive rage that can verge on madness. i.e. in her fury she accused everyone around her of betrayal. INDIGNATION stresses righteous anger at what one considers unfair, mean, or shameful i.e. a refusal to listen that caused general indignation. WRATH is likely to suggest a desire or intent to seek revenge or punish i.e. rose in his wrath and struck his tormentor to the floor.

Indignation, as described above, is what could be called righteous anger - anger at wrongdoing. This is Jesus' anger, for Jesus is angered by wrongdoing. Let's go deeper by examining Father Morris's statements.

"Many liberation theologians in Latin America had good objectives. They were personal witnesses of the great disparity between the rich and the poor and refused to stand by with their arms folded. They saw how some indigenous peoples, blacks, Mestizos, and the poor rural and urban masses were being manipulated and abused by the powerful. But their horizontal and materialistic vision of man led them to adopt elements of Marxist philosophy, including "class struggle" — the pitting of the poor against the rich. In this theological context, the victim status of the lower classes justifies in some cases the use of force to rectify social inequality."

When you hear Rev. Jeremiah Wright talk about social and racial inequality in America, the influence of liberation theology is painfully evident. It is of a different stripe (not violent), but it is there. His unconditional support for Louis Farrakhan (Nation of Islam leader) and other alleged militants, his crude language, the selective content of his preaching, and his conspiracy theories against the government, are divisive. And they are divisive in a similar way as followers of liberation theology in Latin America.

Even though Rev. Jeremiah Wright has now retired as pastor of Trinity United Church of Christ, the language of black liberation theology is still detectable in the church's literature. Here, for example, is the first sentence of the church's mission statement on its official Web site.

Trinity United Church of Christ is called by God to be a congregation that is not ashamed of the gospel of Jesus Christ and that does not apologize for its African roots! As a congregation of baptized believers, we are called to be agents of liberation not only for the oppressed, but also for all of God's family.

"Like the good people at Trinity, I believe strongly in the need to turn faith into action in our common struggle against social injustice and inequality. However, I do not believe anger, hatred, and a clinging to victim status are proper and effective tools to achieve this goal. That is what we saw in their former pastor. I cannot picture Jesus like that. And that has nothing to do with Jesus not being black." After hearing these words, then examining the previous scriptures, notwithstanding his racially insensitive comments on Jesus' race, one has to wonder, "What Jesus does Father Morris know?"

4) Elitist: During this grueling campaign with the media continuously hanging on Senator Obama's every word, the Presidential race moved to the state of Pennsylvania, and again ignored the authenticity and truthfulness of his comments and decided to attack him with a new code word of being "Elitist". As both Senator(s) McCain and Clinton have stated and I quote, "I think that Senator Obama's comments are Elitist". The interesting thing about their comments was the hypocrisy of them. Here we have these two Presidential candidates being backed by very wealthy lobbyists (McCain) and the Bilderberg Group that consists of a conglomerate of multi-billionaires which gives them ulterior motives for making such a ludicrous comment.

However, to place these statements into their proper context, an Elitist is defined as "a belief that certain persons or members of certain classes or groups deserve favored treatment by virtue of their perceived superiority, as in intellect, social status, or financial resource. Now if you deconstruct this definition, you will observe that the term Elitist argues that its use pertains to the description of certain persons or groups who possess certain characteristics. (Webster's dictionary) These characteristics include a certain socioeconomic class, a superiority complex to include intellect, an exclusive social standing (they are considered to be the blue bloods of society), and superior financial resources (they are filthy rich). In addition, "Socioeconomic status (SES) is a combined measure of an individual's or families economic and social position relative to others, based on income, education, and occupation. However, in a socioeconomic context, income will be the dominant factor determining Elitism.

Income: Income refers to any flow of earnings received. Income can also come in the form of unemployment or workers compensation, social security, pensions, interests or dividends, royalties, trusts, alimony, or other governmental, public, or family financial assistance. Income can be looked at in two terms, relative and absolute. Absolute income, as theorized by economist, is the relationship in which assets increases, as well as consumption, but not at the same rate.

"Ashamedly there is a wealth gap, like income inequality, that is very large in the United States. Specifically, there exists a racial wealth gap due in part to income disparities and differences in achievement. According to Thomas Shapiro, in his 2004 book entitled, The Hidden Cost of Being African American: How Wealth Perpetuates Inequality, "there are differences in savings (due to different rates of incomes), inheritance factors, and discrimination in the housing market lead to the racial wealth gap."

Shapiro claims that savings increase with increasing income, but African Americans cannot participate in this, because they make significantly less than whites. Additionally, rates of inheritance dramatically differ between African Americans and whites. The amount a person inherits either during a lifetime or after death, can create different starting points between two different individuals or families.

These different starting points also factor into housing, education, and employment discrimination. A third reason Shapiro offers for the racial wealth gap are the various discriminations African Americans must face, like redlining and higher interest rates in the housing market. These types of discrimination feed into the other reasons why African Americans end up having different starting points and therefore fewer assets.

When analyzing a family's SES, the spouse and the subject's economic and social positions are examined, as well as combined incomes, versus economic inequality with an individual, when their own attributes are assessed.

As evidenced by their research, there are definite divides in this country that is delineated according to occupation, income, and education which encompasses SES or Socioeconomic Status. Socioeconomic status is typically broken into three categories, high SES, middle SES, and low SES to describe the three areas a family or an individual may fall into. For the sake of argument, when placing a family or individual into the elitist category, all of these categories are assessed. So in the contextual parameters of this deconstructed definition, let us consider the incomes, education, and occupation of the three presidential candidates that places them in a certain socioeconomic class that will assist us in our analysis of who actually exemplifies the term Elitist which transcends a mere statement, for it is a way of life:

The Candidates

Senator Hillary Clinton and her husband, former President Clinton. Senator Hillary was educated at Wellesley College, B.A. and Yale University, J.D., her husband, William, attended Georgetown and Oxford Universities, B.A. and Yale University, J.D. respectively. They have earned more than $100 million since he left office, much of it from his speeches, her campaign said. The couple earned more than $20 million in 2007. (Source: AP) Combined Income: $120 million dollars Senator McCain was educated at the exclusive, prestigious U.S. Naval Academy, B.S., although he touts honesty, straight talk, he had political aspirations that needed funding. Therefore in 1979, 24 year old Cindy Hensley (sole heir to the Anheuser Busch fortune), now McCain, met and mutually pursued an affair with a 42 year old married man with 3 children.

McCain dumped his family and married Hensley less than a year later. Unfortunately, for Carol Shepp, his wife of fourteen years, his adopted two young children Douglas and Andrew, and their daughter Sidney, when McCain made this selfish decision to abandon them, they did not factor in to his political aspirations. One thing that I failed to mention was for some persons, if you did not have the fortune of being born into money and socioeconomic status, you can marry in to it!

Senator John McCain earlier reported earnings of $405,409.00 in 2007. That amount did not account for his wife's income. Under a prenuptial agreement, the McCain's have separate assets and file separate tax returns. Cindy McCain, the heiress of a large Arizona beer distributorship, is said to be worth $100 million. However, as of July 13, 2008 and unreported during this election cycle, InBev agreed to buy Anheuser-Busch for a total value of $52 billion, which would create a new company to be named Anheuser-Busch InBev. McCain's wife, Cindy, owns the third largest Anheuser-Busch distributor in the country - which means she would stand to profit by partnering with a company that is in business with the Cuban Government. Look for a covert call from Senator McCain for the President to loosen American restrictions and embargos on Cuba.

Combined Income: $100,405,409.00 dollars plus proceeds from the InBev deal (estimated) Senator Obama was educated at Occidental College and Columbia University respectively, B.A. And Harvard Law School, J.D., Michelle Obama graduated from Princeton University, B.A. and received her J.D. from Harvard University. You will agree that the Obama family both have solid educations, which should have positioned them to raise their socioeconomic status to the level of the other two candidates, however, there is a characteristic that separates the two in the purpose of them obtaining their degrees. This decision transcends wealth, prestige, status, or elitism. Both persons decided to forego their Golden Parachutes, for public service in the inner cities of Chicago; Senator Obama as a community organizer, and Lady Michelle as a manager at the University of Chicago hospitals.

Economically, then Senator Barack Obama and his wife, Michelle, paid $1,396,772 in federal taxes after earning $4,139,965 in adjusted gross income in 2007. Most of their earnings came from book sales.

Combined Income: $4,139,965.00 dollars When consideration is given to the average salaries of the Clintons and McCains, it appears that the Obama family comes short by about $106,000,000.00 dollars. By most standards, one would consider them to be in the middle class. Indicative of these salaries, it provides a testament of the economical disparity between the rich and the middle class. Important to note, is the fact that these disparities occur regardless to the fact that they have law degrees from Ivy League schools. How does one explain these disparities? Moreover, how does one even make an association to the elite where Senator Obama is concerned when he fails the litmus test of elitism? Remember, elite suggests certain characteristics. These characteristics include a certain socioeconomic class, a superiority complex to include intellect, an exclusive social standing (they are considered to be blue bloods of society), and superior financial resources (they are filthy rich). In addition, Socioeconomic status (SES) is a combined measure of an individual's or families economic and social position relative to others, based on income, occupation, and education. Therefore, when one considers the fact that although the Obama family possesses the education, they do not possess the income which would have led to the exclusive social standing that is commonly referred to as the Elite of our society. Counter opposing the arguments of the media pundits coupled with the postulations of the two candidates and their families, there are but two families who rise to this level, and it is not the Obama family. Consequently, one must ask why Senator Obama would be charged with such a ludicrous label. As we talked about earlier, People often times are conditioned to view reality on the content of the labels, messages and situations they encounter, the subjective interpretation of these interactions, and how they make decisions, and shape future behavior. There is no objective reality. People interpret the reactions of others, and this interpretation assigns meaning.

Social Reaction is said to pick up on these concepts of interaction and interpretation.

Throughout our lives, we as a people, are given a variety of symbolic labels as "pretty," "smart," "most likely to succeed," "unpatriotic," "un-American," "Elitist," "angry," "lacking judgment as a leader," "soft," "inexperienced," "Marxist," "Capitalist," "Socialist," and these labels are given to represent and define not just one trait but the whole person. Now you remember the "Media Game" of assigning labels? However, always remember that for every media perception, there is an intelligent reality of the reader based upon research. Let's go deeper.

5) Marxist: The latest buzz in the Republican circles began with yet another attempt to define then Senator Obama when disgraced and not yet convicted former Senator Tom DeLay referred to Senator Obama as a "Marxist!" To further quote the oxymoronic news website "The American Thinker," and its author, Lance Fairchok whom I will refer to as simply "moronic," who states that Barak Obama has a thing for Marxists. "He befriends them, listens to their counsel, and he even hires them to work in his campaign."

Perception: The attempt here again is to try and create an image based upon the labeling of Senator Obama as someone who is unscrupulous. This is derived from the perception of this country to allow persons with ulterior motives, and who have no relationship with him define him. Their success in utilizing this code word against President Obama is dependent upon the public's ability to classify the term "Marxist" interchangeably with the term "Communist" based upon past media subliminal messages. Interestingly enough, the words lobbyist, capitalist, and oligarchic never made the cut.

Reality: In spite of the attempts by the right to label Senator Obama as a Marxist, let us realistically consider the terminology used to describe him, and the fundamental differences between communism and Marxism. The basic difference between Communism in general and Marxism in particular, is that Communism aims at the realization of a "Communist society," while Marxism is a theoretical-practical framework based on the analysis of "the conflicts between the powerful and the subjugated." While there are many theoretical and practical differences among the various forms of Marxism, most forms of Marxism share:

- A belief that capitalism is based on the exploitation of workers by the owners of capital.

- A belief that people's consciousness of the conditions of their lives reflects the dominant ideology which is in turn shaped by material conditions and relations of production.

- An understanding of class in terms of differing relations of production, and as a particular position within such relations.

- An understanding of material conditions and social relations as historically malleable.

- A view of history according to which class struggle, the evolving social conflict between classes with opposing interests, structures each historical period and drives historical change.

- A belief that this dialectical historical process will ultimately result in a replacement of the current class structure of society with a system that manages society for the good of all, resulting in the dissolution of the class structure and its support.

CAPITALISM IN ACTION

I am sure that by now you know that we have elected a President (Barack Obama) who has been an advocate of re-empowering the Middle Class with an economic stimulus package that will include tax relief. Unfortunately, this timely message has been shrouded and corrupted by a message sponsored by a capitalist system, who has accused and labeled the President elect and those politicians who have concurred with the President's message, as socialists who want to "spread the wealth around." Translated, President-elect Obama understands what he has lived. He has risen from the desolate paths of poverty to the top executive position in the United States of America, but what makes him unique from other success stories is that he did not forget where he came from and he has accomplished the first kingdom rule of being a public servant that the Christian right should grasp; to "place the care of people before the selfish interests of himself and his friends!" He did not take the elevator to the penthouse and refuse to send it back down to pick up others. He did not become a Supreme Court justice through quotas and then dismantle affirmative action programs. He simply had the character and possessed the altruism to never forget his experiences and struggles. However, for several more weeks, he remained the Presidential elect and not the President, that is George W. Bush Jr. and he is still a republican in charge of our country. So currently, as it has been during his final term in office, Anything Goes! Unfortunately, he and his republican colleagues' free-wheeling, laissez-faire managerial style has managed to collapse the economy world-wide and crash wall street which has sent rippling effects throughout our economy causing a recession that we can only hope we can recover from.

However what I find equally alarming is how this crisis is being addressed by our elected public servants; bailing out all of the capitalist institutions who exploited the middle and working class citizens of this country, while they became very wealthy and we were foreclosed on, lost our jobs, could not feed our families, and remained shackled with debt. To some of you, this is seemingly not problematic! After all, they argue that the people should not have been so fiscally irresponsible and they would not have ended up in this crisis! Normally I would agree with you, however, there are several realities that I cannot get past that leaves me in emotional contempt towards our alleged public servants.

Reality One: The money that is being spent so freely belongs to We the taxpayers. You know the ones who get taxed 11 months out of the year, and mysteriously owe more money in the 12th month. (April 15) It would be refreshing to have access to some of our money when we truly need it.

Reality Two: Our elected Public Servants are stewards of the taxpayers or the United States citizen's money. So as stewards, they have a fiduciary duty to cut governmental costs, and to assist every American citizen to reach a period of self-sufficiency in this society. So in case many of our representatives do not recognize this picture, it is commonly referred to as Public Service.

Reality Three: The United State's citizenry transcends Wall Street, the Federal Reserve and the financial institutions that many of our public self-servants in Washington D.C. hold near and dear to their hearts! Our citizenry are also comprised of the poor, the middle class, and the auto industry that employs more of our citizens than the financial institutions. After all, when the smoke clears, we are the only groups who continue to drown in debt with no relief in sight.

Reality Four: The reluctance of our representatives to bail-out the Big Three automakers is related to their economic infrastructure being tied to many unionized middle and working class citizens in this country. As I said before and I will reiterate, the objective is never to address the needs of the taxpayers who placed them into office, and afforded the lifestyles that they enjoy today. The objective is to keep the taxpayers shackled in debt, while they keep the oppressive financial institutions solvent. Their rationale is to keep the taxpayers paying into a credit based capitalist system, making the owners rich, while the taxpayers die in poverty. For example, the headlines in the 11/26/08 Atlanta Journal Constitution that read "An $800 Billion Commitment: Feds try to make borrowing easier." You read correctly and this is not a typographical error. Under this Capitalistic system, everything is aimed to create opportunities to place the consumer further in debt as the federal government who is supposed to represent the taxpayer, is giving our money to financial institutions with the objective of increasing "consumer lending." I have an idea! Why doesn't the federal government give the consumers money to spend at these institutions? I mean we the people would love to be rescued from credit card, student loan, mortgage, and automobile loan debt that is overwhelming us. Create a rescue plan for the taxpayers so that we can gain confidence in the economy and begin spending again and traveling again. Anything absent a relief plan for the people is going to keep the economy stagnant because spending will continue to decrease.

Reality Five: As stewards of the taxpayer's money, there should be an expectation or desire by our representatives to allocate to the citizens of this country money for assistance with our outstanding debts. However, it appears that in spite of the fact that everyone acknowledges that the money belongs to the "taxpayers," the monies have only been allocated to capitalist institutions that consist of many of our representative's wealthy friends who pay less taxes than we do. Yet they receive multi-billion dollar bail-outs? I sincerely hope that the affected citizens of this country who have been systematically "left behind" now realize that it has never been about addressing their interests as a constituency! On the contrary, it has always been about empowering, and then re-empowering the capitalists of this country. On its face, these bail-outs are simply socialist programs and corporate welfare for the wealthy. This clannish behavior transcends Racial, Democratic, Republican, or Independent party lines, as the common denominator of its enactment is motivated by money, position, and power, simply put, it is Capitalism in action. What will you do to ensure your place at the table during the next election cycle?

6) Socialist: The current trend among the Capitalists in this society to include the Rupert Murdoch's Fox News, New York Post, Rush Limbaugh, and other non-journalist, tabloid media personalities who represent America's secret society is to refer to President Obama with the code word of socialist. Important to note, is that these baseless accusations are being made by persons who are content with the unregulated Oligarchy form of government that they have flourished under. It is no wonder that Mr. President is experiencing such resistance, racial slurs, undermining, innuendo, distractions, and false labeling while he is attempting to curtail the destruction of this country at the hands of the Grand Ole Party (G.O.P.). However, because this label is so far out of scope in the description of Mr. President, it deserves to be addressed in this section. **Perception:** The selfish and greedy capitalists who were instrumental in destroying this economy create the imagery here. Their goal is to paint the picture of a socialist President who is totally opposed to anyone who has worked hard to become successful in life. Seemingly, due to President Obama's contempt to their successes, he has somehow sought to penalize the wealthy by taking money from them through taxation, and redistributing the money to persons and groups who were fiscally irresponsible thus rewarding undeserving citizens. **Reality:** Socialism defined is a broad set of economic theories of social organization advocating public or state ownership and administration of the means of production and distribution of goods, and a society characterized by equal opportunities for all individuals, with a fair or egalitarian method of compensation. Socialists mainly share the belief that capitalism unfairly concentrates power and wealth among a small segment of society that controls capital, creates an unequal society, and does not provide equal opportunities for everyone in society. Western European social critics were the first, modern socialists – Robert Owen,

Charles Fourier, Pierre-Joseph Proudhon, Louis Blanc, Charles Hall and Saint-Simon, who criticized the excessive poverty and inequality consequence of the Industrial Revolution, and advocated reform via the egalitarian distribution of wealth and the transformation of society to small communities without private property. Important to note and what the G.O.P. has fully embraced, is that from the nineteenth century onwards, Capitalism has developed immense productive forces. The problem here is that it has done so at the cost of excluding the great majority of citizens from influence over production. It put the rights of ownership before the rights of Man. It created a new class of wage earners without property or social rights. It sharpened the struggle between the classes. Although the world contains resources, which could be used to provide a decent life for everyone, Capitalism and its advocates has been incapable and disinterested in satisfying the elementary needs of this country's population. It proved unable to function without devastating crises and mass unemployment. It has produced social insecurity and glaring contrasts between rich and the now working poor, which is the linchpin of the class struggle between the G.O.P., the secret society and our President. It resorted to the Grand Ole Party's imperialist expansion and colonial exploitation of the masses, thus making conflicts, between nations and races more bitter. That is the essence of socialist policy and the description of capitalism, which leads me to debunk the compelling argument concerning my President being labeled as a socialist. The manner in which I will argue my point is through the description of socialism compared with President Obama's policy. I believe that the presentation of this empirical data will debunk the capitalist label that has been imposed upon Mr. Obama by these selfish miscreants.

Definition: Socialism advocates public or state ownership and administration of the means of production and distribution of goods, and a society characterized by equal opportunities for all individuals with a fair method of compensation. **Reality:** The focal point of President Obama's economic stimulus plan is to take American taxpayers' money and to disburse it in such a way as to allow the masses to reap the benefits of a return on their investment in America (paying taxes) over decades. An investment from the perspective that if anyone has been taxed all of their lives, then they have literally invested into America's economy. Considering the fact that the accusers of the President have never paid their fair share of taxes in to America's economy, then they should not really have any objections to rendering unto Caesar what belongs to Caesar. It is the least they can do since they have utilized the taxpayers' money to become wealthy. In addition, when one considers the fact that most Americans have lost their jobs, are facing foreclosures, cannot feed their families, are dying each day for lack of healthcare, and cannot retire, distributing money to the respective States so that they can make our streets safe by hiring law enforcement/firefighters/teachers, and to assist the States who are facing lay-offs, budget shortfalls, and high levels of unemployment; then this investment in the American people is well worth the return. I understand that many Republicans do not recognize a President who takes his appointment by the people, and service to the people seriously, so they continue to obstruct progress. I suspect that we all understand that this Bush administration did everything they could, with the support of John McCain and his fellow republicans, to hand over as much of the federal government to these top-tier corporate elites, by paying them from the pockets of ordinary Americans furthering their wealth, while the economy never expanded except through the gains acquired through the financial sector, which then invested their Treasury obtained wealth in these "new-fangled", sure-fired, 99.9% guaranteed exotic (but toxic) securities. These rich oligarchs would throw a few temporary jobs to the "peasants" below making it appear like they were "creating" new jobs through Trickle-Down economics. Where are those jobs now? Gone, my friends! "But there will be more wars, my friends."

If President Obama were a socialist, then he would simply bypass the State's government officials stonewalling and their political posturing, and send checks to the American people directly through a method of direct and fair compensation, but he did not. He is also opposed to the many Republican Governors request to become sovereign entities, which debunks the socialism premise of public and state ownership.

Definition: Socialism advocates criticizes the excessive poverty and inequality consequence of the Industrial Revolution, and advocated reform via the egalitarian distribution of wealth and the transformation of society to small communities without private property. **Reality:** Part of the President's economic plan is not only to address the extreme poverty in our nation (Katrina), but also to invest $275 billion dollars to help Americans to retain their homes and properties while allowing the mortgage companies who manipulated mortgages and sold these mortgages to insolvent clients without prosecution. This does not sound like a man who is interested in transforming society into small communities without private property, as he is actually investing in America's opportunity to own private property. He also plans to increase the monies to unemployment benefits nationwide while he creates jobs to restore Americans dignity thus prompting them to contribute to our economy. Such forward and progressive thinking by the leader of the free world debunks the foundation of socialism that advocates an equal distribution of wealth without that wealth being earned. Therefore, to label President Obama a socialist has to make a person wonder. Where does that accusation come from when right before our eyes the Republican Party has delivered those very clear and bountiful socialist goods to the elites? Under a democracy, the government's general fund is to be used for public good and not handed over to a bunch of corporate elite oligarchs. As a result of this transfer of the government tax dollars to these privileged top-tier elitists, either through the war machine, Homeland Security spying, surveillance programs, Wall Street bail-outs, etc. A result of these decisions have caused ordinary Americans to drive over poorly maintained roads and bridges, send their kids to decaying and overcrowded public schools, continue to watch health care expenses skyrocket and become more inaccessible to nearly 50 million of us, the dismissal of a national alternative energy nationwide network, as well as a global warming solution pushed aside, our food supply becoming more and more dangerously depleted, while being consolidated into the hands of the rich corporate elites, and finally, college educations becoming unattainable for many very bright and competent students. These same (wink wink) fiscally responsible Republicans from the Bush administration have said that there is no money for anything related to the ordinary family, but there is darn plenty for the crooks and thieves who committed fraud through our financial sector.

In Summation, President Obama understands that this country was built upon the premise of greed and exploitation of the middle class for profit. He also understands that over the last eight years, the middle class of this country were an afterthought, experienced a political shakedown, and needed restoration. That is why he has been making bold and authoritative decisions after seeking counsel from the best economic minds of this country. The Rights' attempt to place the President in a box through the use of code words has only served to exacerbate the problem; it gives me great pride to see that most intelligent people in this country are not listening to their divisive rhetoric.

7) Un-American: According to bibleanswer.org, an investigative journalist and a national defense analyst accused then Democratic Presidential nominee and front-runner Barack Obama of once having ties with members of the Communist Party USA.

Cliff Kincaid, president of America's Survival, has teamed up with Herbert Romerstein, a former investigator with the U.S. House Committee on Un-American Activities. Both have compiled evidence of Obama's past ties with Communist Party figures. Kincaid says while a teenager in Hawaii, "Obama was mentored by a Communist Party USA member known as Frank Marshall Davis." "He was a Stalinist agent. And this is a fellow who clearly had a major influence over a young Barack Obama," he points out.

"Davis most likely filled Obama with un-American thoughts and ideas", Kincaid contends. Kincaid says their evidence then documents how Obama went off to college where he became friends with various Marxist professors and attended socialist conferences. After college, Obama returned to Chicago and began his political career. "And lo and behold, he lands right in the middle of another communist network," he continues.

According to Kincaid, this new association involved the former members of the Communist Students or a Democratic Society, and the Weather Underground terrorists Bernadine Dohrn and Bill Ayers.

"[These people] … launched Barack Obama's political career in their own home," he details. Kincaid hopes the media will ask Obama to explain his past associations with these individuals.

Perception: If one is said to be un-American, it is most often used by a person commenting on the beliefs or actions of others that they believe are contrary to American values. It implies a substantial deviation from US norms and may extend to internal subversion, espionage, treason and attacking the American way. If one is said to be un-American, he or she is thought to be unfit to work in any capacity that is related to government.

Reality: Un-American? President Obama? Wow! Before we address this code word, we must first determine what the definition of American is. According to definitions, an American is anyone who is a citizen of the United States. Therefore, President Obama by birth is an American. This begs the question of why would a citizen be questioned about his citizenship. In other words, why would President Obama be called "Un-American" when by definition he is indeed a citizen and an American? Simple! This is yet another label or code word that is being used by the Republican Party and supporters of the status quo, to elicit a negative response from the citizens of America. If I can continue to interject subliminal messages into the minds of Americans that suggest that one of its citizens is somehow "against America," or is "un-American," then perhaps there may be a shifting in the way President Obama is viewed and perceived with the question that follows: Can Barack Obama be trusted as a President? You know, President of the U. S. is about as American as you can get! The term "un-American" may be used in ad hominem attacks, meant to quash the arguments of American opponents by depicting them as subversive, unpatriotic or deviant. As a result, it is often used in a satirical or sarcastic manner; similarly, its frequent appearance in situations that do not merit its use has further diluted its original, pre-McCarthyism meaning. In other words, people' using the code word "Un-American" uses it as a diversionary tactic, which takes the attention away from the issues that they are disinterested in addressing. For example, the housing crisis, the economy, the Katrina debacle, the high gas prices, the rich becoming richer, the capitalist bail-out, Bush clandestine contractual CEO bonuses, while the rest of the nation continues to struggle financially and economically, are all issues that demand our attention. However, instead of discussing these issues, the media attacks with this diversionary code word, which is insulting to our intelligence. To further bolster my claims and concerns over these journalistic miscreants' accusations of President Obama, is the independent research that I embarked upon concerning who Frank Marshall Davis actually was. In Dr. Kathryn Takara's eloquent depiction, she stated that Frank Davis was a journalist, labor activist, poet, ex-patriate, and resident of Hawaii for almost forty years. As an outsider looking in, he functioned as a significant voice in documenting the progress of the social movement in Hawaii from a plantation to a tourist based economy. In his weekly column, "Frankly Speaking," in the union newspaper The Honolulu Record, he acted as a commentator on the impact of the union movement on the plantation economy in the post war Honolulu scene. As a major national journalist and former editor of the Associated Negro Press, Davis was able to analyze the changing configurations of ethnic groups, class structures and strategies of control. His keen observation of the imperialist forces and his subsequent fall in status due to his outspoken editorials seem a paradox in a "so-called" paradise. His was a voice that inspired and threatened the status quo much like his alleged protégé President Obama. Additionally, like his protégé, Mr. Davis' uniqueness as a black journalist and his middle class status showed that Hawaii was indeed one of the few places in the 1940s and 50s where blacks held roles other than agricultural or service workers in a multi-ethnic setting. Interestingly enough, during my analysis of Mr. Davis, President Obama, the republican code word un-American, and their relationship to one another; I found it necessary to expound upon the glaring parallels to the 60's Hawaii and the current U.S.A.

Striking Similarities

There were class systems in Hawaii, changing configurations of ethnic groups, class structures and strategies of control of the people by their government much like our Oligarchic form of government in the United States.

There was a conflicting parallel of laws and influences between the southern plantation system and plantations in Hawaii, as well as parallels between Blacks and Hawaiians. There were colonial techniques and strategies utilized for dividing the minorities/oppressed groups (aka Willie Lynch techniques of division), binary racism so common, that there are many documented cases of discrimination and racism in Hawaii, much like the good ole U.S. of A.

An Outspoken Gadfly

Anytime a private citizen speaks out against a system of injustice, they are considered as a gadfly that must be neutralized. Malcolm X was murdered, oh excuse me, neutralized; Marcus Garvey was deported, oh I apologize, neutralized; Dr. Martin L. King, Jr. was murdered, again, please forgive me, neutralized. I believe that is the politically correct term to use. Now do not get me wrong, the powers that be have the presence of mind to do whatever they can to neutralize their perceived power-broking opponent, and their connection with the masses. First, they will attempt to dismiss any controversial comments by the Gadfly as fodder. If they are unsuccessful, then they will solicit the cooperation of the governmental system at-large to entrap them somehow in legal jeopardy, through the fabrication of charges against them. They would then solicit political entities such as the I.R.S. to threaten you with an audit, see Brother Al Sharpton, and the government's shenanigans that took place recently with him at the hand of the New York government, as he challenged the cronyism of the court system that seemingly rubberstamped the murder, execution, and legalized lynching of Sean Bell, an unarmed black man by the New York Police department. Or ask Brother Jack Johnson who was finally arrested and convicted of transporting a white woman, (who happened to be his fiancée, Lucille Cameron) across state lines, or I'm sorry, he was arrested for violating the bogus and mean-spirited Mann Act. Or ask Muhammad Ali who was outspoken against the Vietnam War, and was suddenly drafted into the military which is significant when one considers all of the draft dodgers who work in our government and are on our airwaves, it's just un-American. Although he was clearly a "conscientious objector" which was a legal defense, he was convicted and jailed! Interesting!!! Next, there will be an oppositional mainstream media barrage that will release negative articles, innuendoes, sex, lies, and videotape against the Gadfly in an attempt to impeach that gadfly's credibility as a viable, serious, and trustworthy candidate or spokesperson for the masses. Finally, if all else fails, a decision is made to permanently silence you or Murder You which is affectionately referred to as an assassination.

To that end, let us fast forward to the current Presidential race. A race where then Senator Barack Obama (I will refer to Mr. Obama in this book by both titles) had become the odds on favorite to win a seat in the oval office. Ask yourself at this juncture, in this present campaign, which one of these aforementioned areas has not been covered at this point in our 2008 presidential journey? I challenge you before we go any further, as you read this work, To Think for Yourself and Not Let Anyone That You Do Not Know Tell You How to Think. In common terms, do not allow any group control the conversation. Make sure that you do your own research and draw your own conclusions.

8) Unpatriotic: The Supremacists at the Tennessee Republican Party "welcomed" Michelle Obama's visit for a fundraiser Thursday night with an online video that takes the Democratic presidential candidate's wife to task for a comment some considered to be unpatriotic. Michelle Obama was campaigning in Wisconsin last February for her husband, Barack Obama and stated that "For the first time in my adult life, I am proud of my country." Of course this caused a firestorm with the mainstream media with Senator McCain's arm Barbie taking a shot at Senator Obama's wife. "I have always been proud of my country," she so adamantly proclaimed. Well I guess she has always been proud of her country, especially since she has always had the luxury of being treated like a citizen.

Perception: The smoke and mirrors here involve the usual "Guilt by association" game that the G.O.P. continues to play with then Senator Obama. In this case the attempt is to paint a deceptive portrait of a Presidential nominees' wife who is unpatriotic and does not love her country. In the event that they can somehow convince the electorate that his wife does not particularly care for her country, then it only stands to reason that her husband feels the same way. This will translate into mistrust towards then Senator Obama and ultimately cost the Senator the election, after all perception often shrouds reality but let's talk about what's really going on.

Reality: I would somehow imagine that not only is McCain's Barbie proud of her country, but I would argue that her entire subculture is proud of their country! I mean when you have all of the money that you can ever spend in a lifetime, when your background is blue blood, when you have a man who realized this reality early and ditched his wife for a new sponsor of his political ambitions, when you control much of the political powerbase that you are a part of, to the extent that you choose who to help and who to leave in harm's way, coupled with a media group who moonlights as your public relations representatives, then yes I would always be proud of my country. However, if you live in a society where you are oftentimes rendered invisible and impotent; when you are a part of a society that requires brilliance from you, but mediocrity from the rest; when your future, predicted address is Lockup, and your deferred address should have been the university; when you are thought to have the propensity for violence, when you are stereotyped as intellectually inferior, when you are perceived as a threat who walks around with a target on their back; and to add insult to injury, you are said to be whining and imagining your insidiously designed circumstances, (Phil Gramm) and are looked down upon for displaying any emotions so you can't be natural, then you may begin to have thoughts as to who you are and why you believe the way that you do. This leads me to ask, "How can I be proud of a country that has never welcomed me as a citizen?" Be that is may, what we are witnessing during this one-sided media conversation, is that the accusations from the power base contextually, is somehow wielding patriotism as a weapon of the right with the litmus test being the wearing of an American "flag pin" on ones lapel. Need I not remind America that when the bar has been set to such epically low levels to determine patriotism, it relegates this symbol to simply that of a lapel ornament. After all, if this pin is the standard of patriotism, tell us why Klansman and white supremacist David Dukes, whose organizational affiliates once "hung blacks" from trees wears a flag pin? Why does Sean Hannity and Rush Limbaugh who are committed to the destruction of this country and to the demise of our President wears a flag pin? Why does Rudy Giuliani, John McCain, and Newt Gingrich who violates the American and spiritual institution of marriage through adultery and while they were hypocritically leading the charge for impeaching Bill Clinton wears flag pins? And finally, why does the U.S. Republican Senators who have completely undermined the success of the Big 3 American automakers, as they -legislated failure that subsequently led to   bankruptcy of the American car companies Ford and General Motors wear flag pins? You see, when I think of patriotism, I always find myself as a Black man going back to Frederick Douglass's definition of patriotism, the great abolitionist. Douglass says that "a true patriot is a lover of his country who rebukes and does not excuse its sins." A true patriot is a lover of his country. A lover of his country who rebukes and does not excuse its sins, in short, that is what President Obama and Lady Michelle Obama are doing. Perhaps if the Right's attempts to label them are not being conducted with an undercurrent of hate and divisive rhetoric, then perhaps they would understand this reality.

The Telecommunications Act: Giving Hate and Division a Voice

For several years now, I have wondered how the airwaves could have allowed so much vile, hateful language to be aired. I mean this is not just simple unobtrusive language that makes one feel good, or that raises ones spirit. In fact, it is quite the opposite! It is language that continuously defames, debases, attacks ones character, espouses racism and division, and it is done without having to verify any information as factual, and it is without any consequences. It is almost as if the Ku Klux Klan has placed their sheets and hoods in the closet, and has been given microphones and was allowed to spew their venom while cloaked behind a radio frequency and a television signal. However, there are also those persons who are cut from the same cloth, who have been trained well in the art of bigotry and racial warfare. They have been trained on how to successfully assassinate the character of any person who has the audacity to think and speak for themselves. But how did we get to the point where we were relegated to listening to these media bullies and seeing our Intelligence Quotient points decrease on a daily basis? We have the Telecommunications Act of 1996 to thank for this. But what is the telecommunications act of 1996? I am glad that you asked. The Telecommunications Act of 1996 was the first major overhaul of telecommunications law in almost 62 years. The goal of this new law is to let anyone enter any communications business, and to let any communications business compete in any market against any other. However, what it accomplished was violations of all monopolistic laws as a few corporations began to purchase as many radio and television networks as their money could buy, ala Rupert Murdoch.

The Telecommunications Act of 1996 has the potential to change the way we work, live and learn. It will affect telephone service -- local and long distance, radio, cable programming and other video services, broadcast services and services provided to schools. Quite frankly, the Federal Communications Commission (FCC) has a tremendous role to play in creating fair rules for this new era of competition.

Why did this happen? In some cases, industries agreed to the terms of the Act and then went to court to block them. By leaving regulatory discretion to the Federal Communications Commission, the Act gave the FCC the power to issue rules that often sabotaged the intent of Congress. Control of the House passed from Democrats to Republicans, more sympathetic to corporate arguments for deregulation.

And while corporate special interests all had a seat at the table when this bill was being negotiated, the Public did not. Nor were average citizens even aware of this legislation's great impact on how they got their entertainment and information, and whether it would foster or discourage diversity of viewpoints and a marketplace of ideas, which is crucial to democratic discourse. The impact of these laws and the commitment to silence dissent in the conservative State of Georgia has reached critical mass. For in the month of February and during black history month, black talk radio was rendered a serious blow when Magic-FM purchased 92.5 and 107.5, in which the gospel station 92.5 moving to 102.5. These decisions, station movements, and subsequent purchases laid the groundwork for unceremoniously cancelling the Warren Ballentine and Al Sharpton shows respectively. Now Magic-FM has chosen to entertain us while decreasing by 30%, our ability to remain socially conscious on liberal political issues that affect our families on a daily basis with the morning slots consisting of the Steve Harvey, Frank and Wanda, and Tom Joyner shows, and the evening slots consisting of the Michael Baisden show. Do not get me wrong, these are strong line-ups, but these personalities do not possess a primary political and current events format on their shows. However, on every other AM radio station one hears conservative bigoted and hateful rhetoric without opposition. Is this the "dumbing down" of Georgians and if so, then what do we have to look forward to in the 21st century?

Now, as Congress once again takes up major legislation to change telecommunications policy, and as it revisits the Telecom Act, major industries have had nearly a decade to reinforce their relationships with lawmakers and the Administration through political donations and lobbying:

- Since 1997, just eight of the country's largest and most powerful media and telecommunications companies, their corporate parents, and three of their trade groups, have spent more than $400 million on political contributions and lobbying in Washington, according to a Common Cause analysis of Federal records.

- Verizon Communications, SBC Communications Inc., AOL Time Warner, General Electric Co./NBC, News Corp./Fox, Viacom Inc./CBS, Comcast Corp., Walt Disney Co./ABC, and the National Association of Broadcasters, the National Cable & Telecommunications Association, and the United States Telecom Association together gave nearly $45 million in federal political donations since 1997. Of that total, $17.8 million went to Democrats and $26.9 million went to Republicans.

- These eight companies and three trade associations also spent more than $358 million onlobbying in Washington, since 1998, when lobbying expenditures were first required to be disclosed. (Common Cause)

And study after study has documented that profit-driven media conglomerates are investing less in news and information, and that local news in particular is failing to provide viewers with the information they need to participate in their democracy. How the

Telecommunications Act of 1996 got passed, and its unexpected consequences, offer vivid lessons in what happens when public policy is made largely without either informing or consulting the public, and when big corporations, spending millions on political contributions and lobbying in Washington, get to skew the policy debate and make promises they do not intend to keep. The story of the Telecom Act also demonstrates what can happen when a federal agency, the Federal

Communications Commission is permitted to issue rules that flout what Congress intended. But the most damaging impact has been to democracy, as citizens confront a media universe that has become less and less diverse and offers them fewer real choices. This universe is dominated by a handful of giant corporations that own radio and TV stations, newspapers, cable systems, movie studios, and concert venues.

The Act prompted a wave of media mergers, reducing the number of diverse voices in radio and television. The creation of radio monoliths such as Clear Channel Communications has driven out minority Radio Station owners, and has made it more and more difficult for new artists to get airtime on commercial radio. It also has meant that in many communities throughout the country, only a small number of radio stations are locally owned. Not able to compete with huge corporations, minority owners in many communities have been driven out of business. Obeisance to the bottom line has meant that local TV stations, increasingly owned by out-of-town corporations, are producing less local news or none at all. And network news staffs have also been shrinking, as the "Project for Excellence in Journalism" noted in 2004: "Most sectors of the media are cutting back in the newsroom, both in terms of staff and the time they have to gather and report the news; journalists face real pressures trying to maintain quality."

The law extended the terms of broadcasters' TV licenses, and made it much more difficult for those licenses to be revoked, making broadcasters far less accountable to the viewers they serve, and much more concerned about the shareholders who want to see them as profitable as possible. Thus creating the opportunity for the employment of the racist, unpatriotic, sacrilegious, atavistic Neanderthals that they portray as journalists, whose sole purposes are to divide the races and incite hate, division, and mistrust among the masses in our country.

Race Dividers and Hatemongers

A Hatemonger is defined as a person who kindles hatred, enmity, or prejudice in others. In this section I will be analyzing and revealing to you the reader, those persons who have been hired in order to exploit Americans unreported illness of racism, hired to keep this country divided along racial lines as they systematically target their viewing audiences and consistently incite feelings of hate, fear, violence and bigotry thus keeping the secret society of the elite and the powerful in control and while maintaining the status quo.

DIVIDER ONE: SEAN HANNITY

Sean Hannity is a conservative political hack and character assassin of limited intelligence, who first gained national recognition as co-host of Fox News Channel's Hannity & Colmes, and he has since began hosting the high-rated talk-radio show in the US, The Sean Hannity Show, as well as another show on Fox News Channel, Hannity's America. In a society that utilizes ghostwriters, he is also the author of two New York Times bestselling books.

Early Life

Hannity is the son of Hugh J. and Lillian F. Hannity. Both his paternal and maternal grandparents were non-U.S. immigrants from Ireland. He has two sisters, Joanne S. Hannity and Therese Grisham (Hannity). He grew up in Franklin Square, New York. During the late 1980s, Hannity worked in construction in Santa Barbara, California, and also as a bartender.

He has lived a nomadic life, wandering aimlessly and residing in Roswell, Georgia; Athens, Alabama; Lloyd Harbor, New York; and Santa Barbara, California respectively. He married Jill Rhodes, a columnist for The Huntsville Times, on January 9, 1993. They have two children, Patrick and Merri Kelly Hannity.

Education

Hannity graduated high school in 1980 from St. Pius X Preparatory Seminary in Uniondale in Long Island, New York. This must be the only alleged "Seminary" that he claimed to have attended when he interviewed Dr. Jeremiah Wright, an actual seminarian which calls his integrity into question. After all, why would you state on national television that you graduated from Seminary when you only graduated from Seminary High School? I will leave the conclusions up to the pundits. Described as "an indifferent student," Hannity dropped out of New York University and another college numerous times for an alleged lack of funds which seems illogical when one considers available financial aid for students in good standing. A more logical premise would be that he was academically inferior, and could not measure up to the numerous universities' standards. But we will soon see how GOP corporate affirmative action began to work on his behalf. After failing in college, he later decided to pursue a radio career. Being given a "hand up" in 2005, he spoke at a graduation ceremony of Jerry Falwell's Liberty University, who awarded him an honorary degree, not an earned degree from an accredited university.

Professional

This grandson of immigrants without a degree in any field let alone journalism, somehow finagled his way into currently becoming a nationally syndicated radio talk show host broadcasting from flagship station WABC (AM) in New York City, co-host of Hannity & Colmes, a Fox News political debate program, and host of Hannity's America, also on Fox News. Wow!

Only in America.

Oh do not get me wrong, of course he was given every opportunity without a higher education, to host his first talk radio show in 1989 at the volunteer college station at UC Santa Barbara, KCSB-FM, while working as a general contractor and despite being enrolled there academically. The show aired for 40 hours of air time; Hannity has since called the show "terrible." Hannity's weekly show was cancelled after less than a year when KCSB management first identified his bigotry and accused him of "discriminating against gays and lesbians" after two shows featuring the book The AIDS Cover-up: The Real and Alarming Facts about AIDS by Gene Antonio. Bailed out again and being the recipient to legalistic affirmative action, the station reversed its decision to dismiss Hannity despite his racism and bigotry, and due in part to a campaign conducted by the Santa Barbara Chapter of the American Civil Liberties Union. Hannity decided against returning to KCSB.

After leaving KCSB, Hannity placed an ad in radio publications lying about his sordid dark background, and presenting himself as "the most talked about college radio host in America," and WVNN in Athens, Alabama (part of the Huntsville market) hired him to be the afternoon talk show host. From Huntsville, he moved to WGST in Atlanta in 1992, filling the slot vacated by Neal Boortz, who had moved to competing station WSB. In September 1996, Fox News founder Roger Ailes hired the then relatively unknown Hannity to co-host the television program Hannity & Colmes with Alan Colmes. Finally, Hannity had a home that gave him the creative freedom to spew his venom, and to spread his gospel of hate, racism, bigotry, supremacy, and separatism without any fears of retribution, thanks to the Telecommunications Act.

Later that year, Hannity left WGST for New York, where WABC had him substitute for their afternoon drive time host during the week of Christmas. In January 1997, WABC put Hannity on the air full-time, giving him the late night time slot. WABC then moved Hannity to the same drive time slot he had filled temporarily a little more than a year earlier. Hannity has been on WABC's afternoon time slot since January 1998.

Important to note, is that Journalist Max Blumenthal, in a June 2005 article published in The Nation, claimed that Hannity had a friendly off-air relationship with white nationalist/supremacist Hal Turner which lasted from 1998 to 2000. While the relationship claims were seconded by Turner himself in a posting on his personal blog, they were denied by Hannity himself and by the program director at WABC, Larry Boyce, who disputed the factual accuracy of many of the allegations.

This begs the question as to what reason did Mr. Turner have to lie? I believe that the public has a reasonable expectation for Hannity to "Man Up" and admit to his relationships, and to be proud of them. After all, he never has a problem exposing anyone else's relationships!

Hannity's radio and television shows draw praise from conservative politicians: "He has a great personality, and the tone counts for a lot," said Texas Sen. John Cornyn. "He's willing to ask questions and challenge the assumptions that many in the mainstream news media are not." He also has been vocally critical of and has drawn criticism from progressive and liberal groups such as Media Matters for America.

In 1995, Fortune magazine reported that Hannity made $5 million per year from his radio show, "and undoubtedly more from Fox" and his related ventures.

However, he has received a neocon standard pay raise of $20 million per year which brings his yearly salary to $20 million per year after signing his contract with Fox for $100 million over 5 years. Do not ever tell me that racism, bigotry, and dumbing down the working class does not pay. However, I wish that I could understand why the average American who is broke, facing foreclosure, and cannot feed their family, would listen to this wing nut and allow him to influence them, when he is paid handsomely to influence public opinion and perception. Whereas the average worker is facing bankruptcy! However, I do find it encouraging to see that you now do not need a college education, or even a journalism degree to be successful. Just be a white supremacy sympathizer. God Bless America and even Fox.

Let Us Examine his Mind and Modus Operandi

I have always believed that if one wants to determine who someone is, then they should examine that person's mind, thoughts, and beliefs, for absent a true relationship these will be your points of reference. However in this case, examine his works, which most persons refer to as his "Intellectual Property" or should I say his literary works, television shows, or public displays of hate, anti-Semitism, and demagoguery.

Literary Works

Hannity is the author of two books, published through the now-defunct <u>Regan Books</u>, which was owned by <u>Rupert Murdoch</u>, <u>owner of Fox News</u> and focused on celebrity authors and controversial topics, sometimes from <u>tabloids</u>. Hannity has stated that he is too busy to read many books, and that he dictated a lot of his own two books into a tape recorder while driving in to do his radio show. Both books reached the <u>nonfiction bestseller list</u>, his second quickly to number one and for five consecutive weeks. Not bad for a college dropout and mental pygmy!

Let Freedom Ring

Hannity's 2002 book, <u>Let Freedom Ring: Winning the War of Ideas in Politics, Media, and Life</u>, has been described as "an unapologetic diatribe against liberalism, questioning its logic and posing questions about the outcome of its agenda for Americans". A reviewer for <u>People</u> magazine stated it is "an amusing tour guide of an imaginary Museum of Modern Left-Wing Lunacy", while noting that Hannity's "outrage is entertaining."

Deliver Us from Evil

Of both of his works, this is perhaps the most telling of the two, and is the most revealing of his deeply rooted hatred that Rupert Murdoch has given a voice to. Hannity's 2005 book, <u>Deliver Us from Evil: Defeating Terrorism</u>, <u>Despotism</u>, <u>and Liberalism</u>, <u>Business Week</u> stated that "Hannity's <u>biases</u> and <u>rhetorical style</u> are revealed from the outset," and that the book is "full of <u>name-calling</u> trumped up as intellectual debate, <u>one-sided history lessons</u> designed to <u>deceive</u> the ill-informed, and good old-fashioned war-mongering", and that it "isn't a good sign that millions of Americans are lapping up copies of this and similarly <u>simple-minded</u> and intemperate books." The <u>St. Louis Post-Dispatch</u> complimented the book for its style of <u>prose</u> that "steers clear of the dully academic" or dumbs down the people, and then continued, "But that's the kindest thing to be said of Deliver Us From Evil. It reads like a long, long transcript of his television and radio shows, with their <u>Manichaean</u> monologues." <u>Publishers Weekly</u> said of the book, "Many readers...will find Hannity's 'irrefutable' evidence to be anything but," and that "his <u>selective use of history</u> and <u>circular logic</u> raise far more questions than it settles." The magazine of the <u>World Future Society</u> summarized, "The <u>polarization</u> typified in this oneeyed rant is a further complication in seeking <u>security</u> in today's world," while the conservative magazine <u>National Review</u> summarized it as providing a "compelling <u>conservative</u> perspective."

Arguing concerning the politically-wedded religious elements in Hannity's book, lawyer and author Jason Carter stated that the book is "an example of not only <u>'us against them'</u> piety but also the inappropriate use of religious language." He stated that "Hannity compares American <u>liberals</u> to <u>terrorists</u> and <u>despots</u> and categorically calls them 'evil'." Carter states that Hannity "sacrilegiously takes a line from <u>the Lord's Prayer</u>, praying for God to deliver us from evil, and uses it to make a political statement as though his argument, his party, or his President would do the delivering." Anyone who graduated from Seminary would never commit this faux pas.

Television

Hannity is a host of <u>Hannity & Colmes</u>, an American political "point-counterpoint"-style television program on the <u>Fox News Channel</u> featuring Hannity and <u>Alan Colmes</u> as co-hosts. Hannity presents the conservative point of view with Colmes providing the liberal viewpoint. Hannity has had on air clashes with show guests such as <u>Fr. Thomas J. Euteneuer</u> of <u>Human Life International</u>, who challenged Hannity on his public dissent from the <u>Catholic Church</u> on the issue of <u>contraception</u>. Hannity has stated that if the Catholic Church were to <u>excommunicate</u> him over the issue, he would join or fall back on <u>Jerry Falwell's</u> <u>Thomas Road Baptist Church</u>, the church associated with <u>Liberty University</u>, who awarded Hannity his honorary <u>bachelor degree</u>. In <u>January 2007</u>, Hannity began a new Sunday night television show on Fox News, <u>Hannity's America</u>. Hannity's America, now that's a scary notion; living in a country with a racist at the helm.

Freedom Concerts

Hannity has hosted <u>country music</u>-themed Freedom Concerts since 2003, billed to help benefit the Freedom Alliance Scholarship Fund, a charity created by <u>Oliver North</u> to provide college scholarships to children with a parent severely disabled or killed in military action. Appearing artists have included <u>Sara Evans</u>, <u>Martina McBride</u>, <u>Lee Greenwood</u>, <u>LeAnn Rimes</u>, <u>Montgomery Gentry</u>, <u>Darryl Worley</u>, <u>Charlie Daniels</u>, and <u>Michael W. Smith</u>.

The Freedom Concerts were held annually in the Northern Star Arena at the <u>Six Flags</u> Great Adventure Amusement Park in <u>Jackson</u>, <u>New Jersey</u> through 2006. In 2007, the annual concert was expanded to a summer series held at locations across the <u>United States</u>, culminating with the September 11 event at Great Adventure marking the sixth anniversary of the September 11, 2001 attacks.

Speakers at the Sept 11, 2007 concert included Oliver North, Newt Gingrich, Republican Presidential candidate Rudy Giuliani and several conservative talk show hosts from WABC Radio, a real Grand Ole Party love fest.

STRANGE RELATIONSHIPS OR NOT?

Having developed an art form out of creating "guilt by associations" allegations without any responsible journalism research having been conducted, which tears down his designated opponent's character; I feel that it is only appropriate to provide the reader with a front row seat into his associations. After all, you can tell a lot about a person by the company that they keep.

From the Teletype of the A.D.L.
Updated: March 22, 2005

According to the Anti-Defamation League this man, White supremacist Hal Turner named three federal court judges with connections to the Matt Hale case as public officials who "need to be reined in." Turner also posted the judges' full names and addresses on his Web site, and read their names during a March 5, 2005, appearance on the Fox News program "Geraldo."

Turner, of North Bergen, New Jersey, has a history of explicitly encouraging extreme violence against Jews, other minorities and government officials. Turner shut down his shortwave radio show in early 2004, allegedly for lack of funds, and has confined his activities since then to posting violent and racist political and societal commentary on his Web site, which he updates frequently. Some of his more recent statements include:

On February 28, 2005, Turner advocated assaulting and killing African-Americans on March 15 to commemorate his birthday: "I think a full day of violence against blacks . . . would be a really nice thing . . . complete with lynchings, church burnings, drive-by

shootings and bombings to put these subhuman animals back in their place."

On January 3, 2005, Turner posted the presidential inauguration parade route on his Web site, saying "it seems to me there can be no protection against a 'Turner Diaries' type of mortar attack or a Hezbollah-type rocket attack launched from outside the security zone. Rest assured, if the fed's [sic] get wiped out, I'll be cheering the TV set!"

In addition to his activities in the United States, Turner recently returned from a trip to Brazil to help generate support for his efforts and those of other white supremacist organizations.

Posted: November 7, 2002

White supremacist radio talk show host Hal Turner, known for incendiary anti-Semitic and racist rhetoric, has caused concern in recent weeks by explicitly encouraging extreme violence against Jews, other minorities, and government officials. Among other measures, Turner has advocated bombings and assassinations.

Turner hosts the "Hal Turner Show" (apparently from his home in North Bergen, New Jersey, although he has a New York City mailing address). The show is broadcast on weekday evenings by shortwave radio station WBCQ out of Monticello, Maine, and reaches most of the country. It is also simulcast on the Internet.

Turner's language and message are often extreme, and in recent months Turner has repeatedly urged acts of violence and terrorism. On September 25, for example, Turner suggested to his audience that "it is time to start killing Jews in the United States, cut their throat as they walk down the street, drive by and blast them with a shotgun...throw Molotov cocktails through their jewelry store windows and then Israel can ask us to stop.

Turner encouraged his audience to "BOMB their synagogues, BOMB their businesses, let's BOMB their homes, that's what I SAY because maybe when these filthy Jew, mother f--- start dying en masse here in the United States, they will pay attention over in Israel." And they talk about Al Qaeda!

Jews are not the only target of Turner's exhortations toward violence.

On October 22, Turner told listeners that "if the INS can't do its job, and round up these illegal aliens, then in my opinion, we people who are here legally should maybe think about drive-by shootings with machine guns in front of every Mexican Consulate and kill every single one of these invaders."

On October 28, when a caller alleged that a federal judge stopped expenditure for a new courthouse because the town was not diverse enough, Turner opined, "I hope somebody assassinates that Federal Judge."

On Halloween, after hearing that "international observers" were coming to monitor the upcoming election in Florida, Turner called on the people of Florida to go to the polls armed and demand that the observers leave - or kill them on the spot if they refuse.

Although Turner claims no formal affiliation with any white supremacist group, his "Hal Turner Radio Network" broadcasts Aryan Nations programs and provides air time to other white supremacist guests such as Matt Hale, leader of the World Church of the Creator. Turner also sponsors other race-baiting programs, among them Michigan white supremacist James Wickstrom's "Yahweh's Truth." As I consider the "modus operandi" of Hal Turner, I am astounded by the striking similarities that the rhetoric of Hannity, Limbaugh, Beck, and the other supremacists have with him!

In the event that you have been anywhere in America during the Presidential campaign, you have viewed the poli-tricks that have been taking place in the media outlets against Democratic frontrunner, then Senator Barack Obama. These all out deceptive tactics by Fox News have involved the airing of a 30-second clip by Senator Obama's Pastor Dr. Jeremiah Wright, the question of race, and the guilt by association argument.

As Roland Martin, one of our preeminent journalists of the 21st century put it so eloquently in a piece on his Essence Blog on March 21, 2008.

The full story behind "Wright's 'God Damn America' sermon."

I just finished listening to the nearly 40-minute sermon Rev. Jeremiah Wright gave on April 13, 2003, titled, "Confusing God and Government."

For those of us watching and listening to the media in the last week, it is better known as the "God Damn America" sermon.

Wright's scriptural focus was Luke 19:37-44 (reading from the New Revised Standard Version).

In this sermon, Wright spoke about the military rule during biblical days, led by Pontius Pilate. It was clear, through his language, such as "occupying military brigade" that he was making an analogy to the war in Iraq.

"War does not make for peace," he said. "Fighting for peace is like raping for virginity.

"War does not make for peace. War only makes for escalating violence and a mindset to pay the enemy back by any means necessary," he said.

He then gets to the thesis of his sermon, saying, "y'all looking to the government for only what God can give. A lot of people confuse God with their government."

Wright criticizes the Bush administration and it supporters for using Godly language to justify the war in Iraq. He equates using God in America as condoning the war in Iraq to the same perspective of Islamic fundamentalists.

"We can see clearly the confusion in the mind of a few Muslims, and please notice I did not say all Muslims, I said a few Muslims, who see Allah as condoning killing and killing any and all who don't believe what they don't believe. They call it jihad. We can see clearly the confusion in their minds, but we cannot see clearly what it is that we do. We call it crusade when we turn right around and say that our God condones the killing of innocent civilians as a necessary means to an end. We say that God understands collateral damage. We say that God knows how to forgive friendly fire.

"We say that God will bless the shock and awe as we take over unilaterally another country, calling it a coalition because we've got three guys from Australia, going against the United Nations, going against the majority of Christians, Muslims and Jews throughout the world, making a pre-emptive strike in the name of God. We cannot see how what we are doing is the same thing that Al-Qaeda is doing under a different color flag – calling on the name of a different God to sanction and approve our murder and our mayhem."

He continues on his thesis of equating government with our God, saying that God sent the early settlers to America to take the country from Native Americans; ordained slavery; and that "we believe that God approves of 6 percent of the people on the face of this earth controlling all of the wealth on the face of this earth while the other 94 percent live in poverty and squalor while we give millions of tax breaks to the white rich."

He also criticizes the "lily white" G-7 nations for controlling the world's capital.

Then Wright speaks to:

1. Governments lie. "This government lied about their belief that all men were created equal. The truth is they believed that all white men were created equal. The truth is they did not even believe that white women were created equal, in creation nor civilization. The government had to pass an amendment to the Constitution to get white women the vote. Then the government had to pass an equal rights amendment to get equal protection under the law for women. The government still thinks a woman has no rights over her own body, and between Uncle Clarence (Thomas), who sexually harassed Anita Hill, and a closet-Klan court, that is a throwback to the 19th century, handpicked by Daddy Bush, Ronald Reagan, Gerald Ford, between Clarence and that stacked court, they are about to un-do Roe vs. Wade, just like they are about to un-do affirmative action. The government lied in its founding documents and the government is still lying today. Governments lie."

"The government lied about Pearl Harbor. They knew the Japanese were going to attack. Governments lie. The government lied about the

Gulf of Tonkin. They wanted that resolution to get us in the Vietnam War. Governments lie. The government lied about Nelson Mandela and our CIA helped put him in prison and keep him there for 27 years. The South African government lied on Nelson Mandela. Governments lie.

"The government lied about the Tuskegee experiment. They purposely infected African American men with syphilis. Governments lie. The government lied about bombing Cambodia and Richard Nixon stood in front of the camera, 'Let me make myself perfectly clear…'" Governments lie. The government lied about the drugs for arms Contra scheme orchestrated by Oliver North, and then the government pardoned all the perpetrators so they could get better jobs in the government. Governments lie.

"The government lied about inventing the HIV virus as a means of people of color.

Governments lie. The government lied about a connection between Al Qaeda and Saddam Hussein and a connection between 9.11.01 and Operation Iraqi Freedom. Governments lie.

"The government lied about weapons of mass destruction in Iraq being a threat to the United States peace. And guess what else? If they don't find them some weapons of mass destruction, they gonna do just like the LAPD, and plant them some weapons of mass destruction. Governments lie.

2. Governments change. He said long before the United States colonized the world, so did Egypt.

"All colonizers are not white. Turn to your neighbors and say that oppressors come in all colors."

He then went back to the Bible and spoke about the changing of kings in Babylonia.

"Prior to Abraham Lincoln, the government in this country said it was legal to hold Africans in slavery in perpetuity…when Lincoln got in office, the government changed. Prior to the passing of the 13th, 14th and 15th amendments to the Constitution, government defined Africans as slaves, as property. Property, people with no rights to be respected by any whites anywhere. The Supreme Court of the government, same court granddaddy of the court that stole the 2000 election. Supreme Court said in its Dred Scott decision in the 1850s, no African anywhere in this country has any rights that any white person has to respect at any place, any time. That was the government's official position backed up by the Supreme Court – that's the judiciary; backed up by the executive branch – that's the president; backed up by the legislative branch and enforced by the military of the government. But I stopped by to tell you tonight that government's change.

"Prior to Harry Truman's government, the military was segregated. But governments change. "Prior to the Civil Rights and equal accommodation laws of the government in this country, there was backed segregation by the country, legal discrimination by the government, prohibiting blacks from voting by the government, you had to eat and sit in separate places by the government, you had sit in different places from white folks because the government said so, and you had to be buried in a separate cemetery. It was apartheid, American style, from the cradle to the grave, all because the government backed it up.

"But guess what? Governments change. Under Bill Clinton, we got a messed up welfare to work bill, but under Clinton blacks had an intelligent friend in the Oval Office. Oh, but governments change.

"The election was stolen. We went from an intelligent friend to a dumb Dixiecrat. A rich Republican who has never held a job in his life; is against affirmative action (and) against education – I guess he is; against healthcare, against benefits for his own military, and gives tax breaks to the wealthiest contributors to his campaign. Governments change. Sometimes for the good, and sometimes for the bad."

"Where governments change, God does not change. God is the same yesterday, today and forever more. That's what his name I Am means. He does not change.

God was against slavery on yesterday, and God, who does not change, is still against slavery today. God was a God of love yesterday, and God who does not change, is still a God of love today. God was a God of justice on yesterday, and God who does not change, is still a God of justice today.

God does not change."

3. He then speaks of the government in his Biblical text and said the Romans failed. Then he said the British government failed even after it colonized the world. He said the Russian government failed. The Japanese government failed. The German government failed.

"And the United States of America government, when it came to treating her citizens of Indian descent, she failed. She put them on reservations.

"When it came to putting her citizens of Japanese descent fairly, she failed. She put them in interment prison camps.

"When it came to putting the citizens of African descent fairly, America failed. She put them in chains. The government put them on slave quarters. Put them on auction blocks. Put them in cotton fields. Put them in inferior schools. Put them in substandard housing. Put them scientific experiments. Put them in the lower paying jobs. Put them outside the equal protection of the law. Kept them out of their racist bastions of higher education, and locked them into positions of hopelessness and helplessness.

"The government gives them the drugs, builds bigger prisons, passes a three strike law and then wants us to sing God Bless America. Naw, naw, naw. Not God Bless America. God Damn America! That's in the Bible. For killing innocent people. God Damn America for treating us citizens as less than human. God Damn America as long as she tries to act like she is God and she is Supreme.

"The United States government has failed the vast majority of her citizens of African descent. Think about this. Think about this. For every one Oprah, a billionaire, you've got 5 million blacks that are out of work. For every one Colin Powell, a millionaire, you've got 10 million blacks who cannot read. For every one Condi-Skeezer Rice, you've got 1 million in prison. For every one Tiger Woods, who needs to get beat at the Masters, with his Cablanasian hips, playing on a course that discriminates against women, God has this way of bringing you up short when you get too big for your Cablanasian britches. For every one Tiger Woods, we've got 10,000 black kids who will never see a golf course. The United States government has failed the vast majority of her citizens of African descent."

"Tell your neighbor he's (going to) help us one last time. Turn back and say forgive him for the God Damn, that's in the Bible though. Blessings and curses is in the Bible. It's in the Bible."

Where government fails, God never fails. When God says it, it's done. God never fails. When God wills it, you better get out the way, 'cause God never fails. When God fixes it, oh believe me it's fixed. God never fails. Somebody right now, you think you can't make it, but I want you to know that you are more than a conqueror through Christ. You can do all things through Christ who strengthens you."

He then went on to talk about the salvation of Christians through the death of Jesus Christ. The sermon ended with a song proclaiming, "God never fails."

In this piece, not only does Mr. Martin debunk the vicious rhetorical venom that was spewed by Fox contributors, but he places back into perspective, the heart of Pastor Wright in this fiery message that spoke truth to power. However, there is a more telling issue present at work here. The foundational premise of white supremacy in this country that dares any Black Man or dissenter to challenge the deeply entrenched establishment of supremacy at all costs. If you dare to do so, then our media machine will crush you by first calling you a racist, by planting seeds of doubt about your patriotism, by then planting seeds of doubt concerning your genuine love and interest for this country through the subliminal messages of 30 second sound bytes that distort the truth of God's word.

But apparently Mr. Hannity had questionable relationships of his own. Consider the following revelation.

Jason Linkins
The Huffington Post
Sean Hannity Confronted Over His Relationship
With Neo-Nazi Hal Turner
March 23, 2008 01:39 PM

The folks over at News Hounds have been watching their Fox News Channel quarry dither over Senator Barack Obama's associations with pastor Jeremiah Wright, and noted Fox's own Sean Hannity getting himself tripped up in the guilt-by-association tango. Seems that one of Hannity's former close chums is a neo-Nazi named Hal Turner who used to be a radio host, is apparently the top man in Bergen, NJ white-supremacist circles, and probably spends a lot of his time in his basement with Star Wars action figures acting out Holocaust-denier versions of The Return of the Jedi. In short, just the sort of person with whom you'd imagine Sean Hannity spends a lot of formational time with. Anyway, a few days ago, Hannity brought Malik Shabazz of the New Black Panther Party on the show. Shabazz and his organization had previously chosen to endorse Barack Obama, who subsequently rejected the endorsement. It was up to Hannity to make some hay out of this, but the tables got turned very quickly.

From News Hounds:

Hannity added, "What I don't think you're understanding here, Malik, is that when you hear the minister of him for 20 years, when you hear the associations with Louis Farrakhan, one of the biggest racists and anti-Semites in the country, what you're not understanding is, America hears extremism at its worst."

Shabazz responded, "Let me ask you this. Are you to be judged by your promotion and association with Hal Turner?"

Hannity waved his arm around. "I don't know anybody named, Hal Turner, this is nonsense. I don't know him." Then Hannity changed his tune. "Sir, sir... That was a man that was banned from my radio show ten years ago, that ran a Senate campaign in New Jersey."

Then, as Shabazz refused to stop talking or back down, Hannity, in a tacit admission, said, "I'm not running for president."

"A neo Nazi, you backed his career," Shabazz said.

Hannity answered, "That is an absolute, positive, lie and you've been reading the wrong websites…, my friend. Good try."

Well, there's plenty of evidence to the contrary (Max Blumenthal's piece in Nation is good for a start), but it hardly matters, because don't you know, days later, Turner himself was doing his pal a total solid by coming out and stating, "Oh, yeah! We're best of buds!"

I was quite disappointed when Sean Hannity at first tried to say he did not know me and then went on to say that I ran some senate campaign in New Jersey. In fact, Sean Hannity does know me and we were quite friendly a number of years ago.

When Hannity took over Bob Grant's spot on 77 WABC in New York City, I was a well-known, regular and welcome caller to his show. Through those calls, Sean and I got to know each other a bit and at some point, I can't remember exactly when, Sean gave me the secret "Guest call-in number" at WABC so that my calls could always get on the air.

I mean, Hannity gave Turner his Super Secret Little Anti-Semite Annie Decoder Ring so he could call him up whenever he wanted to! If the two men had been younger - and mentally eligible for a high school education they surely would have gone to prom together!

Anyway, Turner and Hannity have a nice, long, intimate, chummy history, and Turner offers the essential blow-by-blow. "I can tell you from my firsthand, personal experience that Sean Hannity does, in fact, agree with many of my political and social views. I can also tell you that Sean Hannity disagrees with some of my political and social views. I won't go subjectby-subject to say which he agrees with and which he disagrees with. You can figure that out easy enough on your own!" Can we? What if we're not enthusiastic fans of the thought processes of nimrods, though?

Naturally, Turner has got a blustery warning for us all: "Another big difference is that I am perfectly willing to use force and violence against my enemies while Sean Hannity and others are not. Those using me as a prop to attack Sean Hannity would do well to remember this fact. Rest assured I will remember them when the opportunity presents itself; especially as it pertains to that douche bag sodomite Max Blumenthal for the falsehoods and total trash he wrote about me in 'The Nation' magazine."

More specifically, it was also learned that, Newshounds have updated its Hannity/Turner post, pointing out a comment signed by Phil Boyce, Program Director of WABC, Hannity's radio station, disputing many of the facts, especially the dates, in Turner's account (Boyce's comment has been posted here as well. See first comment below). Newshounds responded to Boyce's criticisms, saying: "the real issue is what was Turner allowed to say on the air, how often and what was Hannity's reaction? We have an article in a national magazine plus one of the parties involved who say that Hannity was a welcoming, friendly and encouraging host for Turner's views for a good while. Neither Boyce nor Hannity has specifically denied that."

In addition, consider these statements in Hal's own words:

Neo Nazi/White Supremacist Hal Turner Confirms Friendship and Kinship with Sean Hannity

Reported by Ellen Magazine - March 23, 2008

Earlier in the week, Sean Hannity denied, albeit in contradictory terms, ever having a relationship with neo-Nazi/white supremacist Hal Turner. As I posted the night Hannity was confronted about Turner, the evidence conflicts with Hannity's claims. Now Turner has confirmed their friendship and their simpatico views in a blog post called, "About Sean Hannity and Me. . . . . Yes, we were friends and yes, Sean agreed with some of my views." H/T Dave from queens.

UPDATED: Comments received from someone claiming to be Hannity's Program Director

In his post (**Warning: not for the faint of heart**) that reveals just what kind of guy he is, Turner writes:

"In my opinion, based on my first hand experience, I believe Sean Hannity is, in fact, a Hal Turner sort of guy. It seems to me that a big difference between Sean and me is that I am willing to say publicly what I think about savage Black criminals, diseased, uneducated illegal aliens and the grotesque cultural destruction wrought by satanic Jews while Sean and many others keep quiet to protect their paychecks.

We have cited many times an article in "The Nation" as evidence that Turner and Hannity were palsy. In his post, Turner calls the author, Max Blumenthal, a "douche bag sodomite," but Blumenthal's account is essentially confirmed by Turner's:

When I utilized that call-in number, Sean would very often come onto that line during commercial breaks so we could chat before I went on the air. Our off-the-air chats grew to an exchange of other phone numbers, me giving Sean my home and cellular number and Sean giving me his direct dial-in number at Fox News channel.

In 1993, my wife got pregnant and around a month later, Sean reported that he and his wife were expecting their first child. We got to talking about things expectant dads talk about and the relationship grew.

…Over the course of the next three or four years, Sean and I spoke regularly off the air about our kids, politics and news of the day. My on-air calls to his show remained regular and welcome. Turner concludes his blog post by threatening to use "force and violence" against his enemies. "Those using me as a prop to attack Sean Hannity would do well to remember this fact. Rest assured I will remember them when the opportunity presents itself."

Last Wednesday (3/19/08), Hannity & Colmes guest Malik Shabazz asked Hannity, in response to his continual attacks on Barack Obama regarding his pastor, "Are you to be judged by your promotion and association with Hal Turner?"

Hannity at first denied knowing Turner, then asserted that Turner was someone running a campaign in New Jersey whom Hannity had banned from his radio show. Then in what sounded like a tacit admission to me, Hannity told Shabazz, "I'm not running for president."

Will the Real Sean Hannity please stand up?

Two nights later (3/21/08) on Hannity & Colmes, Hannity professed to be saddened by the racial divisiveness engendered by the controversy about Obama and his pastor. But Hannity seems to have directly participated in far more divisiveness than Obama. Now that the evidence has been presented to you, it is my hope that you now have a clearer picture of whom Sean Hannity is and what he represents. By knowing this, you will be able to gain more insight into the associations and the support systems that he has developed with the Fox News network, etal. More specifically, it is my contention that if a person is found to be racist, and the professional network who hires him, has the foreknowledge that we the people have about their employee and rewards him with a hefty raise, then we understand Fox News philosophy towards minorities, Jews, and Immigrants. Oh, his views have not changed, and no doubt his relationships with Supremacists still remain! However, they have become more covert and clandestine, due to his position as a well-compensated public figure. However, there is one major difference between Hannity's current employer, Fox Network, and his former employer, KCSB. KCSB demonstrated high ethical standards by terminating his employment for his racist views; whereas, the Fox Network made a conscious decision to capitulate to capitalism by allowing him to continue to damage lives, create strife, and division with the spewing of his racially tinged venom. Most people, even if they do not agree with a man's point of view, can respect that man for standing on his principles in the midst of controversy without compromise. To that end, "Will the Real Sean Hannity please stand up?"

DIVIDER TWO: RUSH LIMBAUGH

Rush Hudson Limbaugh III is yet another racial divider that wreaks havoc on our societal fabric. He has the dubious distinction of reviving AM radio in the United States, and is considered to have been a kind of "national precinct captain" for the Republican Parties' Congressional victories in 1994. In a 1993 cover story, "The National Review" an ultra-conservative magazine called him "The Leader of the Opposition" during the Clinton and Obama administration.

Education and draft status

Limbaugh graduated from Cape Central High School, in 1969. His father and mother wanted him to attend college, so he enrolled at SE Missouri State University. Being the underachiever that he is, he dropped out after two semesters and one summer; according to his mother, "he flunked everything," even a modern ballroom dancing class. In other words, he should have ridden on the short yellow school bus. As she told a reporter in 1992, "He just didn't seem interested in anything except radio." Be that as it may, doesn't one need to be educated and credentialed in order to work in the professional realm? At least that is what I was reared to believe. For example, a doctor cannot practice medicine without a Medical degree. An Engineer cannot practice their craft without an engineering degree and or a P.E. certification It stands to reason that before an individual can be assigned to a radio program as a personality, he must complete a curriculum in broadcast journalism or communications. Perhaps traditional workplace qualifiers do not apply to him!

Limbaugh's birth date was ranked as 175 in the Vietnam War draft lottery. No one was drafted above 125. However, he was classified as "1Y" (later reclassified "4F") due to either a football knee injury or a diagnosis of Pilonidal disease, a chronic infection in the skin slightly above the crease between the buttocks. How convenient! Be that as it may, when one considers the fact that Rush could not decide on which health condition he would use to divert the draft, one cannot help but wonder if he had a legitimate reason for not serving his country, and does this make him a "Draft Dodger and Unpatriotic?"

1970s

For the rest of the decade Limbaugh moved around to several radio stations before settling in Kansas City, Missouri. In 1979, after several years in entertainment, he took a break from radio and accepted a position as director of promotions with the Kansas City Royals baseball team all without a college degree; Wow, Affirmative action and nepotism at its best. Retired star, George Brett is one of his best friends.

In 1984, Limbaugh returned to radio as a talk show host at KFBK in Sacramento, California, where he replaced Morton Downey Jr. The repeal of the Fairness doctrine which had required that stations provide free air time for responses to any controversial opinions that were broadcast by the FCC in 1987, meant stations could broadcast editorial commentary without having to present opposing views. Oh how times have changed! Daniel Henninger wrote in an editorial, "Ronald Reagan tore down this wall (the Fairness Doctrine) in 1987, and Rush Limbaugh was the first man to proclaim himself liberated from the East Germany of liberal media domination." This ushered in the dark ages of lies, bigotry, and race baiting that is led by this Unpatriotic Draft dodger!

1990s

The program gained in popularity and moved to stations with larger audiences eventually growing to over 650 radio stations nationwide. When the Grand Ole Party won control of Congress in 1994, one of the first acts by many freshmen (calling themselves the "Dittohead Caucus") was to award Limbaugh the title of "honorary member of Congress" in recognition of his support of their efforts during this period.

Humor columnist and journalist Lewis Grossberger acknowledged that Limbaugh had "more listeners than any other talk show host" and described Limbaugh's style as "bouncing between earnest and political." Wow, let us recap, not intelligent enough to complete college, dodged the military draft, yet he still received the blessing of radio producers nationwide and was given a platform to spew his venom of racial hatred, bigotry, supremacy, and division all without the benefit of a journalism degree. Then he is rewarded for his loyalty to the conservative movement. Man talk about racial preferences!

A LOYAL FOLLOWING

The tragedy of this facade is that the many people who follow Rush are no different than you and I are. They want a quality education for their children-Rush has access to it, they want to be safe within their homes/neighborhoods-Rush is safe in his gated exclusive subdivision, they would like to have lower gas prices-Rush does, they want to take more money home to feed/cloth/care for their families without being taxed exclusively and separate from the wealthiest Americans-Rush does, they need to be able to work without the threat of having their jobs outsourced overseas-Rush has his job making millions, and they would like to be able to have health insurance for their families in case of sickness-Rush is insured. As strange as it may seem, none of these obvious common threads that bind us together as American people are not even considered by them as they blindly follow Rush thus making him a very wealthy man while they continue to struggle on a day-to-day basis to make ends meet. It often reminds me of Lazarus and the rich man.

Nevertheless, this perpetual following by the calculations of Arbitron ratings has increased significantly. This indicated that The Rush Limbaugh Show had a minimum weekly audience of 13.5 million listeners, making it the largest radio talk show audience in the United States.

POSITIONING HIMSELF FOR SUCCESS

In spite of Rush's vast limitations, and the following of the Rush-heads, who has made a role model for themselves and their kids from someone who flunked out of college, who deceptively used tactics to avoid serving his country in the military, and who espouses racist, divisive, and supremacist doctrines; he was not successful yet. Now the road to success was a little tricky, but when one considers the capitalistic nature of this society coupled with a deeply entrenched good ole boys network, Rush's success was inevitability.

Come with me while we follow the trail, and watch the golden boy of the good ole boys network position himself for success. In reality, his show was co-owned and first syndicated by Edward McLaughlin, former president of ABC who founded EFM Media in 1988, with Limbaugh's show as his first product. In 1997, McLaughlin sold EFM to Jacor Communications, which was ultimately bought up by Clear Channel Communications. Today, Limbaugh owns a majority of the show, which is syndicated by the Premiere Radio Networks. According to a 2001 article in U.S. News & World Report, Limbaugh had an eight-year contract, at the rate of $31.25 million a year. And while many of the Rush-heads are continuously following him around, talking like him, making life-altering decisions based upon the poisonous and divisive rhetoric that he spews without logic, thought, or as we definitely know education; little do they know is that their beloved demagogue is being paid an exorbitant amount of money to rant and rave about how bad life is because of certain groups of people, and ultimately keep Americans "dumbed down and living in fear." "Those people are taking all of our jobs, those people are bringing all of the crime into this nation, how we must take our country back from all of those minorities who are lazy, and living off of welfare", and many are actually believing him. Just how many are believing him you may ask? Well figure this, on July 2, 2008, Matt Drudge reported that Limbaugh signed a contract extension through 2016 that is worth over $400 million, breaking records for any broadcast medium television or radio. Wonder how much money will Limbaugh give to the Rush-heads to help them from avoiding foreclosure, $0; I wonder how many bags of groceries will Limbaugh purchase for the Rush-heads to assist them in avoiding starvation, $0; I wonder how many trips to the doctor, how many prescriptions, how much dental work, or eyeglass benefits will Rush sponsor for his beloved Rush-heads, $0, I really wonder how many gallons of gas Rush will buy for his beloved Rush-heads, again $0. Why because there is no relationship between Rush and his Rush-heads! The Rush-heads are simply a means to an end, but it is a most significant means! Because most network markets depend upon the ratings of a media personality, and when the people stop tuning in to listen, then the ratings plummet, and when the ratings plummet, then the sponsors terminate their contracts, and when the contracts are terminated, then Rush cannot be paid, and therefore, he must go. So yes, the people are more significant than many people realize.

Hopefully the people will awaken from their blind stupor before it is too late and they lose everything.

JUDGE A MAN BY HIS SYSTEM OF BELIEFS

Paraphrased, the late Dr. Martin L. King Jr. stated that we should judge a man not by his personal god-given appearance, but by the character that he or she displays. I would venture to say that a man can be judged by his belief system, and by the way that he treats other people who he has judged to be inferior to him.

A message to the Rush-heads

Don't you think that it would have been a better idea to examine a man to see if he is worthy of your trust and faith? That being said, How many of you know this man, and how many simply out of frustration for the way that our government, the wealthy, and corporations/lobbyists have destroyed the quality of life in this country, have simply designated him as the voice for this society? You may want to reconsider the anointing of a member who at least has a college education and is not a member of the very capitalistic group that has pilfered America of her resources through the exploitation of their pain and frustration. Continue this journey with me.

Rush's belief system:
Listen to the words of this consummate hypocrite and a translation of those words

"I love being a conservative. We conservatives are proud of our philosophy. Unlike our liberal friends, who are constantly looking for new words to conceal their true beliefs and are in a perpetual state of reinvention, we conservatives are unapologetic about our ideals." (Limbaugh)

We are confident in our principles and energetic about openly advancing them (or openly running over anyone who challenges them). We believe in individual liberty (lawlessness), limited government (an oligarchial society), capitalism (where the rich get richer through the exploitation of the working class), the rule of law (as interpreted by conservative judges), faith (where money and power replaces God), a color-blind society (where the rich rule and the working class stay in their place) and national security (all other nations stand aside and support our quest for imperialism).

We support school choice (creating private, elitist charter schools for the affluent while the less fortunate are forced to attend underperforming and financially strapped public schools), enterprise zones, tax cuts (for the rich), welfare reform (bail outs for the rich and corporate welfare), faith-based initiatives (church bribes for Pastoral influence of congregations for election support), political speech (media driven hatemongering and division), homeowner rights (the freedom to murder anyone on your property and hide behind Castle laws) and the War on Terrorism (no civil rights, more police brutality, and incarceration for all dissenters).

"And at our core we embrace and celebrate the most magnificent governing document ever ratified by any nation — the U.S. Constitution. Along with the Declaration of Independence, which recognizes our God-given natural right to be free, it is the foundation on which our government is built and has enabled us to flourish as a people (the US Constitution is void where prohibited by law). We conservatives are never stronger than when we are advancing our principles (when they are in the attack mode and disregarding the rule of law when they constitute a political majority)."

Can any of the Rush-heads say that they genuinely are greedy people who do not believe in obeying the law of the land, and helping those who are less fortunate than they are? Then you are not one of him, and you should reconsider remaining in this one-sided relationship where the people remain impoverished, exploited, and Rush is the only person who is benefitting.

How Rush treats his fellow man who has a
life threatening disease

Michael J. Fox incident

On the October 23, 2006 edition of his radio show, Limbaugh imitated on the "DittoCam" (the webcam for website subscribers to see him on the air) the physical symptoms of actor Michael J. Fox, who has Parkinson's disease and has appeared in political campaign ads for candidates who support a form of embryonic stem-cell research, and has stated that he sometimes doesn't take his medicine explicitly to show the effects of the disease. Limbaugh imitated Fox's Parkinson's symptoms as displayed on the commercial, stating that "(Fox) is exaggerating the effects of the disease. He's moving all around and shaking and it's purely an act. This is really shameless of Michael J. Fox. Either he didn't take his medication or he's acting." Fox was offended, as were people on both sides of the political spectrum who felt Limbaugh's parody of Fox was unfair or in poor taste. The possibility of a reasoned and civil discussion of stem-cell research was quickly overshadowed by dueling website and blog attacks. Proponents of stem-cell research immediately used this incident to raise funds for several Democratic candidates running for Congress, while detractors accused Fox of being just another partisan of Democratic candidates. Fox himself appeared on numerous news programs to explain his condition and to defend his advocacy for stem-cell research.

Phony soldier's controversy

(Taken from the Main article: Phony soldiers controversy)

Another controversy occurred during the September 26, 2007 broadcast of Limbaugh's radio show, when he used the term "phony soldiers," allegedly referencing a September 21 Associated Press story about individuals falsely claiming to be veterans in order to receive benefits. A caller, after saying he was currently serving in the Army and has been in 14 years, said, "They never talk to real soldiers. They like to pull these soldiers that come up out of the blue and spout to the media." Limbaugh interrupted, "The phony soldiers." The caller continued, "The phony soldiers. If you talk to a real soldier, they are proud to serve. They want to be over in Iraq. They understand their sacrifice, and they're willing to sacrifice for their country." Several minutes later, after the caller had hung-up, Limbaugh read from the AP story describing the story of Jesse Macbeth. Jesse Macbeth joined the Army but did not complete basic training, yet claimed in alternative media interviews that he and his unit routinely committed war crimes in Iraq. On June 7, 2007, Macbeth pleaded guilty to one count of making false statements to the U.S. Department of Veterans Affairs and was sentenced to five months jail and three years probation. Media Matters noted Limbaugh's use of the term "phony soldiers" in an article on their website. The article alluded that Limbaugh was saying that all soldiers who disagree with the Iraq War were "phony soldiers," and their article received substantial press coverage after it was discussed in speeches by Presidential candidates John Edwards and Chris Dodd. Limbaugh argued that, when he had made the comment about "phony soldiers," he had been speaking only of Macbeth and others like him who claims to be soldiers and are not, and that "Media Matters takes things out of context all the time." Media Matters disputed the accuracy of Limbaugh's claim and defended its story, yet there is a principle that is even more telling here. Here we have Limbaugh, a draft dodger and phony journalist, calling someone a phony soldier! What utter hypocrisy is being displayed here at the expense of others for ratings, if any soldier at least attended basic training, they served more time in the military than Rush did. What a bastion of character.

Among Limbaugh's detractors were members of VoteVets.org who produced a series of ads that ran on their website and on YouTube taking Limbaugh to task for insulting veterans who opposed the war. The members of Vote-Vets, a number of whom asserted they were conservative politically, told reporters that protesting the current war policy should not be a partisan issue, but most of the support they received after the Limbaugh controversy came from congressional Democrats.

On October 19, 2007, Limbaugh announced the winning bid in an eBay auction of a letter sent to Clear Channel Communications Chief Executive Officer Mark Mays by U.S. Senate Majority Leader Harry

Reid. "We call on you to publicly repudiate these [phony soldier] comments," the letter said, ". . . and to ask Mr. Limbaugh to apologize for his comments." The auction's high bid of $2,100,100.00 by Betty Casey of the Eugene B. Casey Foundation set a new eBay record for largest charity bid. Shortly before the auction closed, Senator Reid addressed the Senate, saying, "I don't know what we could do more important than helping to ensure that children of our fallen soldiers and police officers who have fallen in the line of duty have the opportunity for their children to have a good education." In his radio broadcast later in the day, Limbaugh was critical of Reid's speech, saying Reid had tried "to horn in and act like he's part of this whole thing, folks." Limbaugh also said, "Senator Reid, you did not mention that I am penitently matching whatever the final total is." (Paraphrased)

Matching funds from Limbaugh would increase the total donation to the charity benefiting children of Marines and law enforcement personnel killed in the line of duty to $4,200,200.00.

Operation Chaos

Limbaugh has stated that there is nothing wrong with Republicans voting in the Democratic primary, as Democrats voted for John McCain in Vermont, New Hampshire, Florida, and other states. "This is getting absurd. If it weren't for independents and Democrats crossing over, Senator McCain would not be our nominee!" Dubbing the effort "Operation Chaos," Limbaugh says he intends to continue to encourage his listeners to vote for whoever is behind in the Democratic primary, to sow chaos and disunity among Democrats during a divisive primary battle. Limbaugh then began to advocate that his Republican listeners vote for Clinton, something the rules of the Texas primary permitted. According to a county volunteer, one voter declared "Rush Limbaugh sent me," another "I am voting for Hillary Clinton but I want to see the Democrats implode," and a great many others mentioning Limbaugh.

In Ohio, Limbaugh circumvented federal election laws and similarly encouraged his listeners to do the same unethical thing and re-register as Democrats and vote for Clinton. Although Ohio does not use an open primary, voters who change their registration must attest that they support the principles of the party to which they switch. About sixteen thousand Ohio Republicans switched parties for the election. The Cuyahoga County Board of Elections announced that, at the urging of Democrat Sandy McNair, the cross-overs would be investigated. Later, the Ohio Attorney General's office stated that it would be hard to prosecute anyone for falsifying a change of registration, because of the difficulty of proving a voter's fraudulent intent. Limbaugh has said that "The dream end of this "Operation Chaos" is that this keeps up to the Convention, and that we have a re-creation of Chicago 1968 with burning cars, protests, fire, and literal riots and all of that, that is the objective here."

Unfortunately for Rush, and fortunately for America, when "We the People" converged on Denver, Colorado for the Democratic National Convention, there was no disunity, much to the Rush-heads chagrin. On the contrary, there was peace, love, and unity behind the nominee, as we transcended the hypnotic Oligarchic stronghold of this country, to once again move towards our common goal of a Government "of," "by," and "for" the People.

An Un-American Icon

Rush Limbaugh is arguably an icon in the media circles, although when he speaks one does not know if you will hear coherent arguments or a Oxy Contin induced divisive diatribe. To that end, he has solidified his hypocrisy, selfishness, and hate for America by making the comments on the first day of President Barack Obama's presidency. Yes in spite of America's maturity in bridging the gap of racism, and as we celebrated our commonality of being a free people who exercised their freedom to choose their own leaders; he has decided to ignore America's choice to love one another, and descend to the sewers of supremacy, division, and hateful rhetoric as he unapologetically decided to speak ill of America's future, by stating that he "hoped that President Obama failed." Now I could choose to talk about the subtle innuendoes of racism, jealousy, bigotry, and supremacy that this statement suggests, but that would be counterproductive to all of the progress that we have made as a people in this current election. However, as "we the people" consider this statement and realize that we are all Americans first, and that our destinies are inextricably tied together, so much so, that if Our President failed then America would fail. Therefore, to that end, Mr. Limbaugh has in essence told each and every one of us that it is his wish and desire that the United States of America fails. What an un-American comment from one who has lived in the lap of luxury due to the freedoms that America has afforded him as he signed an American media contract, and spends American millions while many of our citizens struggle to survive. Anyone who follows him at this point can be accused from the "guilt by association" gospel that the right preaches, of being un-American as well. However, it is par for the course from a consummate hypocrite who ignores the basic freedoms of life, liberty, and the pursuit of happiness that each American is entitled to, and readily wishes that America should fall like Bin Laden and Al Qaeda wishes. It begs the question as to whether Rush is hiding his turban in the closet, and does he espouse the terrorist's doctrine of hate. Moreover, does he have these men on speed dial? Who would follow such a vile man? Maybe someone who wants to see America fall as well.

DIVIDER NUMBER THREE: WILLIAM O'REILLY

Many of you refer to him affectionately (not all of us) as Bill O'Reilly. He is an American television/radio host, author, syndicated columnist, and self-proclaimed "traditionalist" political commentator. But I call him a pseudo-intellectual chameleon who changes his colors at a moment's notice and has transformed "race baiting" into an subliminal art form. He is the host of the cable news program The O'Reilly Factor. Prior to hosting The O'Reilly Factor, he served as anchor of the entertainment program, Inside Edition. O'Reilly also hosts The Radio Factor, a talk radio program syndicated by Westwood One, and is the author of seven books.

Early life/Education

Bill O'Reilly was born September 10, 1949 in New York City to parents William and Angela O'Reilly, from Brooklyn, New York and Bergen County, New Jersey. His father was an accountant for the oil company Caltex which gave Bill his connection to big oil at an early age. In addition, Bill was reared in an environment of privilege from the onset of his life. In 1951, his family moved to Levittown on Long Island. After graduating from Chaminade High School, a private, exclusive Catholic boys high school in Mineola, in 1967, O'Reilly attended Marist College. While at Marist, a private, exclusive liberal arts college, O'Reilly played punter in the National Club Football Association, and was also a writer for the school's newspaper, The Circle. An honors student, he majored in history. He spent his junior year of college abroad, attending Queen Mary College at the University of London. O'Reilly received his B.A. in History in 1971. He played semi-professional baseball during this time, as a pitcher for the Brooklyn Monarchs. After graduating from Marist College, O'Reilly moved to Miami, Florida at age 21, where he taught English and history at Monsignor Pace High School for two years. O'Reilly later returned to school and earned a M.A. in Broadcast Journalism from Boston University (where he attended school with Howard Stern) in 1976. While attending Boston University, he was a reporter and columnist for various local newspapers and alternative news-weeklies, including The Boston Phoenix. O'Reilly did his broadcast journalism internship in Miami during this time and was also an entertainment writer and movie critic for The Miami Herald. O'Reilly also earned a Master of Public Administration from Harvard's John F. Kennedy School of Government.

Broadcasting career

O'Reilly's early television news career included reporting and anchoring positions at WNEP-TV in Scranton, Pennsylvania, where he also reported the weather. At WFAA-TV in Dallas, Texas, O'Reilly was awarded the Dallas Press Club Award for excellence in investigative reporting. He then moved to KMGH-TV in Denver, Colorado where he won a Local Emmy Award for his coverage of a skyjacking. O'Reilly also worked for KATU-TV in Portland, Oregon, as well as TV stations in Hartford, Connecticut (WFSB-TV), and in Boston, Massachusetts.

In 1980, he anchored his own program on WCBS-TV in New York where he won his second local Emmy for an investigation of corrupt city marshals. In 1982, he was promoted to the network as a CBS News correspondent and covered the wars in El Salvador and the

Falkland Islands from his base in Buenos Aires, Argentina. He later left CBS over a dispute concerning the uncredited use in a report by Bob Schieffer of riot footage shot by O'Reilly's crew in Buenos Aires during the Falklands conflict. (A 1998 novel by O'Reilly, Those Who Trespass: A Novel of Television and Murder, depicts a television reporter who has a similar dispute over a Falklands War report. The character proceeds to exact his revenge on network staff in a series of graphically-described murders.)

In 1986, O'Reilly joined ABC News as a correspondent for ABC World News Tonight. O'Reilly began his journey away from responsible and ethical journalism, when in 1989, O'Reilly joined the nationally syndicated King World (now CBS) program Inside Edition, a tabloid/gossip television program in competition with A Current Affair. He started as senior correspondent and backup anchor for British TV host David Frost, and subsequently became the program's anchor after Frost's termination. In addition to being one of the first American broadcasters to cover the dismantling of the Berlin Wall, O'Reilly also obtained the first exclusive interview with murderer Joel Steinberg and was the first television host from a national current affairs program on the scene of the 1992 Los Angeles riots.

O'Reilly was replaced by former NBC News and CBS News anchor Deborah Norville on Inside Edition. He then enrolled at the Kennedy School of Government at Harvard University, where he received a Master's degree in Public Administration. After Harvard, he finally sold his soul to the devil, when he became the cornerstone for journalistic white supremacy in 1995, when he was hired by Roger Ailes, chairman and CEO of the then startup FOX News Channel, to anchor "The O'Reilly Report." The show soon moved to a new time slot, and was renamed, "The O'Reilly Factor."

O'Reilly's radio program reaches 3.25 million-plus listeners and is carried by more than 400 radio stations. According to the talk radio industry publication Talkers Magazine, O'Reilly is #11 on the "Heavy Hundred," a list of the 100 most important talk show hosts in America. Conservative Internet news site News Max's "Top 25 Talk Radio Host" list selected O'Reilly to the #2 spot as most influential host in the nation!

Personal life

O'Reilly married Maureen E. McPhilmy, a public relations executive, in 1995. They have a daughter and a son. O'Reilly currently resides in suburban Manhasset, New York.

The O'Reilly Factor

O'Reilly's television show, The O'Reilly Factor, is routinely the highly-rated show of the three major U.S. 24-hour cable news channels and began the trend toward more opinion-oriented prime-time cable news programming. The show is taped late in the afternoon at a studio in New York City and airs every weekday on the FOX News Channel at 8:00 p.m. Eastern Time. However, after President Obama's inauguration, his program is shown six days per week to further FOX News supremacist agenda of impeaching the credibility of our President, while undermining the success of America.

Political beliefs and points of view:
Main article: Politics of Bill O'Reilly

The O'Reilly Factor and O'Reilly's talk-radio program, The Radio Factor, focus on news and commentary related to politics most of the time. He has coined the deceptive term "traditionalist," when describing his points of view on various topics, saying the term is not limited to the normal party lines.

O'Reilly being the chameleon that he is, said that he was not affiliated with any political party; in 2000, however, The New York Daily News determined that he was registered with the Republican Party in the state of New York. His excuse was that it was a clerical misunderstanding and has since been registered as an independent. However, as the truth has a way of coming out, in the lead up to the 2008 presidential election, The Daily Telegraph ranked O'Reilly 82nd on its list of the "100 most influential conservatives in America."

In a 2003 interview on NPR, O'Reilly determined not to reveal his clandestine political motives, said:

"I'm not a political guy in the sense that I embrace an ideology. To this day I am an independent thinker, an independent voter, I am a registered independent ... there are certain fundamental things that this country was founded upon that I respect and do not want changed. That separates me from the secularists who want a complete overhaul of how the country is run" (Bill O'Reilly)

Controversy, criticism, and parody

Over the years, O'Reilly has been criticized by or had disputes with many public figures including Al Franken, Bill Moyers, George Clooney, Ludacris, 50 Cent, Rosie O'Donnell, Ariana Huffington, Mark Cuban, Joe Scarborough, and Keith Olbermann, sometimes in response to commentary by O'Reilly. Progressive media watchdog organizations like Media Matters for America and Fairness and Accuracy in Reporting have criticized O'Reilly's reporting on a variety of issues, in particular his alleged distortion of facts and use of misleading or erroneous statistics on his nationally shown television program.

O'Reilly is considered the main inspiration for comedian Stephen Colbert's satirical character on the Comedy Central show The Colbert Report, which features Colbert in a "full-dress parody" of The O'Reilly Factor. On the show, Colbert is deferential to O'Reilly, affectionately calling him "Papa Bear."

The Dark Side of Bill… That Fox Network refused to report

Fox Network and Bill O'Reilly, who stands behind his "no spin zone" moniker to describe his character and integrity in news reporting, appears to be a term that he should use loosely. For on October 13, 2004, O'Reilly fired the proverbial first shot when he filed a lawsuit against O'Reilly Factor producer Andrea Mackris, her lawyer Benedict P. Morelli, and Morelli's law firm for extortion, contending Mackris had privately threatened to charge O'Reilly with sexual harassment unless he paid her more than $60 million (USD) which is a stretch in my opinion. But that is not the entire story. Andrea Mackris, 33, who was a producer on the show, filed a lawsuit against the top-rated TV host Oct. 13, alleging O'Reilly made a series of explicit phone calls to her, advised her to use a vibrator and told her about his sexual fantasies involving her.

The New York Daily News, citing unidentified sources, reported that the admittedly innocent O'Reilly had agreed to pay Mackris anywhere from $2 million to $10 million. Separately, the New York Post said it was believed that O'Reilly paid "multimillions of dollars" to settle the suit, whereby both lawsuits were dismissed, but this has not been confirmed as the terms of the agreement are conveniently confidential as his "No Spin zone" at Fox News conspicuously failed to run this story! Yet according to news sources, O'Reilly made this statement while hiding behind his lawyer, "Mr. O'Reilly denies that he has done anything that rises to the level of unlawful sexual harassment." Let's examine that statement. It says that there was a denial to "anything" that rises to the level of "sexual harassment! At best this statement is debatable, but mostly I noticed that there was not a denial of her specific claims. Well you know, if you do not address it, it will just go away.

The lawsuit was subsequently dismissed on <u>October 28, 2004</u>. What I find so particularly disconcerting is the fact that this same man, who went to great lengths to avoid being publicly labeled as a "sexual predator" for his alleged actions, continues to assassinate the character of men of high moral standards. But I am not fooled one bit. Mostly because I understand that like Woody Allen and Robert Kelly, for most intents and purposes, the ability to pay to conceal your transgressions does not absolve you from the reality of who you are. Fox News, made a decision as they always do, to protect would be, potential criminal activity for the sake of partisanship, camaraderie, and capitalism. I just hope that the tapes of conversations between the alleged victim and O'Reilly do not one day surface. But then again, he probably paid for those as well.

DIVIDER NUMBER FOUR: GLEN BECK

Hear Ye, Hear Ye, Let It Be Hereby Known that in the Two thousand and tenth year of our Lord, Glen Lee Beck is hereby crowned the "King of Racial division and Hatemongering." Yes that is correct! Without this man, America would be in a better position to love one another, to accept one another for their differences, to work together towards rebuilding this country, and to look at the character of our President in his attempting to address the needs of the "body politic" as a whole, and not inciting America to judge him by the "color of his skin." Has he always been this hateful? Is there a method to his madness? Let us take a closer look at this misogynic demagogue and develop a better insight of this divider.

Glenn Lee Beck was born February 10, 1964 and is an American conservative radio and television host, political commentator, author, and entrepreneur. He is the host of The Glenn Beck Program, a nationally-syndicated talk-radio show that airs throughout the United States on Premiere Radio Networks. Beck is also the host of a self-titled cable-news show on Fox News Channel. As an author, Beck has gained success with five #1 New York Times best selling books. Beck is also the founder and CEO of Mercury Radio Arts, a multi-media production company through which he produces content for radio, television, publishing, the stage, and the Internet.

Beck has become a well-known and polarizing public figure, whose provocative and racially tinged views have afforded him media recognition and popularity in conservative circles, along with controversy and criticism. To his supporters, he is a conservative champion, defending traditional American values from liberalism, while to his detractors he is notorious for conspiracy theories and incendiary rhetoric. He epitomizes the prevailing double-standard that dichotomy of living in two different societies affords him. He attended as many high schools as Sarah Palin did colleges before graduating, which can explain his consistent incoherent belligerence on his television show.

Glenn Lee Beck was born in Everett, Washington, on February 10, 1964, to William and Mary Beck. His parents lived in Mountlake Terrace, Washington at the time of Beck's birth and sometime later moved their family to Mount Vernon, Washington where they owned and operated City Bakery in the downtown area. Beck was raised as a Roman Catholic and attended the exclusive Immaculate Conception Catholic School in Mount Vernon. At age 13, he won a contest that landed him his first broadcast gig as a disc-jockey for his hometown radio station, <u>KBRC</u>.

Apparently substance abuse runs in his family, for in 1977, William Beck became an absentee father as he filed for divorce against Beck's mother, Mary due to her increasing <u>alcoholism</u>.

Suddenly finding themselves homeless, Glenn and his older sister moved with their mother to <u>Sumner</u>, <u>Washington</u>, and attended an exclusive <u>Jesuit school</u> in <u>Puyallup</u>. On May 15, 1979, his mother allegedly drowned in <u>Puget Sound</u>, just west of <u>Tacoma</u>, <u>Washington</u>, along with a man who had taken her out in a small boat. Attempting to preserve her image, a Tacoma police report stated that Mary Beck "appeared to be a classic drowning victim," but a <u>Coast Guard</u> investigator speculated that she could have intentionally jumped overboard. Beck has described his mother's death as a suicide in interviews during television and radio broadcasts. After their mother's death, Beck and his older sister moved to their father's home in <u>Bellingham</u>, <u>Washington</u>, where Beck graduated from <u>Sehome High School</u> in June 1982. In the aftermath of his mother's death and subsequent suicide of his stepbrother, Beck has said he used "Dr. <u>Jack Daniel's</u>" to <u>cope</u>.

Being a quintessential nonconformist since his teens, at 18, following high school graduation, Beck relocated to <u>Provo</u>, <u>Utah</u> and worked at radio station <u>KAYK</u>. Feeling he "didn't fit in," Beck quit the Utah station after six months, taking a job at Washington D.C.'s <u>WPGC</u> in February 1983. While working at WPGC, Beck met his first wife, Claire. The couple married and had two daughters, Mary and Hannah; Mary was born in 1988 with <u>cerebral palsy</u>, the result of a series of strokes at birth. Following in his mother's footsteps, the couple divorced in 1994 amid Beck's struggles with <u>substance abuse</u>. To further exacerbate his problems, along with being a recovering alcoholic and drug addict, Beck has been diagnosed with <u>Attention Deficit Hyperactivity Disorder</u>. He cites the help of <u>Alcoholics Anonymous</u> (AA) in his sobriety and attended his first AA meeting in November 1994, the month he states he stopped drinking <u>alcohol</u> and smoking <u>cannabis</u> which is quite a feat when one considers the scientific studies that identify the perpetual struggles that alcoholics and drug addicts face throughout the span of their lives. His denials remind me of Rush Limbaugh proclamations that he freed himself of his prescription "drug addiction" in a record five weeks. What men! In spite of his alcoholism, drug addictions, and attention deficits, Glen Beck, in 1996, while working for a New Haven-area radio station, Beck was admitted to Yale University through a special "affirmative action" program for non-traditional students. Beck took one theology class, "Early Christology," but found himself to be intellectually inferior, and then dropped out. Unfortunately his lack of intelligence could not allow him to be a successful beneficiary of the quota system that he benefitted from with this special Yale University "admissions program."

In 1999, Beck married his second wife, Tania. Her love changed his religion, as they joined The Church of Jesus Christ of Latter-day Saints in October 1999, partly at the urging of his daughter Mary. The couple has two children, Raphe (who is adopted) and Cheyenne. Beck's "on-air" vitriolic hate speech has afforded him the opportunity to live in a multimillion dollar home in Connecticut with his wife and four children.

Political views

Beck has called himself a conservative with libertarian leanings. Among his core values Beck lists personal responsibility, private charity, the right to life, freedom of religion, limited government, and family as the cornerstone of society, all while he selfishly utilizes his national platform to spew vitriolic hate, racial division, and incoherent conspiracy theories. Beck also believes in low national debt while excluding his multi-million dollar salary, and has said "A conservative believes that debt creates unhealthy relationships. Everyone, from the government on down, should live within their means and strive for financial independence." Beck supports individual gun ownership rights and is against gun control legislation. Beck believes that there is a lack of evidence that human activity is the main cause of global warming thus refuting the empirical findings of doctoral experts in the environmental field with no college degree. He has "tried to do his part by buying a multimillion dollar home "prop" with a 'green' design." He also views the American Clean Energy and Security Act as a form of wealth redistribution, and has promoted a petition rejecting the Kyoto Protocol.

Influences

Seeking to legitimate himself intellectually, according to Joanna Brooks, a scholar of American religion, one pre-eminent influence on Beck's political ideology has been W. Cleon Skousen (1913–2006). Skousen was an anti-communist, a supporter (though not a member) of the John Birch Society, and limited-government conservative whose works involve a wide range of subjects (including the Six-Day War, Mormon eschatology, New World Order conspiracies, and even parenting). Beck praises Skousen's "words of wisdom" as "divinely inspired", referencing Skousen's The Naked Communist and especially The 5,000 Year Leap (originally published in 1981), which Beck said in 2007 had "changed his life." According to Skousen's nephew, financial and political commentator Mark Skousen, Leap reflects Skousen's "passion for the United States Constitution," which he "felt was inspired by God and the reason behind America's success as a nation." The book is touted by Beck as "required reading" to understand the current American political landscape and become a "September twelfth person." Beck authored a foreword for the 2008 edition of Leap and Beck's on-air recommendations in 2009 propelled the book to number one in the government category on Amazon for several months.

9-12 Project

Beck put together a campaign, the 9-12 Project, that is named for nine principles which he says embody the spirit of the American people on the day after the September 11 attacks and speaks volumes on his attitude towards government that borderlines on "treasonous." His nine principles are as follows:

The Nine Principles: (Interpretation mine)

1. America is good. (Good to me, the hell with anyone else)

2. I believe in God and He is the Center of my Life. (As long as he continues to allow me to display my racist, supremacist views, while encouraging Governmental treason)

3. I must always try to be a more honest person than I was yesterday.

4. The family is sacred. My spouse and I are the ultimate authority, not the government. (Either my family obeys me, or I will trade them in for more obedient models)

5. If you break the law you pay the penalty. Justice is blind and no one is above it. (Unless you are member of the power-base like Scooter Libby)

6. I have a right to life, liberty and pursuit of happiness, but there is no guarantee of equal results. (To hell with the poor)

7. I work hard for what I have and I will share it with who I want to. (Government cannot force me to be charitable)

8. It is not un-American for me to disagree with authority or to share my personal opinion. (Even though that personal opinion incites violence)

9. The government works for me. I do not answer to them, they answer to me. (But I can spend American money that the government prints)

Beck has supported and incited the tea party protests from their inception, justifies the random acts of violence and threats against our representatives and private citizens and held a broadcast from one of the April 2009 rallies in San Antonio, Texas.

In September 2009, the conservative political activism group FreedomWorks organized the Taxpayer March on Washington, to rally against President Barack Obama's policies. The event was inspired by Beck's 9/12 project.

Media career and income

In 2002 Beck, anticipating his inevitable skewed views causing controversy, created Mercury Radio Arts, a media platform which produces his broadcast, publishing and online projects, as well as his live performances. In addition to broadcasting, Beck allegedly has written five New York Times-bestselling books, and is the publisher of Fusion Magazine. Alleged when one considers the role of ghostwriters in our society where many successes are fabricated. He also stars in a one-man stage show that tours the US twice a year.

Spewing racially insensitive and divisive views thus creating media controversy has served Beck well. In June 2009, estimators at Forbes calculated Beck's earnings over the previous 12 months at $23 million, with 2009–2010 revenues on track to be higher. Although the majority of his revenue results from his radio show and books, his website's 5 million unique visitors per month also provides at least $3 million annually, while his salary at Fox News is estimated at $2 million per year. Additionally, Beck's online magazine Fusion sells an array of Beck-themed merchandise.

Beck's controversial views is said to have potentially hurt his earning potential, however; despite millions of viewers, more than 200 companies have joined a boycott of Beck's television program, making it difficult for Fox to sell ads. The time has instead been sold to smaller firms offering such products as Kaopectate, Carbonite, 1-800-PetMeds and Goldline International. Network executives say they believe they could charge higher rates if the Beck were more widely acceptable to advertisers. Beck's radio show is also sponsored by Goldline International, a fact that has brought Beck criticism; Goldline was listed as the exclusive sponsor of Beck's comedy tour last summer.

Radio

Radio historian Marc Fisher has argued that Beck is "first and foremost an entertainer, who happens to have stumbled into a position of political prominence." However, I believe that Beck is deliberate, calculating, greedy, and has an underlying current of racist and supremacist views that guides his dialect, interpretation, and dialogue.

Beck began his radio career in 1977, at age 13, when he won a local radio contest on station <u>KBRC</u> in Mount Vernon, Washington, to be a disc jockey for an hour. It was then that Beck and his school classmates produced old-time radio with live scripts and sound effects for radio station, <u>KGMI</u>, in <u>Bellingham</u>. In his junior year of high school, he began working part-time at Seattle station <u>KUBE</u> 93 (FM) having to take a <u>Greyhound Bus</u> from Bellingham to Seattle in order to get there. After hosting a show midnight to dawn on Fridays and Saturdays, Beck would sleep in the station's conference room following his show.

Following high school graduation, Beck pursued his career as a <u>Top 40 DJ</u>. He moved to Provo for six months and worked at FM 96.1. Beck left the station in February 1983 to go to <u>WPGC-FM</u> in Washington, D.C., another First Media radio station. Later that year, he moved to <u>Corpus Christi</u>, <u>Texas</u>, to work at radio station <u>KZFM</u>.

In mid-1985, Beck was hired away from KZFM to be the lead DJ for the morning-drive radio broadcast by <u>WRKA</u> in <u>Louisville</u>, <u>Kentucky</u>. His four-hour weekday show was called Captain Beck and the A-Team. Beck had a reputation as a "young up-and-comer." The show was not political and not surprisingly included off-color humor. One of his competitors, <u>Terry Meiners</u>, was critical of Beck's bigotry for jokes regarding another competitor who was overweight. The show slipped to third in the market and Beck left abruptly in 1987 amid a dispute with WRKA management.

Months later, Beck was hired by <u>Phoenix</u> <u>Top-40</u> station <u>KOY-FM</u>, then known as Y-95. Beck, then 23, was partnered with a 26-year-old <u>Arizona</u> native Tim Hattrick to co-host a local "<u>morning zoo</u>" program. During his time at Y-95, Beck cultivated a rivalry with local pop radio station <u>KZZP</u> and that station's morning host <u>Bruce Kelly</u>. Through <u>practical jokes</u> and <u>publicity stunts</u>, Beck drew criticism from the staff at Y-95 when the rivalry culminated in Beck telephoning Kelly's wife on-the-air, mocking her recent <u>miscarriage</u>. In 1989, Beck resigned from Y-95 to accept a job in Houston at <u>KRBE</u>, known as Power 104. Beck was subsequently fired in 1990 due to poor ratings. He would later deflect his inadequacy as a radio host to the <u>Houston Chronicle</u> stating that his stint at Power 104 "was the worst time in [his] broadcasting career."

After leaving Houston, Beck moved on to <u>Baltimore</u>, <u>Maryland</u> and the city's leading <u>Top-40</u> station, <u>WBSB</u>, known as B104. There, he partnered with <u>Pat Gray</u>, a 27-year-old morning <u>DJ</u>. During his tenure at B104, Beck had a relapse and was arrested for <u>speeding</u> in his <u>DeLorean</u> with one of the car's <u>gull-wing doors</u> wide open. According to a former colleague, Beck was "completely out of it" when a B104 manager went down to the station to <u>bail</u> him out. After a year of struggling personally with his recurring addictions and professionally, Beck found himself working alone when Gray's contract was canceled. When Beck was fired also, the two men spent six months in Baltimore living off of their severance, unemployed and planning their next move. Then, in early 1992, Beck and Gray both moved on to <u>WKCI-FM</u> (KC101), a <u>Top-40</u> radio station in <u>Hamden</u>, Connecticut.

At WKCI, Beck and Gray co-hosted the local four-hour morning show, billed as the Glenn and Pat Show. On a 1995 broadcast of the show, Alf Papineau, a "man after Beck's heart," pretended to speak <u>Chinese</u> during a taped comedy skit. When an <u>Asian-American</u> listener called to complain, Gray and Beck made fun of the caller and played gongs in the background while Papineau spoke in a mock-Chinese accent. The listener contacted a number of human rights organizations, four of which formed the Connecticut Asian American Coalition Against KC101 Racism. The station manager read an apology on the air and the station issued a written pledge to refrain from offensive activities and instituted cultural sensitivity training for employees.

When Gray left the show to move to Salt Lake City, Beck continued with co-host Vinnie Penn. At the end of 1998, Beck was told that his contract would not be renewed when it expired at the end of the 1999.

The Glenn Beck Program first aired in 2000 on <u>WFLA (AM)</u> in <u>Tampa</u>, Florida, and took their afternoon time slot from eighteenth to first place within a year. In January 2002, <u>Premiere Radio Networks</u> launched the show nationwide on 47 stations. The show then moved to <u>Philadelphia</u>, Pennsylvania, broadcasting from new flagship station WPHT. On November 5, 2007, <u>The New York Times</u> reported that Premiere Radio Networks was extending Beck's contract. By May 2008, it had reached over 280 terrestrial stations as well as <u>XM Satellite</u>. It was ranked 4th in the nation with over six and a half million listeners.

Television

In January 2006, CNN's Headline News announced that Beck would host a nightly newscommentary show in their new prime-time block Headline Prime. The show, simply called Glenn Beck, aired weeknights at 7:00 p.m., repeating at 9:00 p.m. and midnight (all times Eastern) from May 8, 2006 to October 16, 2008. CNN Headline News described the show as "an unconventional look at the news of the day featuring his often amusing perspective on the top stories from world events and politics to pop culture and everyday hassles." At the end of his time at CNN-HLN, Beck had the second largest audience behind Nancy Grace. On July 21, 2008, Beck filled in for Larry King on the show Larry King Live. In 2008, Beck won the Marconi Radio Award for Network Syndicated Personality of the Year.

On October 16, 2008, it was announced that Beck would join the Fox News Channel, leaving CNN Headline News. A news hour with Jane Velez-Mitchell filled Beck's former slot, with subsequent slots filled by Lou Dobbs Tonight encores. Chris Balfe, president of Beck's company, Mercury Radio Arts, said that the reason Beck came to Fox was because of president Roger Ailes, remarking that they "have a fantastic relationship!" No doubt a relationship built upon "dead presidents that fold."

After moving to the Fox News Channel, Beck began to host Glenn Beck airing weekdays at 5pm ET, beginning January 19, 2009, as well as a weekend version. His first guests included Alaska Governor Sarah Palin and the wives of Jose Compean and Ignacio Ramos. He also has a regular segment every Friday on the Fox News Channel program The O'Reilly Factor titled "At Your Beck and Call." As of September 2009 http://en.wikipedia.org/w/index.php?title=GlennBeck&action=edit Beck's program drew more viewers than all three of the competing time-slot shows on CNN, MSNBC and HLN combined.

However, his show's high ratings have not come without controversy from both outside and inside Fox News. The Washington Post's Howard Kurtz reported that Beck's use of "distorted or inflammatory rhetoric" has given him a "lightning-rod status," that in turn, has complicated the channel's and their journalist's efforts to neutralize White House criticism that Fox is not really a news organization. Television analyst

Andrew Tyndall echoed these sentiments, calling Beck an "activist" and "comedian" whose incendiary style has created "a real crossroads for Fox News," stating "they're right on the cusp of losing their image as a news organization." Befitting of an organization that has benefitted from the exploitation of America's unreported illness, and it will be interesting to see if Fox News chooses the people's interest over their capitalist self interests. Stay tunes America!

Media controversies

The word of God states that "out of the heart, the mouth speaketh." I humbly make that statement to you the reader as I delve into this category on Beck as his words and deeds serve to give the reader a clearer picture of the character of this media demagogue.

The Anti-Defamation League special report referred to Beck as America's "fear monger-in chief" and said "Beck and his guests have made a habit of demonizing President Obama and promoting conspiracy theories about his administration." Beck responded by claiming that the ADL was, "as responsible for the plight of Jewish people as the National Organization for Women is for the plight of women. It is nothing, I believe, nothing but a political organization at this point." Beck has continued to deny being a conspiracy theorist in response to allegations from politically left bloggers. Concerns have been raised from political commentators that his echoing of far right theories and on-air rants could lead to violence. The head of Beck's media company has dismissed this and said that he "clearly, repeatedly and unequivocally denounced violence and promoted peaceful, nonviolent expression". In 2006, Beck remarked to Muslim congressman-elect Keith Ellison, a guest on his show, "I have been nervous about this interview with you, because what I feel like saying is, 'Sir, prove to me that you are not working with our enemies.' And I know you're not. I'm not accusing you of being an enemy, but that's the way I feel." Ellison replied that his constituents "know that I have a deep love and affection for my country. There's no one who's more patriotic than I am, and so you know, I don't need to — need to prove my patriotic stripes." Beck's question, which he himself suggested was "quite possibly the poorest-worded question of all time," resulted in protests from several <u>Arab-American</u> organizations.

During the 2009 <u>Henry Louis Gates controversy</u>, Beck argued that President Barack Obama has repeatedly shown "a deep-seated hatred for white people or the white culture," saying "I'm not saying he doesn't like white people. I'm saying he has a problem. This guy is, I believe, a racist." These remarks drew criticism, and resulted in a boycott promulgated by <u>Color of Change</u>. The boycott resulted in 80 advertisers requesting their ads be <u>removed from his programming</u>, to avoid associating their brands with content that could be considered offensive by potential customers. Due to the show's high ratings, broadcast industry observers believe Beck's potential earnings remain unharmed.

In July 2009, Glenn Beck began to focus what would become many episodes on his TV and radio shows on <u>Van Jones</u>, Special Advisor for Green Jobs at President <u>Barack Obama</u>'s <u>White House Council on Environmental Quality</u>, . Beck was critical of Jones' involvement in <u>STORM</u>, a communist non-governmental group, and his support for hotly debated death row inmate, <u>Mumia Abu-Jamal</u>, who had been convicted of killing a police officer. Beck spotlighted video of Jones referring to Republicans as "assholes," and a petition Jones signed suggesting that Bush knowingly let the 9/11 attacks happen. Among other things, Beck referred to Jones as a "communist-anarchist radical". It has been speculated that Beck's criticisms may have been motivated in part by Jones' prior involvement in <u>Color of Change</u>, the organization that had previously convinced advertisers to pull their support from Beck's TV show. In September 2009, Jones resigned his position in the Obama administration, after a number of his past statements became fodder for conservative critics and Republican officials. Time magazine credited Beck with leading conservatives' attack on Jones while a writer for New York's <u>Daily News</u> called it Beck's "first knockout punch." Jones would characterize the attacks from his opponents as a "vicious smear campaign" and an effort to use "lies and distortions to distract and divide."

In 2009, Beck and other conservative commentators were also critical of <u>Association of Community Organizations for Reform Now</u>

(ACORN) for various reasons including claims of voter registration fraud in the 2008 presidential election. In September 2009, he promoted a series of undercover videos portraying community organizers offering inappropriate advice to undercover independent journalists James O'Keefe and Hannah Giles who posed as a pimp and prostitute while visiting various ACORN offices. Following the videos' release the U.S. Census Bureau severed ties with the group while the U.S. House and Senate voted to cut all of its federal funding.

In 2009, lawyers for Beck brought a case (Beck v. Eiland-Hall) against the owner of a satirical website named GlennBeckRapedAndMurderedAYoungGirlIn1990.com with the World Intellectual Property Organization (WIPO). The claim that the domain name of the website is itself defamatory was described as a first in cyberlaw. Beck's lawyers argued that the site infringed on his trademarked name and that the domain should be turned over to Beck.[128] The WIPO ruled against Beck, but Eiland-Hall voluntarily transferred the domain to Beck anyway, saying that the First Amendment had been upheld and that he no longer had a use for the domain name.

On March 11, 2010, Glenn Beck noted on his TV show that social justice had been a theme of the controversial Father Charles Coughlin, as well as of American Nazi sympathizer Fritz Julius Kuhn who in 1939 called for a "socially just white gentile ruled United States." The media reported Beck was asking Christians to leave their churches if they hear preaching about social justice because they were code words for Communism and Nazism. This prompted outrage from some Christian bloggers such as the Rev. Jim Wallis, leader of a Christian social justice organization, who blogged "What he has said attacks the very heart of our Christian faith, and Christians should no longer watch his show." Beck later clarified that he meant that if confronted with a Black liberation theology church such that of Rev Jeremiah Wright, one should find another parish, and noted that Wallis had served as a spiritual adviser to President Obama.

In his keynote speech at the 2010 Conservative Political Action Conference (CPAC), Beck "stirred controversy within conservative ranks" when he took pains to criticize the Republican Party as "addicted to spending and big government."[43] As a result, fellow conservative radio host <u>Mark Levin</u> told Beck to "stop dividing us" and "stop acting like a clown", while Republican icon <u>Rush Limbaugh</u> questioned why "the only people who can stop Obama should be excoriated for being just as bad."

The Commonality Of These Four Well Paid Media Darlings

The commonality of these four well paid journalistic hit-men is that they are symbolic of a neo-white supremacist movement that has infiltrated the American landscape. A movement shrouded in intellectual mediocrity, limited credentials, with its experiential component being limited to academic underachievement professionally and racist views personally! You may ask what is meant by the term, "White Supremacy."

Helan Page, an African American anthropologist, defines white supremacy in the US as an "ideological, structural, and historic stratification process by which the population of European descent has been able to intentionally sustain, to its own best advantage, the dynamic mechanics of upward or downward mobility or fluid class status over the non-European populations (on a global scale), using skin color, gender, class or ethnicity as the main criteria for allocating resources and making decisions."

"This complex definition explains the substance of white supremacy and its ability to mutate like a virus to meet constantly changing conditions. Since neither white supremacy nor the European nationalism that is its base is recognized as an expression of group interests, it is difficult for other groups to defend themselves against it. Even many who benefit from its existence fail to recognize its current manifestation as institutionalized racism or homophobia."

These common group interests need no conscious manipulation to be expressed; they are based on color, class, sexual orientation, and Christianity. From far right groups like the Ku Klux Klan to liberals who deny the pervasiveness of anti-Black racism on the left, white supremacy privileges all people of European descent: a sort of affirmative action for whites. This is how one explains the free passes, the absence of degrees in journalism that were not required to receive multimillion dollar media contracts, the blatant hypocrisy and irreverence towards hardworking American professionals, and the continued support of diatribes of division, fear, hate, and supremacy.

Although many hard-working white Americans do not espouse to such close-minded, insidious, arrogant, and selfish doctrines. "The words of a few defenders of white supremacy make these common interests very clear. Thom Robb, national director of the Knights of the KKK, speaking at a 1993 Klan rally in Pulaski, Tennessee, declared: "Politicians, teachers, professors, and religious leaders. None of them speak out for the defense of white Christian America." ("Christian" in an irreverent, satanic sense) Robb's speech was no more threatening than the militaristic rhetoric offered by failed presidential candidate Patrick Buchanan at the 1992 Republican National Convention: "If your leaders have lost the stomach and the will to fight, then you go out and find new leaders… Our culture is superior to other cultures, superior because our religion is Christianity."

"The connection between a far right marginal figure like Thom Robb and a national mainstream politician like Pat Buchanan is a shared belief in white supremacy. Robb is less successful at disguising his fundamental prejudices. While the Klan is seen as being against all who are not white, radical conservatives like Pat Buchanan or religious leaders like Pat Robertson of the Christian Coalition prefer to advocate for Western civilization and Christianity. All see themselves as threatened by a non-white, non-European-dominated future America."

"White supremacist beliefs, though largely invisible to the majority of the American public, regardless of race, are at the heart of the American experience. The persistence of these beliefs suggests that the racial myths and stereotypes common to white supremacy are integral to the maintenance of the US social order. Sometimes the tenets of white supremacist groups can be helpful when they reflect, epitomize, crystallize, or even clarify the perceptions of a predominantly white Christian society. For example, a December 1990 survey conducted by the National Opinion Research Center revealed that 78 percent of nonBlacks said African Americans are more likely than whites to "prefer to live off welfare" and less likely to "prefer to be self-supporting." Such studies prove the enduring nature and widespread acceptance of white supremacist beliefs. These beliefs help to explain why the majority of white Louisianans voted for Ku Klux Klansman David Duke."

"Each of these beliefs is a reassertion of European nationalism and its successor, American nationalism. White supremacy, assuming its own universal value and superiority, justifies the aggressive imposition of its own assumptions on other peoples and cultures. This is its response to the movements of "we the people of color, women, lesbians and gays, and minority religions when they defend themselves against the aggression of white supremacy." Robb and Buchanan simply seek to redefine America's Manifest Destiny, to abridge its multicultural reality, and to continue the dominance of white supremacy. As Theodore Allen points out in The Invention of the White Race, "in critical times, the thrust for freedom and democracy is thwarted by the reinvention of the white race."

"The invisibility of white supremacy masks how violence and the threat of violence guarantee its durability. White people assert their moral right to use violent force whenever their group interests are threatened. People of color have no equivalent moral right to defend themselves against European aggression, especially when such aggression is done in the name of "law and order.""

"This paradoxical belief has been a powerful weapon with which to steal and exploit land and other natural resources, to defend slavery and racism, to condemn lesbians and gays, and to deride all who are not Christian. Those who are not white or Christian are expected at best, to merge into the dominant culture and political system, or worst, to remain invisible and not to challenge white Christian hegemony. Outsiders seeking acceptance are constantly pressured to prove themselves, to suppress their indigenous culture, and to assimilate into the "mainstream" to achieve upward mobility."

"White supremacist beliefs are perpetuated through a series of social conventions irrespective of political boundaries. Organized white supremacy makes prevailing attitudes of prejudice appear moderate and reasonable: it normalizes everyday injustice. For example, a 1993 study commissioned by the National Science Foundation found that racist attitudes and stereotypes are rampant among whites, regardless of political affiliation. For example, 51 percent of the respondents who identified themselves as conservatives said they think African Americans are "aggressive and violent." For those who identified themselves as liberals, 45 percent felt that Blacks had those attributes. Furthermore, Blacks are "irresponsible" according to 21 percent of the conservatives and 17 percent of the liberals studied." These examples personify the same Doctrine and practice that this subculture has used to stereotype, and relegate the black male to second-class citizenship by assigning uncorroborated labels to him. Labels, which the candidacy of then Senator Obama has debunked, disarmed, demystified and shattered, which has angered the supremacists. I often thought that I as a black male who was born on August 4, 1961 as Senator Obama was, would have to settle on living vicariously through this transformational figure in his meteoric rise to the pinnacles of success, because of my limited employment opportunities; in spite of my educational background and plethora of experience working in three state criminal justice systems, to include being granted only 3 interviews with the U.S. Bureau of Prisons over a six year period in spite of my 100% rating on their register. Also in spite of being told that my F.B.I. exam scores would be mailed to me in 4-6 weeks from Virginia, I received a rejection letter in 2 days. When the Bureau of Prisons finally and grudgingly granted me an interview, and in spite of my high scores by a Bureau of Prisons interview panel, I was told that my credit had to be checked before I could be considered for an employment opportunity. But in spite of my obstacles, I still continue to rise and I now believe that I have the ability to continue to achieve greatness in this society. Consequently, America has witnessed an unprecedented attempt by this "Invisible Empire" to reassign these labels to the black male once again, so he must be wiser and consider his steps in life. That is why then Senator Obama's many accomplishments has been disregarded, and are rarely spoken about, as the strategy for his opponents, surrogates, and haters are to launch pre-emptive character strikes and to breed mistrust among voters, while they attempt to incite hate and division among our citizens based upon race. Additionally, these attacks have been systematic, vicious, and deceptive! Deceptive from the perspective that the candidate who is initiating these attacks through his surrogates, publicly denied any malicious intent. Funny thing, each time he began to lose in the polls, there was a relentless attack on then Senator Obama's character with the outdated Ayers, Wright, and ACORN weapons of mass distractions, with some uninformed Americans listening to this ignorant and divisive rhetoric as Senator McCain, Governor Sarah Palin, and their surrogates support through their actions "A White Supremacy doctrine," which creates a dangerous environment and resurrects old wounds through our tolerance as a nation.

But as Dr. Page states, "Excessive tolerance of white supremacist activities threatens the culture of pluralism and impairs the practice of democracy in America. White supremacists are America's deepest nightmare because they attack not only individuals, but they assault the legitimacy of our democratic process itself. Their ideology seeks to overturn civil and human rights achieved through open debate and free elections, one of the cornerstones of democracy."

"Because the percentages of whites who actually belong to white supremacist groups are small, there is a general tendency to underestimate their influence. What is significant here is not the number of people actually belonging to hate groups, but the number who endorse their message? Once known primarily for their criminal activities, racists have demonstrated a catalytic effect by tapping into the prejudices of the white majority through the Fox News sponsorship of tea bag rallies, CPAC conventions, and McCain/Palin campaigns.

"Recent polls by the National Opinion Research Center reveal that 13 percent of whites in America have anti-Semitic beliefs; another 25 percent are racist. This noticeably impacts public policy concerning central issues of racism, poverty, crime, reproductive rights, civil rights for gays and lesbians, the environment, and even the elections for our public figures."

White Supremacy in Practice

Most white supremacists in America believe that the United States is a "Christian" nation, with a special relationship between religion and the rule of law. Because racists give themselves divine permission from God to hate, they often do not see that their actions are driven by hate; they claim to "just love God and the white race."(Ala the "Christian Conservatives) However, if they are religious, they distort Biblical passages to justify their bigotry simply because they have no relationship with God. A popular religion called Christian Identity provides a theological bond across organizational lines. Identity churches are ministered by charismatic leaders, who promote racial intolerance and religious division, a more accurate name for these movements are "satanic cults." Even for those who are not religious but conveniently naïve and cunning as a fox, "racist" to them means being racially conscious and seeing the world through a prism of inescapable biological determinism with different races having different pre-ordained destinies. Here lies the foundation and catalyst that fuels the shows that appear on the Fox News network with hosts of Sanity, Beck, and O'Reilly leading the charge. Other media supremacist support groups that fund the likes of Rush Limbaugh; the rhetoric of an academic Jerome Corsi, who chose to forego the accomplishments of academia, for the mindless shame of supremacy by producing a tabloid like book "Obama Nation"; or the "closet skinheads" who create sites like the Urban Dictionary whose subject is not to define words, but for the castigation of all persons who are not of the "Superior Race" through the use of supremacist code-words, or the supremacists who carry bibles but do not practice the tenets of Christianity aka "Christians for Social Justice."

ADDRESSING DENIAL AND FRONTING

Now since I am mindful of the fact that we live in a society where its citizens, its representatives, and the media alike continuously vacillate from intelligent to ignorant at a moment's notice, many of you will say, Well I just think that you are being divisive yourself, and life is not that bad! On the contrary, I do not even know if there is such a term as white privilege, I just think that you are making excuses for why you cannot succeed! Well those of you who choose to accept this conventional and traditional means of absolving yourselves of any guilt or responsibility as Americans suffer daily from government imposed poverty, unemployment, exorbitant gas prices, no-bid contracts for friends, Katrina, white collar crime, bailouts, foreclosures, racial hatred, murder of citizens by the police, sin, pimping God, character assassinations, adulterous leaders, misleading a nation of people, consistently breaking the law, bankrupting a country in eight years while amassing tremendous wealth, executing citizens who are proven innocent while the guilty either do not get prosecuted or have their sentences commuted, and using the media to sponsor hate by abandoning the tenets of journalism, we want to extend our thanks to citizen Tim Wise, a white anti-racist writer and activist who places "White Privilege" into its proper perspective so that All Of Us can understand.

For those who still can't grasp the concept of white privilege, or who are looking for some easy-to-understand examples of it, perhaps this list will help.

"White privilege is when you can get pregnant at seventeen like Bristol Palin and everyone is quick to insist that your life and that of your family is a personal matter, and that no one has a right to judge you or your parents, because "every family has challenges," even as black and Latino families with similar "challenges" are regularly typified as irresponsible, pathological and arbiters of social decay."

"White privilege is when you can call yourself a "f***in' redneck," like Bristol Palin's boyfriend does, and talk about how if anyone messes with you, you'll "kick their f***in' a*s," and talk about how you like to "shoot shit" for fun, and still be viewed as a responsible, all-American boy (and a great son-in-law to be) rather than a thug."

"White privilege is when you can attend four different colleges in six years like Sarah Palin did (one of which you basically failed out of, then returned to after making up some coursework at a Community college), and no one questions your intelligence or commitment to achievement, whereas a person of color who did this would be viewed as unfit for college, and probably someone who only accepted in the first place because of affirmative action."

"White privilege is when you can claim that being mayor of a town smaller than most medium-sized colleges, and then Governor of a state with about the same number of people as the lower fifth of the island of Manhattan, makes you ready to potentially be president, and people don't all piss on themselves with laughter, while being a black U.S. Senator, twoterm state Senator, and constitutional law scholar, means you're "untested."

"White privilege is being able to say that you support the words "under God" in the pledge of allegiance because "if it was good enough for the

founding fathers, it's good enough for me," and not be immediately disqualified from holding office--since, after all, the pledge was written in the late 1800s and the "under God" part wasn't added until the 1950s--while if you're black and believe in reading accused criminals and terrorists their rights (because the Constitution, which you used to teach at a prestigious law school, requires it), you are a dangerous and mushy liberal who isn't fit to safeguard American institutions."

"White privilege is being able to be a gun enthusiast and not make people immediately scared of you."

"White privilege is being able to have a husband who was a member of an extremist political party that wants your state to secede from the Union, and whose motto is "Alaska first," and no one questions your patriotism or that of your family, while if you're black and your spouse merely fails to come to a 9/11 memorial so she can be home with her kids on the first day of school, people immediately think she's being disrespectful."

"White privilege is being able to make fun of community organizers and the work they do-like, among other things, fight for the right of women to vote, or for civil rights, or the 8-hour workday, or an end to child labor--and people think you're being pithy and tough, but if you merely question the experience of a small town mayor and 18-month governor with no foreign policy expertise beyond a class she took in college and the fact that she lives close to Russia— you're somehow being mean, or even sexist."

"White privilege is being able to convince white women who don't even agree with you on any substantive issue to vote for you and your running mate anyway, because suddenly your presence on the ticket has inspired confidence in these same white women, and made them give your party a "second look."

"White privilege is being able to fire people who didn't support your political campaigns and not be accused of abusing your power or being a typical politician who engages in favoritism, while being black and merely knowing some folks from the old-line political machines in Chicago means you must be corrupt."

"White privilege is when you can take nearly twenty-four hours to get to a hospital after beginning to leak amniotic fluid, and still be viewed as a great mom whose commitment to her children is unquestionable, and whose "next door neighbor" qualities make her ready to be VP, while if you're a

black candidate for president and you let your children be interviewed for a few seconds on TV, you're irresponsibly exploiting them."

"White privilege is being able to give a 36 minute speech in which you talk about lipstick and make fun of your opponent, while laying out no substantive policy positions on any issue at all, and still manage to be considered a legitimate candidate, while a black person who gives an hour speech the week before, in which he lays out specific policy proposals on several issues, is still criticized for being too vague about what he would do if elected."

"White privilege is being able to attend churches over the years whose pastors say that people who voted for John Kerry or merely criticize George W. Bush are going to hell, and that the U.S. is an explicitly Christian nation and the job of Christians is to bring Christian theological principles into government, and who bring in speakers who say the conflict in the Middle East is God's punishment on Jews for rejecting Jesus, and everyone can still think you're just a good church-going Christian, but if you're black and friends with a black pastor who has noted (as have Colin Powell and the U.S. Department of Defense) that terrorist attacks are often the result of U.S. foreign policy and who talks about the history of racism and its effect on black people, you're an extremist who probably hates America."

"White privilege is not knowing what the Bush Doctrine is when asked by a reporter, and then people get angry at the reporter for asking you such a "trick question," while being black and merely refusing to give one-word answers to the queries of Bill O'Reilly means you're dodging the question, or trying to seem overly intellectual and nuanced."

"White privilege is being able to go to a prestigious prep school, then to Yale and then Harvard Business school, and yet, still be seen as just an average guy (George W. Bush) while being black, going to a prestigious prep school, then Occidental College, then Columbia, and then to Harvard Law, makes you "uppity," and a snob who probably looks down on regular folks."

"White privilege is being able to graduate near the bottom of your college class (McCain), or graduate with a C average from Yale (W.) and that's OK, and you're cut out to be president, but if you're black and you graduate near the top of your class from Harvard Law, you can't be trusted to make good decisions in office."

"White privilege is being able to dump your first wife after she's disfigured in a car crash so you can take up with a multi-millionaire beauty queen (who you go on to call the c-word in public) and still be thought of as a man of strong family values, while if you're black and married for nearly twenty years to the same woman, your family is viewed as un-American and your gestures of affection for each other are called "terrorist fist bumps."

"White privilege is when you can develop a pain-killer addiction, having obtained your drug of choice illegally like Cindy McCain, go on to beat that addiction, and everyone praises you for being so strong, while being a black guy who smoked pot a few times in college and never became an addict means people will wonder if perhaps you still get high, and even ask whether or not you ever sold drugs."

"White privilege is being able to sing a song about bombing Iran and still be viewed as a sober and rational statesman, with the maturity to be president, while being black and suggesting that the U.S. should speak with other nations, even when we have disagreements with them, makes you "dangerously naive and immature."

"White privilege is being able to claim your experience as a POW has anything at all to do with your fitness for president, while being black and experiencing racism and an absent father is apparently among the "lesser adversities" faced by other politicians, as Sarah Palin explained in her convention speech."

"And finally, white privilege is the only thing that could possibly allow someone to become president when he has voted with George W. Bush 90 percent of the time, even as unemployment is skyrocketing, people are losing their homes, inflation is rising, and the U.S. is increasingly isolated from world opinion, just because a lot of white voters aren't sure about that whole "change" thing. Ya know, it's just too vague and ill-defined, unlike, say, four more years of the same, which is very concrete and certain. White privilege is, in short, the problem."

White privilege "in action" is what you witnessed from Mitt Romney in the first Presidential debate.

But as I have stated on numerous occasions, not every one of our Caucasian brothers and sisters espouse to such a counterproductive doctrine, neither do they foster atmospheres of hypocrisy, mediocrity, and underachievement, and by now it is my hope that this interpretive narrative does not leave you angry and not wanting to continue our discourse because "hate" in any form is shameful and incendiary. Need I not remind you, that there were white brothers and sisters who stood beside people of color as "Freedom Riders!" As many of them were ridiculed, called Negro lovers, while they died together trying to secure the inalienable right of voting for all people, only to now have the above-mentioned vile genre of people pass bills to strip them of this right. Additionally, no truer statement of their character and greatness was made than on Election Day, when white America decided to look beyond race and philosophy in choosing a black man to become their President as well as ours.

Nevertheless, unfortunately and ashamedly so, this type of behavior is actually corroborated and rubber-stamped by persons of the very race that is being mistreated, alienated, and disenfranchised. Yes it pains me to report that White Privilege is not without their associates, I affectionately refer to them as Slaves!!!!!!!!!!

Slaves For Sale

If the title offends you, then you may call them neo-colonial puppets. However for those persons, who are interested in truth and are concerned less with semantics; let us discuss this matter in length. Slavery is defined as a social-economic system under which certain persons known as slaves are deprived of personal freedom and compelled to work. Moreover, in its narrowest sense, the word slave refers to people who are treated as the property of another person, household, company, corporation or government.

According to a broad definition of slavery used by Kevin Bales of "Free the Slaves" (FTS), an advocacy group linked with Anti-Slavery International, there are 27 million people (although some put the number as high as 200 million) in virtual slavery today, spread all over the world. According to FTS, these slaves represent the largest number of people that has ever been in slavery at any point in world history and the smallest percentage of the total human population that has ever been enslaved at once.

FTS claims that present-day slaves have been sold for as little as US$40, in Mali, for young adult male laborers, or as much as US$1,000 in Thailand for HIV-free, young females, suitable for work in brothels. The lower limit represents the lowest price that there has ever been for a slave: the price of a comparable male slave in 1850 in the United States would have been about US$25,800 in present-day terms (US$1,000 in 1850). Today, Fox News pays much more. That difference, even allowing for differences in purchasing power, is significant.

It is probably due to the fact of today's greater population, making human life cheaper. Because of the lower price, the economic advantages of present-day slavery are clear. In addition, the similarities of the slave system and the capitalist system in America are astounding with the common denominator being the exploitation of workers economically to become rich.

After the Telecommunications Act was passed and the Fairness doctrine was repealed, there was a modern day system of economic slavery that reared its ugly head. This system was so enticing that persons of the same race displayed no loyalties to each other but rather sold out to the highest bidder.

Although outlawed in nearly all countries today, forms of slavery still exist in some parts of the world. To make it plain so that everyone may understand, slavery in its simplest form has a few elements that must be present in order for one to be considered as a slave.

1.)   There must be a treating of one person as property.

Meaning that some person, household, company, but for the sake of argument, some government or corporation, or some element or representative of a government sponsored corporation must exist.

2.)   There also must be some socio-economic system in place where the slave is compelled to work.

To that end, we have in our midst several high paid slaves who have been purchased on the free market to engage in black face politics, present themselves as authorities on minority matters, create divisions, to defame, to debunk, and to create a false belief system. Theirs are the platforms of hidden agendas that they stand on, and are supported by the people of their race at times, but by their masters all of the time. One thing that you should never do, is to let the "black faces" fool you; for it is all about the "Benjamins" baby!

SLAVE ONE: JUAN WILLIAMS

Juan Williams, born April 1954 is an accomplished Emmy Award–winning American writer, and radio and television correspondent. He is a Senior Correspondent at National Public Radio, has written at length for The Washington Post, and regularly appears as a contributor on PBS and specifically Fox News.

Education and career

Williams was an immigrant, who was born in Colón, Panama, which is near the Panama Canal Zone (United States territory at the time). His father was a boxing trainer. Williams was raised in the Episcopal branch of the Anglican Church, of which his father was a member.

In 1958, his family moved to the Bedford-Stuyvesant neighborhood in Brooklyn, New York.

Having led a life of privilege and elitism, he graduated from Haverford College with a degree in philosophy. Williams immediately began his tenure at the Washington Post, for which he worked from 1976 to 1999. During his tenure at the Post, he played several roles, including editorial writer, op-ed columnist, and White House correspondent.

In 1996, Williams became host of the syndicated television program America's Black Forum, on which he was the cornerstone of a panel that has included the republican hatchet men, Niger Innis and Armstrong Williams. Important to note, is the fact that he has been a Fox News Channel political contributor since 1997, not someone who is a regular panelist on Special Report with Brit Hume and Fox News Sunday with Chris Wallace. On Fox News Sunday, he is known for his frequent debates with Brit Hume and Bill Kristol, as we can always depend upon him to share his opinion on the people of his race that he seemingly is ashamed of or is simply paid to stereotype and further the agenda of supremacy.

Williams's latest book is "Enough: The Phony Leaders, Dead-End Movements, and Culture of Failure That Are Undermining Black America and What We Can Do about It" (Williams, 2006), which was a critical look at the current generation of black leaders. In it, he echoes themes expressed by Bill Cosby, calling on black Americans to take responsibility for their actions; return to a work ethic that, he contends, has been lost in recent years; and begin to reemphasize stigmatization, at least in certain forms, as a way to promote policies that he sees as conducive to black development, such as renewed focus on education, monogamy and marriage, and self-sufficiency. While Williams begrudgingly acknowledges that the African-American community has made great strides since the civil rights era, he also argues that there have been significant areas, such as the out-of-wedlock birth rate, in which black Americans and families have fallen behind. He expressed these views in an interview about his book that aired on NPR's Morning Edition on August 7, 2006.

In spite of his accomplishments, Mr. Williams has displayed through his rhetoric, a detachment to the challenges and obstacles that plague our society. After all, how can you make an argument about the ills that face a people without there being a discourse concerning a system that has undermined the success of a generation of people? He speaks about there being a need for the creation of policies that are "conducive to black development!" These are policies that specifically focus on monogamy and marriage, education, and finally self-sufficiency. So let us consider the flaws of his argument.

1)   Policies focusing on monogamy and marriage:

Perhaps Mr. Williams did not receive the memo that would have informed him that monogamy and marriage transcends the black race. If he would have simply asked prominent white leaders and Republicans Rudy Giuliani, who trade in mistresses for wives at such an alarming rate that he is now on his third wife! He first married his second cousin, Regina Peruggi, and when he was still married to her and working with U.S. Attorney General's office in Washington, DC, while they were experiencing problems, he began to date Donna Hanover and began to live with her while being married. A few weeks later, Giuliani selfishly filed for a legal separation, thus leading to a annulment based upon his argument that he found out that his current wife was his second cousin. Well Giuliani soon married Hanover, and the relationship lasted for several years, but Giuliani having no moral compass, became estranged from his current wife and became the subject of rumors of yet another extramarital affair with Cristyne Latagano, his communications director. Giuliani then met Judith Nathan, a sales manager for a pharmaceutical company, in May 1999 at Club Macanudo, an Upper East Side cigar bar; he took the initiative in forming an ongoing relationship that was kept secret for almost a year. Abusing his authority as the mayor, Nathan began to be chauffeured around the city by members of New York police department.

At one point, it got so good to him that he began parading his mistress, in the Mayor's mansion in front of his wife and children. He went on to divorce her, and marry his mistress.

What a man!

How about former New York Governor Eliot Spitzer who prosecuted the bad guys on Wall Street as New York Attorney General, who ran on a holier than thou platform, but stepped down in shame when his appetite for secretly buying sex from prostitutes became public knowledge. How about his republican colleague Newt Gingrich, who pressed his first wife Jackie for a divorce, while she was recovering from cancer surgery, and while he was allegedly shacking up with Callista Bisek? I mean, since we are on the subject of "monogamy and marriage" being race-specific. Finally, how about our Presidential candidate John McCain who returned from the war as a hero, but became an adulterer when he left Carol Shepp, HIS WIFE, while she was injured, disfigured, suffering from low self-esteem, and confined to a wheelchair, and began his lusty affair with his multibillionaire wife, Cindy. Moreover, in the midst of the self-righteous maverick's denials, Arizona court records indicate the following:

An examination of court documents states that McCain did not sue his wife for divorce until Feb. 19, 1980, and he wrote in his court petition that he and his wife had "cohabited" until Jan. 7 of that year or for the first nine months of his relationship with Hensley.

Although McCain suggested in his autobiography that months passed between his divorce and remarriage, the divorce was granted April 2, 1980, and he wed Hensley in a private ceremony five weeks later. McCain obtained an Arizona marriage license on March 6, 1980, while still legally married to his first wife. But the American people want to entrust the country to him! Wow!

2)   The relationship between education and self-sufficiency:

Webster's dictionary defines self-sufficiency as having the ability to care for one's own needs. The ability to obtain an education is paramount for one to position themselves to become self-sufficient. As a quality education on the high school level will determine where one will attend college, and where one attends college oftentimes will determine where one will work, which in return determines one's economy, which is in direct correlation to one's ability to become self-sufficient. That is why while "Slave" Williams continuously voted down college admissions programs that will assist lower socioeconomic students and minorities in being admitted to top tier colleges, his republican colleagues and others have continuously shared the luxury of "Legacy Admissions" in the top tier colleges around our nation. What are legacy admissions?

Legacy preferences or legacy admissions are a type of preference given by educational institutions to certain applicants on the basis of their familial relationship to alumni of that institution. (Students so admitted are referred to as legacies or legacy students) There is a long history of this practice at American universities and colleges. The Ivy League institutions are estimated to admit 10% to 15% of each entering class based upon this factor.

Former Harvard University president Lawrence Summers has stated, "Legacy admissions are integral to the kind of community that any private educational institution is." In the 1998 book "The Shape of the River: Long-Term Consequences of Considering Race in College and University Admissions," authors William Bowen, former Princeton University president, and Derek Bok, former Harvard University president, found "the overall admission rate for legacies was almost twice that for all other candidates!"

Although university officials state that legacy preferences are used only as a tipping factor in admissions, the strength of the programme is actually quite strong. According to a study by two Princeton academics, Espanshade and Chung, legacy preference admits are given an equivalent of 160 point boost in their SAT scores (out of 1600) and can account for as much as a 300 point boost. However, this is actually a larger advantage than for recruited athletes or affirmative action, which gave equivalent boosts of between 185 and 230 points, respectively. But wait, wasn't affirmative action ruled unconstitutional in College admissions?

Now we understand about the athletes, and how they are given admissions advantages by their respective schools, mostly due to the fact that their admissions bring revenue to the school. (Ticket sales, television rights, multi-million dollar donations to the athletic department, etc), we do not understand why nor can we justify why Legacy students are given such a clear advantage on admissions requirements simply because they belong to a particular family. This undermines the spirit of academic excellence, and has a correlation to future economic opportunities. Consequently, it begs the question as to why non-legacy students even waste their time disciplining themselves, studying hard, foregoing the party circuit at their respective institutions of higher learning to strive for academic excellence, when their sin is being born into the "wrong family." For I would argue that it appears that it does not matter what grades you make, if you do not have the "complexion of the right connection," then you will find it increasingly more difficult to gain access into those challenging jobs in whatever discipline, service industry, political office, or job that we aspire to that have the prerequisites of one's talents, experience, and education that should transcend any universities' "geographical location." If the argument is that these seemingly exclusive universities better prepare a student for the rigors of certain work environments, then how do you explain a "C" student from Yale such as our former President Bush Jr. who destroyed this country? How do explain a historical and brilliant legal mind in former Supreme Court justice Thurgood Marshall who graduated from Howard University, a "historically black college and university?" More specifically, how do you explain the high school graduates, non-college attendees or academic failures in Rush

Limbaugh and Sean Hannity who make millions, but are "arguably illiterate" from an academic perspective? If it were solely about colleges and not the "complexion of the connection," then how does one explain the graduation with honors of a Joshua Packwood, a white male from Morehouse College, another "historically black college and university" who is employed on Wall Street at Goldman Sachs? I too graduated from a "historically black college and university" at Alabama State University with a Master of Arts in Criminology with honors, yet my opportunities remain limited in spite of my plethora of experience in multiple State systems and with multiple disciplines of human services, criminal justice, criminology, consulting, counseling, probation, pretrial services, management, and education as a professor in academia! Are we as American citizens any less entitled to live in a country that will afford us an "equal opportunity" to succeed? Or do we have to look forward to an establishment in this country that will continue to politically and bureaucratically block opportunities to succeed, and blame me for my failures?

Maybe when "Slave" Williams makes his arguments the next time, perhaps he can perform his due diligence in these areas before attempting to assign blame to a group of people with his rhetoric. While Williams acknowledges that the African-American community has made great strides since the civil rights era, he also hypocritically argues that there have been significant areas, such as the out-of-wedlock birth rate, in which black Americans and families have fallen behind. He expressed these views in an interview about his book that aired on NPR's Morning Edition on August 7, 2006. And inasmuch as I do remember this interview, it left me with the belief that Mr. Williams was not presenting his book from an intellectual perspective, but rather he was posing as a literary bully who was touring the media circuit to castigate a race of people who looked like him, even though he did not know them, and did not care to know them let alone assist in the addressing of the problems that he claims to have discovered that was present in their race. At best and unfortunately, I have to reiterate as from my previous discourse, that Mr. Williams presents yet another flawed argument and concern to the public that does not carry the weight of scholarly research or common sense, which leads me to believe that his intentions are tinged with ulterior motives. Permit me to explain. When Mr. Williams argues that the statistics for out-of-wedlock birth rates for Black Americans and families have fallen behind, he fails to include other races in the conversation which is irresponsible on his part.

For example, according to a National Vital Statistics report, Volume 56, Number 6: In 2005, a total of 4,138,349 births were registered in the United States, 26,297 or 1 percent more than in 2004. After a downward trend from 1990 to 1997, the total number of births has generally increased, but remains below the number in 1990 (4,158,212), the most recent peak. If you have time, (See Tables 1–15 for national and state data by age, live-birth order, race, and Hispanic origin in the aforementioned report.)

The number of births to non-Hispanic white women decreased 1 percent in 2005, whereas births increased by 1 percent for non-Hispanic black women, and 4 percent for Hispanic women. Births also increased for Asian or Pacific Islander (API) women and American Indian or Alaska Native (AIAN) women, by 1 and 2 percent, respectively. Among the specified Hispanic groups, births increased by 2 percent for Mexican, 3 percent for Puerto Rican, 5 percent for Central and South American, and 8 percent for Cuban women.

As you can see by the findings of this report, Mr. Williams' arguments again are flawed. But for the sake of argument, if I decided to agree with his premise, has he included the data for unreported births according to race? What about the statistics of those black births where the father is currently unemployed and is not allowed to live in the house and help raise his child, because the government has indicated that a prerequisite of receiving welfare assistance is contingent upon the father not being present in the home? Does he speak about the plethora of black fathers who were raising their children before they were murdered by an abusive police officer? Let's not even mention the illusion that we call the drug war that locks down our fathers in penitentiaries and jails around America, instead of treating them for addictions, and instead of arresting the Customs, ATF officers who allow drugs to cross our borders, and instead of impeaching the legislators who pass laws that favor users from other races and socioeconomic backgrounds. Mr. Williams my belief is when you add these outliers to your statistical findings, then your argument may not change but your presentation will. Ironically enough, it is unfortunate that Mr. Williams refuses to discuss or use as an example, the Republican's Vice-Presidential candidate Sarah Palin's daughter, Bristol who is five months pregnant and who fits the alleged profile with the exception of her race and although it is always tragic when a baby has a baby, I would argue that this situation was learned about because it was made public. How many baby "Palins" are in America, and how many of them are non-black? Certainly, by listening to Mr. Williams' argument, you would conclude that there are not many which are the foundation of his intent.

Keep in mind that his chameleonic tactics became evident when it was learned that he was a staunch supporter of Justice Clarence Thomas when sexual harassment charges were wielded against him by Anita Hill in his Supreme Court confirmation hearings, while he was under investigation by the Washington Post for making "sexually explicit and hostile" comments against some of his female colleagues. What a hypocrite! However, it is not surprising because it is in step with the Conservative movement. Do as I say, not as I do.

SLAVE TWO: LARRY ELDER

Larry Elder by all intents and purposes is the consummate minstrel man who has been absentia from his race for many years. The answer may very well be in his history. Born Laurence Allen, "Larry" Elder is an African-American radio and television personality. He is a claimed member of two political parties, (conservative/libertarian)and is a talk show host and author whose program The Larry Elder Show is heard on talk radio 790 KABC in Los Angeles, California. Elder has been on 790 KABC since 1994 and was syndicated on ABC Radio Networks from 2002 to 2007. Beginning in 2008, he has been the host of Showdown with Larry Elder on Fox News, there is that name again.

Biography

Larry Elder was born in Los Angeles and grew up in the city's Pico-Union and South Central areas, Elder attended Washington Preparatory High School and later graduated from Crenshaw High School and earned his B.A. in Political Science in 1974 from Brown University, a prestigious Ivy League College which affirmative action allowed him to gain admission into. Elder's affirmative action admission's tour then took him to Ann Arbor, Michigan where he earned his J.D. from University of Michigan Law School in 1977. Following his graduation from law school, Elder took a position with the prestigious Cleveland law firm of Squire, Sanders and Dempsey, which was the ninth-largest law firm in the country at the time, isn't affirmative action great! He excelled there as a corporate trial lawyer, but soon tired of the regimented promotional system. In his own words, "I wanted to make more money and I wanted to make it faster," he explained to Reason magazine. "I thought I was more talented and should be accelerated much faster." In 1980, he founded "Laurence A. Elder and Associates", a business specializing in recruiting experienced attorneys.

From 2002 to 2007, Elder's show was nationally syndicated by ABC Radio Networks and its news-talk network, ABC News & Talk. After Citadel Broadcasting took over most of ABC's radio operations in 2007, syndication of Elder's show was discontinued in favor of Mark Levin, and the show reverted to a local show in August of that year.

Elder, who by his own admission, wanted to make money faster, and was willing to do whatever it took to ensure that he "accelerated", and who fit the neocolonial pedigree, was one of the rotating talk hosts auditioning for the slot vacated by the now-cancelled Imus in the Morning on MSNBC. His audition was on May 7 and 8, and Elder was said to be openly pursuing the permanent position (Orange County Register). However, the job went to Joe Scarborough instead.

Not to let this conservative negro gem get away, on July 5, 2008, Showdown with Larry Elder premiered on Fox News Channel, thus making Elder officially a paid slave and mercenary for the conservative movement.

Family

Elder's mother, Viola, died on June 12, 2006 at the age of 81. His father is Randolph (Randy), who is still living at age 91 during this writing. Elder has one older brother named Kirk. Elder is divorced. He argues that his parents are his role models, but I am not so sure.

First of all, if one considers the background of his parents, then one would understand my reluctance to believe him. Elder's father moved to California, and worked several jobs after World War II to support his family. He also attended night school to earn his <u>GED</u>. By his early forties he had saved enough to open his own café, which he successfully owned and operated near downtown Los Angeles for 30 years. So the father was acquainted with hard work, where his son admittedly wanted to make quick money, the father was all too familiar with discrimination, whereas his son works for the very system that deliberately denied his father an equal employment opportunity. His father displayed no outside signs of ill-will, bitterness, or condemnation of his circumstances, yet it appears that his son is carrying out his self imposed vengeance on the black race on his behalf. On the other hand, his mother, as Elder told Reason in an interview, "My mother had one year of college, which for a black woman of her age was like having a Ph.D. from Harvard. She was an avid reader and she always worked with me. My mother told me that I was going to go to Stanford when I was in the third or fourth grade." When Larry was seven, the family moved to the South-Central neighborhood where they still reside. In spite of Elder's claims of his parents being role models for him, he has not displayed any of their practical teachings concerning character, and respect for all races of people. On the contrary, he is by most practical purposes, the consummate demagogue who only respects these "two" people of color as evidenced by the following belief system.

Elder is a staunch opponent of affirmative action as most hypocrites are who benefitted from it, he also opposes race-based commerce, and the welfare system. He believes that racism is not nearly as prevalent as most African Americans believe, and that there is a tendency of many African Americans to see themselves as permanent victims of racism. Elder routinely blasts African American leaders such as Rep. Maxine Waters (D-Los Angeles) for promoting racial victimization, and is against farm subsidies and milk price supports, gun control, prayer in schools, and patronizing African American-owned businesses simply because they are African American. Finally, Elder believes that the United States should have compensated the freed slaves but did not, and has tried to pay its debt with affirmative action. "And frankly," he stated in Reason, "that's 30 years of failing to hold blacks to the same standards of behavior as they would expect their own sons and daughters to adhere to. What America owes black people is a statement that we are going to evaluate you based on your talents. America owes the commitment not to discriminate." Elder believes that anti-discrimination legislation already in place, along with <u>watchdog</u> organizations such as the <u>NAACP</u>, the ACLU, and the Urban League, are enough to combat discrimination, all of the belief systems that Fox News brass parlayed to their advantage. This is an excellent climax to the denouement of the reporting of our final slave and enemy of racial progress and conciliation, Wardell Connerly.

SLAVE THREE: WARD CONNERLY

Wardell Anthony Connerly was born <u>June 15, 1939</u> and he is supposedly an <u>African-American</u> political <u>activist</u>, businessman, and former <u>University of California Regent</u>. He is also the founder and the chairman of the American Civil Rights Institute (deceptive title), a national non-profit organization in opposition to racial and gender preferences. He is considered to be the man behind <u>California's Proposition 209</u> outlawing race and gender-based preferences in state hiring and state university admissions, widely known as <u>affirmative action</u>. This begs the question as to why would a black man take it upon himself to make it his life's work, to attack a program that was created to correct the systemic racism that has always been prevalent in every area of our society. In the areas of education, hiring, set aside contracts for small contractors, etc., and when I consider the last 8 years of our lives as Americans and the inequities in the distribution of educational funding to different districts, bail-outs of their Capitalist buddies topping 1 trillion dollars; When I consider the current unemployment rate and the studies that reveal that a white male with a prison record will be hired by a company before a black male who is a college graduate, and as I consider our former Vice-President Cheney who receives a stipend from Halliburton of $16,000.00 per month and the multibillions of dollars in no-bid contracts that have been awarded to Halliburton, and the federal/state governments who refuses to allow small minority owned companies to come in to the 9th ward in New Orleans to begin to rebuild it, I cannot help but be confused as to why this ENEMY OF THE PEOPLE would be attacking such a program but let's continue our journey of truth.

EARLY LIFE

Wardell Anthony Connerly was born June 15, 1939, in Leesville, Louisiana, population in July 2007 of 5,957, with an estimated median household income in 2005 being $27,100, so Connerly understands what meager beginnings entail. Being clear about his position on race and being a black man, Connerly has stated that he is one-fourth black, with the rest a mix of Irish, French, and Choctaw. Although it is common knowledge that if your blood has black running through it, then you are considered black. Homer Plessy taught us that! His father, Roy Connerly, left the household when Ward was 2, and his mother died when Ward was 4. The orphaned, young Connerly went to live first with an aunt and uncle and then a grandmother. His life as a black male in America was a struggle. He attended Sacramento State College, eventually receiving a bachelor of arts with honors in political science in 1962.

While in college, Connerly was student body president and actively involved with Delta Phi Omega, later becoming an honorary member of Sigma Phi Epsilon Fraternity. During his college years, Connerly was active in campaigning against housing discrimination and helped to get a bill passed by the state legislature banning the practice; Quite confusing when there is nothing in his early life that would be construed as the catalyst that has made him so mean-spirited towards minorities. On the contrary, it was the complete opposite. He came from meager beginnings, was reared in several familial households, so God gave him a front row seat to the average struggle of the typical minority household. He was given equal employment opportunity; he worked for a number of state agencies and Assembly committees, including the Sacramento re-development agency, the state department of housing and urban development, and State Assembly committee on urban affairs. It was during the late 1960s that he became friends with then-legislator Pete Wilson, who became governor in 1991. At the suggestion of Wilson, Connerly stepped away from his government job in 1973 and started his own consultation and land-use planning company.

The elements of family coupled with opportunities for economic advancement should at least have given Connerly the insight that should have molded his character so he would not be the person that he is today.

In 1993 he was appointed to the University of California Board of Regents, and true to his form, after his appointment to the University of California board of regents in 1993, Connerly began to discuss his views on affirmative action. In 1994, after listening to Jerry and Ellan Cook, whose son had been rejected at the University of California, San Francisco Medical School, Connerly became convinced that affirmative action, as practiced in the University of California, was tantamount to racial discrimination. Never mind the probability that this families' son was academically inferior and just did not get accepted if you consider the following admissions criteria of the University of California. Why do I say that? Consider the following information that I pulled from the University of California website.

What are your chances?

General statements can be made about your chances of acceptance to the University of California based upon your race, academic performance, and undergraduate school attended.

The computations use historical data from thousands of students who applied to the University of California.

Undergraduate (U.C. Berkeley)

Do most of the "underrepresented minorities" who benefit from these preferences come from economically disadvantaged backgrounds?

No, most do not.

For example the American Medical College Application Service states, "The average affirmative action medical school applicant has both parents employed in professions or managerial occupations and average parental income of $51,300.00," to include their white and Asian counterparts.

However, what Connerly did not tell the public was that the affirmative action policies for the University of California system were for the undergraduate institution. The Medical school that the Asian family applied to, had the following criteria form that is described in the below statistical data.

What are my chances?

Based on numerical information about your undergraduate performance, general statements can be made about your chances of acceptance at a University of California medical school. The following computations are based on aggregate data of hundreds of resident students who applied to UC medical schools.

Analysis of this data reveals the following factors to be most predictive of your chances of acceptance:

Numerical information:
MCAT Bio Score (1-15)
Undergraduate BCPM GPA

Indicate the quality of undergraduate institution you attended:
Stanford or East Coast quality private school

University of California

California State University

Finally, consider the admissions statistics for the University of California's Medical School, that Connerly and the Cook family took issue with as it related to the denied admission of their Asian son.

Race	Applied	Accepted	% Accepted	Science GPA*	Ave. MCAT
Asian/White	4754	188	4%	3.83	11.5
Black/Hispanic	464	44	10%	3.59	10.2

(Based upon the 1998 admissions of the medical school) Now if you consider these statistics, you will notice that Connerly chose not to discuss the fact that over 4,700 Asians and whites applied to the school, whereas, only 460 black and Hispanics applied. Of those who were admitted, almost 4 times (188) the Asian and whites were admitted compared to blacks and Hispanics (44)! So where is the racial preference again? And to the Cook family, do you mean to tell me that of the 4,754 Asian applicants, your son did not have the credentials to be accepted? So now, since he could not make the cut within his own race, the other races need to be attacked which symbolizes the character of many Americans. The refusal to "Man Up" and accept personal responsibility for their academic shortcomings. However, what is even more telling is that this is the method that Slave Connerly uses to bolster his argument to strip the few bright minorities in this country who apply to these top tier schools.

Consider his carnage

In 1995, he became the chairman of the California Civil Rights Initiative Campaign and helped get the initiative on the California ballot as Proposition 209. In November of 1996, Proposition 209 passed at the California polls, 54 percent to 46 percent. However, the American Civil Liberties Union immediately filed suit, winning a temporary restraining order which prevented the initiative from taking effect.

On December 21, 1996, Republican Connerly received the opposition of the Democratic White House who announced that it would join the challenge to the constitutionality of Proposition 209, claiming that it violated the equal protection clause of the 14th Amendment.

"By joining the lawsuit against Proposition 209, President Clinton has betrayed his commitment to centrist policies," Connerly told the New York Times. "He recently said he wanted to forge a coalition of the center, yet by this action he joins the radical left."

The Carnegie, Ford, and Rockefeller Foundations, the ACLU, and the California Teachers Association opposed the measure. It passed by a 54% majority. Connerly, in 1997, formed the American Civil Rights Institute, a title that is as deceptive as Connerly's tactics of oppression. Connerly and the ACRI supported a similar ballot measure in Washington which would later pass by 58%. Connerly and his group worked to get a measure on the ballot in the 2000 Florida election. The Florida Supreme Court put restrictions on the petition language, and Governor Jeb Bush later implemented, through a program called "One Florida," key portions of Connerly's proposal, helping to keep it off the ballot by accomplishing some of its key objectives through legislation. During this time, Connerly also became a supporter of an initiative to provide health benefits for domestic partners employed by the UC system which was barely passed by the regents. In other words, take care of everyone's rights but blacks. Thanks Ward, but I know that you are not finished with your work against us, let us go deeper.

In 2003, Connerly helped place on the California ballot a measure that would prohibit the state government from classifying any person by race, ethnicity, color, or national origin, with some exceptions such as the case it is needed for medical research. Critics were concerned that such a measure would make it difficult to track housing discrimination and racial profiling activities. The measure was also criticized by newspapers like the San Francisco Chronicle and Los Angeles Times that claimed it would hamper legitimate medical and scientific purposes. The measure was not passed by the voters.

Following the 2003 Supreme Court rulings in Gratz v. Bollinger and Grutter v. Bollinger, Connerly was invited to Michigan by Jennifer Gratz to support a measure similar to the 1996 California amendment. The Michigan Civil Rights Initiative appeared on the November 2006 Michigan ballot and passed. More racially based carnage as in a great destruction of life (Webster's unabridged dictionary).

POLITICAL AFFILIATIONS AND ULTERIOR MOTIVES

Just like his slave counterpart Juan Williams, Ward Connerly sees himself as a Republican with a libertarian philosophy.

In January, 2008, Connerly endorsed Republican Presidential candidate Rudy Giuliani, a chronic adulterer who the Republican Party portrays as a great leader!

Connerly's opposition to affirmative action has generated controversy. Connerly uses as his platform a belief that affirmative action is a form of racism and that people can achieve success without preferential treatment in college enrollment or in employment. His critics contend that he fails to recognize the problems resulting from past racism, and that he fails to recognize that affirmative action programs can overcome the residual effects of past discrimination on people or minorities. But I would argue that Connerly's primary interest is not racially motivated, but rather he is the neo-colonial puppet who is being controlled by a clandestine, capitalist puppet master. Let us continue.

The Detroit-based pro-affirmative action group <u>By Any Means Necessary</u> (BAMN) claimed that Connerly, as CEO of Connerly & Associates, Inc., his Sacramento based consulting firm; benefitted financially from affirmative action programs in contracting, a claim that was supported by the May 8, 1995 article in the San Francisco Chronicle. California requires state agencies to award 15 percent of all contracts to minority classified firms. Minority owned firms that were not classified as such were not eligible for the set-asides. This created an incentive for organizations to register their ownership by race, in order to compete with similarly owned firms. State agencies may have been reluctant to do business with minority owned firms that were not registered as such, since they would not get full credit for those contracts. Some claim this created a form of state-sanctioned discrimination against nonregistered minority-owned firms. While BAMN's charge is accurate, proper context and background are absent. BAMN also claims that as a spokesman for the American Civil Rights Institute (ACRI), and the American Civil Rights Coalition (ACRC), Connerly earned as much as $400,000.00, by which BAMN questions Connerly's true motives. BAMN seeks a repeal of <u>Proposition 209</u> and a return to affirmative action programs, especially in campus admissions.

BAMN has recently opposed Connerly's efforts to put the <u>Michigan Civil Rights Initiative</u> on the 2006 Michigan Ballot, and recently disrupted a Michigan Board of Canvassers meeting by loudly protesting and overturning a table.

TALKING POINTS OF A REPUBLICAN ACTIVIST

Connerly has made controversial remarks regarding <u>racial segregation</u> on several occasions including the following:

- On a <u>CNN</u> interview in December 2002 he said "Supporting segregation need not be <u>racist</u>. One can believe in segregation and believe in equality of the races," in response to a question regarding former Senate Majority Leader <u>Trent Lott</u>.

- He told the <u>San Francisco Chronicle</u> in September of 2003 "I don't care whether they are segregated or not… kids need to be learning, and I place more value on these kids getting educated than I do on whether we have some racial balancing or not." regarding whether his Proposition 54 could derail school integration efforts in California public schools.

- Firelight Media interviewed Connerly for their documentary video "Arise: The Battle Over Affirmative Action" in which he comments; "If the Ku Klux Klan thinks that equality is right, God bless them," Connerly says. "Thank them for finally reaching the point where logic and reason are being applied, instead of hate."

Connerly issued a written statement clarifying remarks, which some of his critics pointed to as showing a favorable tone towards the Ku Klux Klan's support for his Michigan campaign to outlaw affirmative action quotas and set-asides. Connerly's statement read, "Throughout my life I have made absolutely clear my disdain for the KKK. However, like all Americans, I hope that this group will move beyond its ugly history and agree that equality before the law is the ideal. If they or any group accepts equality for all people, I will be the first to welcome them." The problem here is that from where I sit, I can find no clear distinction between the Klan's philosophy and Connerly's historicity of hate towards the black race.

SLAVES DESERVING HONORABLE MENTION

I do not know which genre of people are worst, the slaves who the networks have paid off to speak for them during this election cycle, or some of the black rap artists (I did say some) who have seemingly been paid to remain a silent partner in this contemptuous attempt by the republicans and many capitalists to derail the candidacy of another black male who is on the verge of history, and who has called for sweeping change in this corrupt, broken, dysfunctional, greedy, hateful, and ungodly government. Oh it is not that you do not understand the mission of Willie Lynch and Jim Crow's offspring to use "divide and conquer" techniques to control our race. I would even imagine that it is not enough for many of you to selfishly enjoy the position of influence that your God-given gifts has placed you in. I guess that you have no conscience or desire to give back to a nation of people who continue to support your work, buy your products, attend your concerts, and scream your names while desiring to be in your presence. Tell me, how do you attack black leaders like Al Sharpton and Louis Farrakhan who protest the unequal treatment of blacks on a daily basis, who struggle to remove the shackles of injustice, who are men enough to speak out against an Oligarchy, and who are disinterested in money, fame, or personal comfort? How does it feel to turn on your own people while you remain conspicuously silent while witnessing the disenfranchisement of our voters, the constant mistreatment, exploitation, and murder of our young men, our girls, our adult men and women? As I consider the exploitation that continues to take place for millions of dollars, the first place that you come to sell your product to is the "Black neighborhood." You are no better or different than the drug dealer that is on the corner, the only difference is, the drug dealer lives in the hood when you have moved out and away from the people that look like you. If you would "Man Up" and just call yourselves neo-colonial puppets/slaves who are owned by a corporation, then you can be respected. So if they tell you to shut up, you shut up; if they tell you to dance when there is no music playing, that is what you do; if they tell you to attack, degrade, and debase your own people, you do it without a thought, and that is why you deserve honorable mention and are spoken of in this context. But again, the Power has never been in your hands, the power is in the hands of the people who support each of you (you know who you are). I wonder where you will end up when, not if, the people stop supporting you. After all, one day everyone will grow tired of being exploited and manipulated and will SHUT YOU DOWN!

BRILLIANCE IN THE NETWORKS' HIRING OF SLAVES TO WORK FOR THEM

There is a deliberate scheme in the Fox Network and many other mainstream media outlets in hiring slaves to speak at critical junctures of this campaign season. First of all, they are black, and in most respects they are capitalists, who are educated, and in most cases are charismatic. Unfortunately, there is no interest in the truth due to their absence of character, and due to their satanic selfishness where they could care less about anyone who looks like them. In addition, these persons further are not interested in giving a hand up to anyone who is of the poor, the working class, the middle class, or who is liberal in their desire to help all people. All of the characteristics of the Oligarchic party better known as the GOP. That is why you will continuously see the brown faces of these slaves on the major networks, especially during the campaign season, and even after Mr. Obama has become President!

The Hypocrisy And Sins Of The Pharisees, Sadducees, and Christian Right

Some call them the "Christian Right" repackaged, the media refers to them as the "Evangelicals", in biblical times they were called Pharisees and Sadducees, but in many cases they should never be called a Christian! Why do I say that? Well first of all, a Christian is defined as one who professes belief in Jesus as Christ or follows the religion based on the life and teachings of Jesus or, One who lives according to the teachings of Jesus. Notice that the emphasis is on the word "lives" to demonstrate that a Christian is based on a profession and a "way of life." Don't be shocked, if you say that you are a Christian, then shouldn't people not be able to look at you, and the way that you live, treat others, and be able to tell that you are a Christian? Why wouldn't people be able to look at you and see Christ? The concern here is that there has been an increasingly significant movement of pious, self-righteousness men with ulterior motives who are attempting to control the conversation on America's political landscape. In the event that you are interested, they are referred to as the "Christian Right" who happen to be "wrong," who are referred to as "Evangelicals" and who are receiving a plethora of respect from the media and political parties by the mere definition of their name, E-V-A-N-G-E-L-I-C-A-L. Wow! Sounds holy doesn't it? I mean it sounds like an angel has been re-assigned to earth. Nevertheless, let us awaken from our stupor and define these subcultures.

Christian Right

The Christian Right is defined as a coalition of right-wing Protestant fundamentalist leaders who have become increasingly active in politics since the Supreme Court's 1972 decision in Roe versus Wade. Among its leaders are Jerry Falwell, James Dobson, (Focus on the Rich Family) and Pat Robertson of the 700 Club. The Religious Right sponsors a network of Christian bookstores, radio stations, and television evangelists. Opposed to carefully select biblical issues such as abortion, homosexuality, pornography, and what it views as the marginalizing of religion in American public life, the Christian Right has also championed prayer in the public schools. In the 1980s it gave strong support to President Ronald Reagan, not Jesus Christ and his teachings.

This term is used by scholars, pseudo-journalists, and journalists alike, to refer to a spectrum of right-wing Christian political and social movements and organizations characterized by their strong support of conservative social and political values. The "Christian Right" as a politically active social movement that runs the gamut, and includes individuals from a wide variety of theological beliefs, ranging from moderately traditional movements within Lutheranism and Catholicism to theologically more conservative movements such as Evangelicalism, Pentecostalism and Fundamentalist Christianity.

Evangelicalism (commonly known as Evangelicals) is a theological movement, tradition, and system of beliefs, most closely associated with <u>Protestant</u> <u>Christianity</u>, which identifies with the <u>Gospel</u>. Although evangelicalism has been defined in a number of ways, most adherents consider belief in the need for personal conversion (or being "<u>born again</u>"), some expression of the gospel through <u>evangelism</u>, a high regard for <u>Biblical authority</u>, and an emphasis on the <u>death and resurrection of Jesus</u> to be key characteristics.

The contemporary usage of the term derives from a 20th century movement which was perceived as the middle ground between the <u>theological liberalism</u> in the <u>Mainline (Protestant)</u> denominations and the cultural separatism of <u>Fundamentalist Christianity</u>. In <u>North American</u> usage of the term "<u>evangelicals</u>" is nearly always used in this sense.

Evangelicalism has been described as "the third of the leading strands in American Protestantism, straddling the divide between fundamentalists and liberals." The terms Christian Right, <u>Religious Right</u>, and Evangelical are sometimes used interchangeably, although this is problematic. Fundamentalists across several religions often share with the Christian Right certain positions on specific issues such as opposition to <u>birth control</u>, <u>abortion</u>, <u>gay rights</u>, <u>separation of religion and government</u>, <u>evolution</u>, embryonic stem cell research, and antipathy for perceived changing moral standards. So while many leaders of the Christian Right are outspoken critics of <u>radical Islam</u>, organizations composed of conservative Christians, Muslim social conservatives, and Orthodox Jews sometimes cooperate in national and international projects, especially through the <u>World Congress of Families</u> and United Nations NGO gatherings.

However, evangelicals seek to distance themselves from stereotypical perceptions of the "fundamentalist" posture, of antagonism toward the larger society, advocating involvement in the surrounding community rather than separation from it.

In North America, evangelicals tend to be perceived as <u>socially conservative</u>. For instance, based on the view that marriage is defined as only between one man and one woman, many evangelicals oppose <u>same-sex marriage</u> and oftentimes ignore <u>polyamory</u> (To have the freedom to love more than one person equally) which in and of itself causes problems. Also, based on the view that an unborn baby's right to live takes precedence over the legal right to terminate an unwanted pregnancy, evangelicals tend to oppose laws permitting abortion. However, they do not seem to take a clear stance on the sins of racism, classism, and adultery, lying, and tearing down another person's character.

Metaphorically, the similarities between these religious subcultures, their political party of choice (G.O.P.) and the Pharisees and Sadducees are fascinating. Consider the Sadducees.

They were a sect of Jews formed around the time of the Hasmonean revolt (c.200 B.C.). Little is known concerning their beliefs, but according to Josephus Flavius, they upheld only the authority of the written law, and not the oral tradition held by the Pharisees. They are believed to have had a small following, drawn primarily from the upper classes. Eventually, they reached an accommodation with the Pharisees, which allowed them to serve as priests in exchange for acceptance of Pharisaical rulings regarding the law. According to my research, they seemed to be associated with the leadership of the Temple in Jerusalem. Possibly, Sadducees represent the aristocratic clan of the Hasmonean high priests, who replaced the previous high priestly lineage that had allowed the Syrian Emperor Antiochus IV Epiphanes to desecrate the Temple of Jerusalem with idolatrous sacrifices and to martyr monotheistic Jews. The Jewish holiday of Hanukkah celebrates the ousting of the Syrian forces, the rededication of the Temple, and the installment of the new Hasmonean priestly line.

Their Beliefs

Sadducees rejected certain beliefs of the Pharisaic interpretation of the Torah. They rejected the Pharisaic tenet of an oral Torah, and interpreted the verses literally. In their personal lives this often meant the perception of a more stringent lifestyle, as they did away with the ability to interpret. In other words, any religious documentation that may interpret any facet of my lifestyle and judge me is unacceptable. The Sadducees emerged as a major force only after the Hashmenite rebellion. The reason for this was not, in fact, a matter of religion. He claims that as complete rejection of Judaism would not have been tolerated under the Hasmonean rule, the Hellenists joined the

Sadducees maintaining that they were rejecting not Judaism but Rabbinic law. Thus, the Sadducees were for the most part a political party not a religious sect. In other words, they disguised themselves as a religious sect when they were actually a well connected political party who pimped God.

Concerning criminal jurisdiction they were so rigorous that the day on which their code was abolished by the Pharisaic Sanhedrin under Simeon ben Shetah's leadership, during the reign of Salome Alexandra, it was celebrated as a festival. The Sadducees are said to have insisted on the literal execution of the law of retaliation in cases that involved them being wronged especially: "Eye for eye, tooth for tooth", which pharisaic Judaism, and later rabbinic Judaism, rejected. On the other hand, they would not inflict the death penalty on false witnesses in a case where capital punishment had been wrongfully carried out, like in cases of Presidents of countries who launch accusations of W.M.D., that led to the execution of Presidents of sovereign nations like Iraq, unless the accused had been executed solely in consequence of the testimony of such witnesses.

On the other hand, the Pharisee is said to be a member of an ancient Jewish sect that emphasized strict interpretation and observance of the Mosaic law in both its oral and written form, or in short, a hypocritically self-righteous person. One of the two great Jewish religious and political parties of the second commonwealth. Their opponents were the Sadducees, and it appears that the Sadducees gave them their name, perushim, Hebrew for "separatists" or "deviants." The Pharisees began their activities during or after the Hasmonean revolt (c.166– 142 B.C.). The Pharisees upheld an interpretation of Judaism that was in opposition to the priestly Temple cult. They stressed faith in the one God; the divine revelation of the law both written and oral handed down by Moses through Joshua, the elders, and the prophets to the Pharisees; and eternal life and resurrection for those who keep the law. Pharisees insisted on the strict observance of Jewish law, which they began to codify. While in agreement on the broad outlines of Jewish law, the Pharisees encouraged debate on its fine points, or debated the loopholes in the law to justify their sinful actions, and according to one view, practiced the tradition of zuggot, or pairs of scholars with opposing views. One supporting and justifying their sinful actions and one who was diametrically opposed to their actions and condemns them. Consequently, they developed the synagogue as an alternative place of worship to the Temple, with a liturgy consisting of biblical and prophetic readings, and the repetition of the basic creed of Judaism. In addition, they supported the separation of the worldly and the spiritual spheres (separation of church and state), ceding the former to the secular rulers of the day. Sound familiar?

Now my bible tells me that we as a Christians "Shall know them by their fruits." Matthew 7:16(a)

This eliminates the confusion of the Christian Right and the Evangelicals who seem to be interested in excluding parts of the Word of God from the national conversation during this election cycle. After all, when one views the news releases, the debates, political pundits, and preachers alike, one would have a tendency to think that only "the right to choose" (abortion) and "gay marriages" are sins. Here we have a Vice Presidential candidate who does not support sex education in schools, who supports abortion even in cases of rape or incest, being exalted by the Christian Right, the preachers, and the Evangelicals, and their position is, "because she chooses to keep the child and abortion is a sin, we choose her." These groups went on to say that anyone who supports a woman's right to choose (Roe vs. Wade) is a wretched sinner, and is unfit to run this country. This argument transformed this election cycle into the contest of "sinner vs. the righteous" even though they omitted one reality about this politically charged manipulatory tactic, that abortion and homosexuality are NOT THE ONLY SINS IN THE BIBLE. That is why I argued earlier in this discourse about the importance of judging a man by "the fruits that they bare." Because if we do not, then the line that separates acceptable sin from unacceptable sin will be more delineated and blurred more than it is now. Why do I say that? Because this election has become about "Choice" Sins, while all other sins have been rendered as acceptable through the silent consent of the Christian ~~Wrong~~ Right, therefore why don't we just throw the bible in the trash if we are not going to read and practice it in its entirety.

How does a Presidential candidate and his GOP supporting cast (Rudy Giuliani, Paul Ryan, John Boehner, Eric Cantor, Fred Thompson, Newt Gingrich), on national T.V. tear down then Senator Obama and impugn his character while proclaiming family values as one of their platforms? How does Catholic Bishops and part-time catholic Pat Buchanan attempt to make the President's invitation to speak at Notre Dame an issue? The last time I checked gentlemen, professed Christians and self-righteous Roman Catholics alike, PEDOPHILIA or so all of you can understand it, school teachers sleeping with their students, priests molesting and raping altar boys (deaf included) and writing checks to make it go away is a sin, ADULTERY, FORNICATION, BEARING FALSE WITNESS AGAINST YOUR NEIGHBOR, MURDERING YOUR NEIGHBOR WITH YOUR TONGUE, are all sins. How does the Christian Right, Preachers and the Evangelicals exalt a Vice-Presidential candidate (Sarah Palin), and prepare her for the sainthood; by talking about how she chose to keep her future grand-child, not abort it, while waging war against then Senator Obama, as they portrayed him as the second coming of Satan for his position on a woman's right to choose? The last time I checked, FORNICATION, PRE-MARITAL SEX, BEARING FALSE WITNESS AGAINST YOUR NEIGHBOR are still sins in the bible and "I betcha" (pun intended) that you are going to have some explaining to do when God pays you a visit and asks you how you managed to overlook such blatant sins and claim to know me? And when he tells you to choose this day who you will serve, The Republican Party and "mammon" (money) or God, he will mean just that. But I suspect that you already understand that.

This is why I told you that being a member of the Christian Right, the Clergy, or if you called yourself an Evangelical, it did not automatically make you a Christian, because Christians adhere to the teachings and characteristics of Christ. What are those teachings and characteristics and what do they look like in action?

1.   They are the Man of One Wife (I Timothy 5:9):

God requires professed Christians who enter into a marital covenant with him in front of man to "Honor" their promise. Unfortunately, these men are so arrogant, pompous, and immoral, that they treat their marriages as any other contract being the lawyers that they are. After all contracts, in their opinion are meant to be broken if they find a better opportunity! Just ask their former wives, it is all about them.

2.   They walk worthy of their calling (Ephesians 4:1):

God requires us to walk before him and represent him with integrity and truth, instead of avoiding the issue, disregarding the truth, blaming others, hiding behind clerical collars, and never giving a straight answer to the people who ask them questions. After all, a lie by any other name is still a lie!

3.   They are more interested in exalting man than tearing him down (Philippians 2:3):

Maybe it is just me, but it appears that during every Presidential election cycle, there is a reckless disregard for the truth by the G.O.P., while there is an all-out attack on the character of innocent men whose desire is to talk about real issues that affect everyday people's lives. There is no regard if their opponents have children who hear the vicious, venomous attacks being waged on their parents, there is no regard as to whether these attacks sadden the children, because the love of God is not in their hearts.

4.   They love ALL Men, as Christ loves all men. Instead of protecting their selfish interests as party members (John 13:35):

It is unfortunate that when I listened to part of the G.O.P. National convention, the tea parties, and the Conservative political action committee convention (CPAC) with Rush Limbaugh as their keynote speaker, all I heard were lies, after attacks, after lies, and attacks, after lies, and attacks with no solutions to our country's current crisis. When I turn to Fox News, all I hear is a hate doctrine being spewed, violence being incited, assassinations being subliminally suggested, and division being perpetuated. All of the dividers and slaves waging all out attacks on anyone who is not a Republican or a Capitalist who supports their political agenda that resists progress at all costs!

5. They rejoice in the truth, instead of trying to conceal it (I Corinthians 13:6):

After media icon Oprah Winfrey, who has been the epitome of political neutrality, went public and told America that Barack Obama was the real deal, you know I was optimistic that this time our political process was going to be different. I actually thought that some of the media outlets were interested in the truth being told in a professional and unbiased manner. Until Joe "the Plumber" Wurzelbacher became an appointed, non-credentialed war correspondent for the republican website PJTV.com, while Keith Olbermann and Chris Matthews were reassigned by MSNBC from political commentary to other assignments during the convention season. I even saw Keith sitting on the stage with NFL commentators! Why? Despite his sports commentator background, because they dared to tell the truth and challenge the political amnesia of the Republican Party as they do not even RESPECT the citizens of America enough to tell them the truth and talk about the issues. Thank God for Ms. Hughes at Radio One who has assembled a stable of truth tellers (Al Sharpton, Steve Harvey, Michael Baisden, and Warren Ballentine) who refuse to be intimidated by these miscreants and refuse to capitulate on standing up for righteousness and truth. Thank God for Charlie King, Soledad O'Brien, Roland Martin, Don Lemmon, Dr. Frederick Haynes, Dr. Michael Eric Dyson, Dr. Cornel West, Tom Joyner, Bashir Jones, Rachel Maddow, Bill Maher, and Tavis Smiley, etal who challenge the media status quo, speak truth to power, and unflinchingly reports the facts. After all, if you care about me you will tell me the truth. You say, "Country First?" Then why does this country lie in ruin, why has the economy collapsed with the federal government Capitalists wanting to bail out and reward their Capitalist friends on Wall Street, and no one in the party wants to discuss the suffering of the American people, how is that for integrity? But they hide behind so-called Evangelicals who hold up their bibles (props), wear their clerical collars, their flag pins, claim patriotism, claim Godliness, yet uphold wrongdoing, never challenge sin, engage in hate politics, reward mediocrity, and expect to be considered holy. WWJD? My guess is that Jesus was judged by his father not on the flag that he bears, but by the fruit that he bears!

6.   They rely on God for vengeance (Romans 12:9):

This one is directly related to number five as Vengeance was taken out on Olbermann, Matthews, and a few other television reporters who dared to stand up for truth. Watch this.

These two worldly men stand up for truth and balanced news reporting, while the so-called Christians looked the other way! I even suspect that the Warren Ballentine and Al Sharpton shows were cancelled in the state of Georgia for these same reasons that I have enumerated above. Should we be concerned? Not really, because the God that they profess to know while they are serving Mammon, will in his season take out his vengeance and right what is wrong with this entire process. So my belief is that all of them should be VERY WORRIED, because God said, "Vengeance is His, and He Will Repay."

7.   They accept responsibility for failures as well as successes (I John 1:9):

Message to the tea baggers, anti-progressives, and the members of the disgruntled Republican Party; YOU LOST the healthcare debate and it is now a law. Before you sink further into your abyss of anger, bitterness, selfishness, racism, and special interests realize one of the characteristics that you should be displaying as a leader. That one of the primary characteristics of a great leader who is of Godly character is in their ability to accept the responsibility for the successes of their leadership as well as the failures under their leadership. If one would simply examine the character of our leadership over the past eight years, there is one common thread that identifies them, there is an inherent and deliberate inability or refusal to accept responsibility for their actions. As America stands at the precipice of destruction, and the American people look for answers from a party of men who held "Absolute Power" for the past eight years, their answer is always the same, "It is someone else's fault." Can someone please tell me why do "We the People" tolerate such mediocrity, incompetence, mean-spiritedness, and lack of integrity from our leaders? Now the leadership who held total power over the past seven years, and ran this country into the ground before "We the People" elected a Democratic House and Senate, have told you that the Democrats have done nothing for the past year! So let's examine this new excuse from the Republican

Party, as they exhibit their normal characteristics of again not accepting responsibility for where this country is at this time. As they traveled around the media circuit, it was continuously stated by these alleged leaders, "that the Democrats have wasted time and have not passed any legislation during this past year!" However, what they did not tell you was as follows:

The G.O.P. Plan: Filibuster and Block all legislation proposed by the Obama administration.

Governor(s) Jindal (LA), Sanford (SC), Barbour (MS), and Perdue (GA), the first wave of obstructionists, are refusing to accept President Obama's stimulus money that would assist the middle class and the working poor who are unemployed by extending their benefits. Interesting enough is that each Governor is representing states that were historically racist, and have continuously passed legislation that oppresses the same multicultural subculture of people that are now taking a back seat to a republican ideology.

Then they shamelessly blamed the Democrats for being ineffective as lawmakers, as they were unable to pass any significant legislation. Remember, they never accept responsibility for anything that they do.

In fact, there was a non-reporting of corruption during the G.O.P.'s control. Since January 1, 2000, in a review of Political Corruption by State and Federal officials by Mole's Progressive Democrat, 102 Republicans have been convicted to 1 Democrat, 5 Republicans have been indicted to 1 Democrat, 21 Republicans have been under federal investigation to 1 Democrat, and 75 Republicans have been implicated in criminal activity to 0 Democrats totaling 203 Republicans to 3 Democrats. If we looked deeper, we would learn that the Republican VicePresidential candidate and her Political party's lawyers have shut down an "Abuse of Power" investigation by influencing all of the witnesses "Not to Testify" in the investigation. Under most circumstances, that would be considered as Witness Tampering.

If you are the minority in the Senate, then you find 60 faithful colleagues to continuously block or filibuster the legislation of your political opponents. That will prevent your opponent from passing any laws that would assist their constituency. But wait, I thought that this was "All about the people who they represent?" Well if that were the case, and it was not about partisanship, then I hardly think that the Republicans would filibuster potential legislation over 72 times. We must never allow these anti-progressive tactics by the Republicans to occur again.

Consider some of the legislation that they filibustered and kept from passing into law.

Here is a summary from AmericaBLOG on the legislation that Republicans filibustered: **The Emmitt Till Unsolved Crimes bill** — Which would help heal old wounds and provide the Department of Justice and the FBI tools needed to effectively investigate and prosecute unsolved civil rights era-murders.

The Runaway and Homeless Youth bill — Which would provide grants for health care, education and workforce programs, and housing programs for runaways and homeless youth.

The Combating Child Exploitation bill — Which would provide grants to train law enforcement to use technology to track individuals who trade child pornography and establish an Internet Crimes Against Children Task Force.

Note: CCE is Senator David "I Like Hookers" Vitter's bill to fight child porn which Republicans just filibustered.

The Christopher and Dana Reeve Paralysis Act — Which would enhance cooperation in research, rehabilitation, and quality of life for people who suffer from paralysis. Coburn put a hold on every single one, and the GOP filibustered the omnibus containing them, in addition to all of these bills which belong to actual Republicans:

Senator Thad Cochran — **Stroke Treatment and Ongoing Prevention Act** (S. 999/HR 477)

Senator Christopher S. Bond — **Vision Care for Kids Act** (HR 507/S. 1117)

Senator Sam Brownback — **Prenatally and Postnatally Diagnosed Conditions Awareness Act** (S. 1810/HR 3112)

Senator Domenici, Pete V — **Mentally Ill Offender Treatment and Crime Reduction Reauthorization and Improvement Act** (S. 2304/HR 3992)

Senator Lugar, Richard G. — **Reconstruction and Stabilization Civilian Management Act** (HR 1084/S. 613)

Senator Coleman, Norm — **Torture Victims Relief Reauthorization Act** (HR 1678/S. 840) Note: The irony of Norm Coleman's bill is obvious, given that the United States tortures prisoners.

Senator Stevens, Ted — **Ocean Exploration, Mapping & Research** (HR 1834/HR 2400/S.39)

Senator Snowe, Olympia J. — **Integrated Coastal and Ocean Observation System Act** (S. 950/HR 2342)

Senator Voinovich, George V. — **Appalachian Regional Development Act Amendments of 2008** (S. 496)

Congresswoman Foxx, Virginia – Matthew Shepard Hate Crimes Bill. Our Republican Congresswoman from the 5th District in North Carolina has expressed her opposition for the passage of this bill due to her belief that the victim, Mr. Shepard, a gay college student who was murdered for that reason, was actually killed during the commission of a robbery. No doubt that she will filibuster this bill's passage.

Special Death Sentence Republican Filibuster

The Americans Healthcare legislation: Imagine if you will, watching a loved one, a spouse, a child, a parent being strickened one morning with a debilitating disease and it causes them extreme pain. You pray, you try to help by giving them over the counter painkillers but their condition only worsens. Because of this unplanned tragedy, you think to yourself, I know, I will take them to the emergency room and get them examined but the company that covers your healthcare has ideas of their own. The Doctors examine your loved one, and they diagnose them, create a treatment plan, and make recommendations to the insurance company whom you have paid high premiums to for years.

Oh and did I tell you that the doctors told the insurance company that "the patient would certainly die if they did not receive these treatments. Since you have a copy of the doctor's report and the treatment plan, you have the confidence and hope that says, "Surely they would not let my loved one die," yet you receive a letter in the mail from the Insurance company telling you that the decision has been made that your loved one was not eligible to receive this type of treatment because "it was not an established method of treatment that is recognized in modern medicine," and they have also decided to discontinue your coverage due to this client having what was considered a "pre-existing condition." Your hope turns to grief, your grief to frustration, your frustration to feelings of helplessness, and your feelings of helplessness turns to anger. Anger because you realize that you are a "taxpayer" and that each one of your representatives are utilizing your tax dollars to provide "comprehensive health, dental, and vision insurance" for themselves and their families. However, when the time presents itself for you, a tax paying citizen to be provided with the same healthcare that your tax dollars pay for, you are said to be ineligible. That is summary of the entire argument. Not the dollar amounts, not the fear tactics of death panels, not the name calling and code words of socialist medicine, but simply, a need for our Representatives to demonstrate the altruism, the selflessness, the courage, the humanity, and the love for their constituents' health and lives that they forego the "special interests" of the healthcare industry and lobbyist donations to their campaign and for once in their lives work together, tell the truth, and place the people's interest FIRST instead of making excuses, filibustering, and fighting a man who asked the question, "Why can't Americans have the same type of healthcare that we in the White House enjoy?" After all, how does one justify using taxpayers' dollars to provide healthcare for themselves while refusing to utilize those same dollars to ensure that the Americans that they are taxing are receiving that same coverage? Think about it and reward your representative in November according to the "level of concern" that their legislation, their filibusters, and lawsuits have demonstrated to you. The explanation by the filthy rich Republicans is that the use of "reconciliation" circumvents the US constitution! Oh does it? Let's examine this premise of reconciliation. Reconciliation is defines as "a legislative process of the United States Senate intended to allow a contentious budget bill to be considered without being subject to filibuster." Because reconciliation limits debate and amendment, the process empowers the majority party." According to an article by the Washington Post, "Republicans complain that reconciliation was never meant for enacting sweeping new programs. But of the 22 reconciliation bills Congress has sent to a president since the process was first used in 1980, 16 were approved by a GOP-controlled Senate, including for President George W. Bush's tax cuts enacted in 2001, 2003 and 2006 that benefitted corporations, the Senate, Wall Street but not Main Street."

8.   They care for and serve tirelessly the needs of the "least of these" (Matthew 25:40):

No truer test of the character of the Republican government was revealed than when Katrina struck New Orleans. Many people and political pundits alike concentrated on the aftermath of the storm while they blatantly attempted to dodge the issues once again, and absolve themselves of any responsibility, but this storm had a much more significant meaning. What God did was strip off the covering of an economically exploitative infrastructure that maintained a lower class system of people who continued to be disregarded and disenfranchised. You see, Katrina represented the "Least of These," it represented people who were systematically locked out of the State's system economically, not given jobs, and were controlled by a welfare system that created a poverty subculture. A group of people who the Government disregarded, ignored, and had no interest in helping. Then to add insult to injury, they politically removed any recourse that the people had to get their lives back through the choosing of leaders that would protect their interests, when the government refused to allow the residents of New Orleans to vote via satellite. Yet the citizens of Iraq were allowed to vote via satellite! Unfortunately evangelicals fail to understand that these people did not commit these shameful acts towards the poor, they did it unto the Lord! That's right! They did it unto the Lord. After all, as Jesus so eloquently stated in his word, "Inasmuch as you have done it to the least of these, you have done it unto me."(Matthew 25:40) WWJD?

9.   They who profess to be Christians gladly submit to Authority (Romans 13:12):

When we deconstruct the Obama Presidency in relation to the racial incidents, the racial tension, the division in this country, the slurs made daily on national television and radio, the utter disrespect of our President, the insidious rhetoric of the Right's political pundits that sparks this countries' anger, the G.O.P. leaders' conspicuous silence and foot dragging tactics in diffusing these life threatening actions by these racist mobs and terrorist cells, and yes the year long opposition to Mr. Obama's agenda that has climaxed with healthcare reform legal challenges, we can conclude that these miscreants possess an inability to submit to the Authority of a Black man who happens to be the United States of America's President. But as we consider the accomplishments of Mr. President and how he is committed to helping the middle class, the working poor, and poor alike. When we consider the fact that he has been consistent in fulfilling his campaign promises to America, it can only be concluded that this countries' anger is being fueled by hate, racism, and supremacy hidden behind a veneer of Christianity. To you, I will attempt to bring to your attention the understanding of who our President is and the consequences that exist for any maltreatment of him as a leader. Paul as he addresses the church (Christians) in Romans 13: 1-2 tells us first that "every soul is to be subject to (submitted to) the higher powers!" Why? Because ultimately these "higher powers" are appointments made by God, as there is no power but of God. Therefore, if you profess to be a follower of the teachings of Christ, you know, a Christian. Then you do not have to trust the appointee (the President). Trust God, the appointer who has All Power. But you do have to submit to the appointee's Authority. Because if you do not, or if you "resisteth the Power, you resisteth the laws of God, and those who resist shall receive to themselves damnation." That is why our President does not sweat it because he understands this one fact and he trusts God to fight his battles. Do you think that Americans wanted to submit to the wars, economic decimation, neglect, photo ops, and law breaking of the Bush administration? No! But we did so because we as Christians who subject ourselves to our God, submitted ourselves to a higher power (President Bush) because we understood that if God appointed him, then it is up to him to correct his chosen leader and vessel.

10.   Christian leaders do not give to the Rich and Oppress the poor (Proverbs 22:16):

In order to understand the bitterness, the resistance, the obstruction, and the hatred towards our current President for helping the poor through legislation, one must understand the average Republican. In an effort to understand and relate to the mentality of the current unrecognized Republican Party one must be able to relate to the not often discussed characteristics of greed, selfishness, exploitation of the working class while oppressing and disregarding the poor with the Katrina disaster being the Party's defining moment. It shocks the conscience, yet is indicative of their Party to watch their leaders utterly disregard the 9th Ward for years and not commit to memory the drowning of babies, grandparents, the elderly, mothers, fathers, and other victims who died in the largest natural disaster in the history of

America and never even blink. It is not coincidental that the Republican Governor Bobby Jindal has yet to find the funds to restore the dignity of the poor by repairing their neighborhoods, but can host a 3 day Republican party Convention in New Orleans in April of 2010 where they will plot and vote for the leader who will devise a plan that will complete the destruction of America.

There Is No Difference Between The Two

Now let us examine the characteristics of the religious organization and movement that Americans have been taught by the Bush administration, clergy, the Christian Right, and Evangelicals to refer to as Islamic Jihadists. Remember this is the group by the Bush administration's standards that must be eliminated, because there was no terrorism before we were introduced to this subculture of people.

Characteristics of an Islamic Jihadist:

1. Jihadists hate based upon the religious affiliation of a person.

2. Jihadists hate based upon the "Skin" color or Race of a person.

3. Jihadists seek to "Murder" and blow up people based upon their skin color and religious affiliation.

Characteristics of the Christian Right, Evangelical, Christians, Clergy, Tea baggers and the Average Joe the Plumber (Professed Christians) abbreviated:

1. These Professed Christians hate based upon a person's religious affiliation (i.e. I can't vote for then Senator Obama because he is a Muslim, even though he is a born again Christian) I want my country back! It's Hate with excuses.

2. These Professed Christians hate based upon the race of a person. (40% of people in America who were polled admitted to having issues voting for then Senator Obama due to his skin color) To you, Jesus wants to know, "How can you say that you love God who you can't see, and hate your brother who you can see?"(1John 4:20 paraphrased)

3. These Professed Christians murder the character of those persons like then Senator Obama and all leaders regardless of color, who help the poor and marginalized population of this country who they hate, on a daily basis with propaganda, innuendo, deliberate lies, and fear tactics that they know are false hoods. Gone is common sense, gone is man's humanity towards man, gone is good faith and intelligent debates; for here in America hate has taken center stage, racial slurs and epithets have become commonplace, with the newly crowned self-appointed Imperial wizard of the tea bagger movement Sarah Palin leading the charge.

And the most compelling truth about this subculture of people whose members include Pat Buchanan, Glen Beck, Sonny Perdue, Nathan Deal, Jerry Falwell, Sean Hannity, Bill O'Reilly, Sarah Palin, Mitt Romney, Paul Ryan, Mitch McConnell, Eric Cantor, John Boehner, Rush Limbaugh, Jim Dobson, Michelle Malkin, Congressional and Senatorial representatives whose media organizations include Fox News, its sponsors and affiliates, is that I can find no difference between the characteristics of the Islamic Jihadists' that we are protecting this country against and the characteristics of these Professed Christians, leaders, militias, and media personalities!

Now that we have applied the "litmus test" for the Evangelical, Clergy, and Christian Right to determine if they are really Christians, there is yet one more issue that deserves our attention. This subculture's Godly judgment and decision-making process as it relates to whom they support.

Realistically, they have made a decision to support and trust characterless Rich men (Gingrich, Limbaugh, O'Reilly, Hannity, Beck) who has problems with telling the truth, yet operates with "Straight Talk" gimmicks. Men who are from a Political party who hates gays, minorities, the poor, the middle class, President Obama, and anyone who is not a loyal member of their "White Boys Millionaires Club." You may ask, "What about White and Black women? They have no problem exploiting you to their advantage. What about White Male millionaires? You are deemed the enemy if you actually possess the character to want to use your influence and power to help all people, look at former President Clinton's alleged impeachable actions and compare them to the accusers (Gingrich, McCain, Sanford, and other GOP leaders) who led the impeachment charge against the President while having been or were currently entangled in nefarious affairs with their own concubines. What about Black Millionaires? They will tolerate you due to the fact that you are a "Means to an end." A "means" to gain votes, a "means" to influence thought and opinion, while they finish destroying this country and pilfering it of its resources. Because it is not enough that people are poverty-stricken while all of them are rich. It's not enough that everyone in the World hates us (U.S.A.) because we hate better than we love, because we exploit better than we assist, because we tear down more than we build up, and we lack the character to accept responsibility for our actions, It's always someone else's fault.

Because it is not enough that hard working Americans cannot afford their mortgages due to exploitative underwriting corporations, the very corporations that the Republican Senators provide security blankets to. Because it is not enough that Americans cannot find jobs so that they can feed their families, while they continue to hire their friends to 6 figure employment deals, and extending to CEOs, million dollar golden parachutes. Because it is not enough that you cannot afford healthcare, yet they receive money to continue to stand for the healthcare giants while they stand against you "The People." It is not even enough that gas prices remain high even though the price of crude oil is low, yet there is veto after veto from the republicans to keep the democrats from attaching a "Windfall Profit tax" to these oil companies. It is not enough for the city of New Orleans to lay in ruin for over two years from Katrina, with the poor having died, having lost everything, yet they have not attempted to rebuild the "Ninth Ward" so that the poor can move back to their generational homesteads. Yet Governor Jindal can present himself as a reformer who stood against bureaucracies during the Katrina debacle, yet the ninth ward remains the victim of ethnic cleansing! What gamesmanship!

Yet the Evangelicals, Christian Right, and some Clergy support this party of people who have demonstrated through their actions that there is nothing God fearing or God(ly) about them. No man can serve two masters, but I am learning that there is an attempt to try. Jesus said that Real Christians should "Love One Another as I Have Loved You. By this shall ALL Men know that you are my disciples, when you have love one for another." This is the true determinant of a Christian, and as I said before, a Christian is not to be confused with the terminology of the Christian Right, Evangelical, or in some respects, Clergy.

An Example Of Godly Love

In spite of the many innuendoes, and the shameless and baseless attacks of the racial dividers Sean Hannity, Bill O'Reilly, and Rush Limbaugh with the help of their fellow journalistic miscreants, concerning then Senator Obama's relationship with Dr. Jeremiah

Wright, the true message of then Mr. Obama's relationship with his Pastor has been lost in translation. The true message of a spiritual father to any son is the impartation of the fruit of the spirit which is what the former Senator from Illinois has displayed before the world, as he has continuously had his character attacked, and his good name under siege through a constant array of shameless tabloid journalism attacks by the infidels of Fox News, and the surrogates of other outlets whose interest is the maintenance of the status quo. My only hope is that his innocent children were not watching and were not exposed to these character assassinations and chants of "arab," "socialist," "anti-christ," "nigger," "terrorist," and "kill him," at the McCain/Palin rallies, and even at the GOP rallies on the Sean Hannity, Rush Limbaugh, Bill O'Reilly, and Glen Beck shows. Yet in spite of these hate-fests, and preemptive media strikes, this man stood his ground and continues to display the Fruit of the Spirit. What is this fruit? I am so glad that you asked.

First of all, defined, the fruit of the spirit is the lists used to describe what a Christian's character grows into, over time. The cultivation of the fruit is achieved through the careful instruction of the spiritual father (Dr. Wright), as he and God teaches and imparts the wisdom to the son (then Senator Obama), concerning how to love the hateful, how to maintain your joy while you are under attack, how to be patient when you are anxious, how to display kindness, gentleness, and goodness in an evil environment, how to remain faithful and always reaching out towards a people who want to destroy you, but most of all, how to maintain your self-control (temperance) when you are tempted to attack your enemies while they are relentlessly attacking you. I should know, because as I followed this election cycle through the debates in the primaries with Senator Clinton, to the debates with Senator McCain, to the hate fest of the Republican National convention, to the current hateful rhetoric that I continue to hear from Senator McCain, Governor Palin, and their media support network at Fox News, and to be honest it angered me to see such public openness in displaying hate, and I am a Christian! However, in spite of it all, President Obama taught me "How to love my enemies," how to suffer long, how not to behave rudely, how to not allow yourself to be provoked, how to remain humble, how to not think evilly or rejoice in sin, but to rejoice in the truth. Trust me I am not naïve to the insurmountable task that is ahead of him as he attempts to unite a country that hates better than it loves. If the current climate is any indication of things to come, he has his work cut out for him. But we cannot afford to leave America in the current state that it is in. Therefore in spite of the resistance, in spite of the hatred, then Senator Obama continues to beareth all things, believeth all things, hopeth all things, and endureth all things, as he displays to the World what an example of Godly love looks like, and that is a testament to the character of God and of his former Pastor, Dr. Jeremiah Wright.

Fearmongers And The Destruction Of America

A Fear monger, commonly known as a "scaremonger" is defined by Webster as one inclined to raise or excite alarms especially needlessly. More specifically and contextually, it means spreading discreditable, misrepresented information designed to induce fear and apprehension. Early in the morning on September 11, 2001, seven and one half years ago and the approximate amount of time that it took to ruin America, nineteen Islamic terrorists affiliated with al-Qaeda hijacked four commercial passenger jet airliners. Hijackers took control of four commercial airliners en route to San Francisco and Los Angeles from Boston, Newark, and Washington, D.C. (Washington Dulles International Airport). At 8:46 a.m.,

American Airlines Flight 11 was flown into the World Trade Center's North Tower, followed by United Airlines Flight 175 which hit the South Tower at 9:03 a.m. Another group of hijackers flew American Airlines Flight 77 into the Pentagon at 9:37 a.m. A fourth flight, United Airlines Flight 93, whose ultimate target was either the United States Capitol or White House, crashed near Shanksville, Pennsylvania at 10:03 a.m. Excluding the 19 hijackers, 2,974 people died in the attacks. Another 24 are missing and presumed dead. The overwhelming majority of casualties were civilians, including nationals of over 90 different countries. In addition, the death of at least one person from lung disease was ruled by a medical examiner to be a result of exposure to dust from the World Trade Center's collapse.

The United States responded to the attacks by launching a <u>War on Terrorism</u>, invading <u>Afghanistan</u> to depose the <u>Taliban</u>, who had harbored al-Qaeda terrorists, and enacted the <u>USA Patriot Act</u>. Many other nations also strengthened their anti-terrorism legislation and expanded law enforcement powers. Stock exchanges closed for almost a week, and posted enormous losses upon reopening, especially in the airline and insurance industries. The economy of <u>Lower Manhattan</u> ground to a halt, as billions of dollars in office space was either damaged or destroyed. To date, eight years later, more countries are more humane, the U.S. primarily occupies Iraq, the U.S. is funding the entire war while Iraq is banking an estimated $40 plus billion dollars per year, the USA Patriot Act continues to strip alleged "enemy combatants" local or foreign, of any of their constitutional rights, secret prisons are opened in the world, prisoners of war continue to be tortured by the U.S., the stock market continues to plunge, and Osama Bin Laden is nowhere to be found. Yet at the most crucial periods when our democracy is on the verge of being shifted and restored back to the people of this country, secret tapes of Bin Laden continue to surface on the television news media circuit warning America that he is planning an attack. What is happening here? It is simply and unequivocally Fear mongering, or in other words, the "Politics of Fear."

CREATING AN ENEMY

The national government used it as a tactic for convincing the American people that the Iraq war was and is a just war, relating weapons of mass destruction (WMD) to Saddam Hussein, Al Qaeda and Iraq. The WMD's never showed up but the war did, as it served as the personal vendetta of Jr. as he avenged the attempted killing of George Bush, his father. Only problem with that was, Saddam did not cause 9-11, Osama did!

The Bush administration is not the first group to use fear-mongering, the Vietnam War is another example. It is a political move, and a good one, because it works. The administration chose issues like WMD, coupled with the uncorroborated fact that the United States was vulnerable to these types of orchestrated deadly attacks to drill into the public's mind and create fear. The general Population, whether for a lack of knowledge or an overwhelming and blind sense of trust (I would bet on the former), believed in what the administration says, "For we all know how they tell the truth!" The Muslims, Al Qaeda, have been portrayed by the Republicans to date as radical extremists, animalistic death warriors, who must be destroyed at all costs as they continue to use the media as their fear machine who portrays the G.O.P. as the only ones who can keep Americans safe. Propaganda or factual basis?

THE U.S. MEDIA AND THE POLITICS OF FEAR

In order for this administration to support their uncorroborated hypothesis, they would need some help from a group of our population who could "Wag the Dog!" Or in other words, from an entity who could create the illusion of fear through periodic Bin Laden sightings, through the re-enaction of 9-11, and through other forms of media trickery. To further illuminate this issue, Dr. Sam Hamod, PHd, a major Muslim scholar and former Director of The Islamic Center in Washington, DC, and the only American to ever hold a major position in the Islamic

World argues, "I was pleased to be on PRI "The World" as a guest, talking about how the Muslim world see Bush, the U.S. and what can be done to improve our image in the Muslim world. However, the section of the show gave 50% of the time to Professor Esposito of Georgetown, he is a Catholic who has made a reputation and a lot of money off of Islam, but can't really grasp its essence; Bill Quandt, a fine political scientist who knows a lot about the secular Arab World, he received 40% of the time; then I, a major Muslim scholar and former Director of The Islamic Center in Washington, DC, and the only American to ever hold a major position in the Islamic World, was allowed 10% of the time.

Of course, since Esposito and Quandt are both bought men, they make a living in Washington, DC by being "politique", they glossed over the real outrage 99% of all Muslims feel about Bush and American foreign policy toward the Muslim world, and 100% of all Muslims are outraged by the desecration by American troops of the Holy Book from God, The Qur'an." I would also argue that they also have grown tired of the Bush administration's preemptive airstrikes that systematically murder innocent children and families with no remorse. They have grown tired of the Bush administration bombing, invading, and destruction of their places of worship as well. But of course, provocation would never be discussed because we are the mighty U.S.A. and God is with us, thus saith the Christian Right and Evangelicals, but not the Christians.

According to Dr. Hamod, as usual, again, "Esposito and Quandt brushed over it, said, "Democracy" is taking hold and will help solve the problem. My point was that this outrage is like a spreading flu virus, an epidemic that will take decades and perhaps centuries, if it is ever forgiven or forgotten in the Muslim world; one must remember that most Muslim children still remember well facts about the Crusades, whereas most American children can hardly tell you who Eisenhower was (this is based on a study done 3 years ago that showed 70% of the American students didn't know who Eisenhower was!)."

"So, even NPR, and PRI are running with fear, CNN, and others have long since capitulated, as has the NY Times and Washington Post, so all we have left are we few on the internet, and at some point, we'll be shut down, and some of us will probably be "persons of interest" and possibly arrested for sedition and speaking out as happened in Nazi Germany as the Hitler Nazis took away more and more rights, freedom of speech, freedom of assembly and every other human thing of value before WWII and during that war."

"We have seen enough of the media cowering before the Bush administration to realize that they are totally cowed. When his journalistic colleagues deserted Dan Rather, when they and he knew he had spoken the basic truth of the draft dodging and lying by GW Bush, Jr. about his National Guard service. It was clear that Dan caved in and so did his professional colleagues and organization. Fear overrode any sense of ethics, courage or anything else in their lives, and they were afraid the Bushies would come after them with anger and zeal." (Dr. Hamod, 2002)

"Actually, if Dan and the others had stood up, they could have defeated the Bushies-but they lacked the courage to stand up. That is the present failure of our media and our societypeople have lost the courage to stand up and demand their freedom of speech and the freedom to speak the truth, they'd rather bow to the Bush team's lies."

Bush has an "endless war" going on, with his slippery use of "terrorism," so that this open ended war will eventually lead him to be able to impose "martial law," for the "sake of safety of our country." It is coming, and there is no major media outlet in the US to speak against it, just as there was none courageous enough to speak against Hitler as he took more and more power and abused the German nation more and more.

"I hope that more people in the media will speak up; if not, then we are doomed to fascism that will make Franco, Stalin and Hitler look like amateurs, because we have technology today that even Orwell could not imagine, technology Franco, Stalin and Hitler would have loved to have had."

WHEN A POLITICAL PARTY HAS COMPLETE POWER AND MEDIA SUPPORT

The Bush regime reaped the benefits of a Fear Campaign and parlayed it to gain a majority in Congress, The Senate, and the White House thus giving the Republican Party "Complete Power" over the legislative decisions, the passage of laws, the appropriation of taxpayers' money, foreign policy (that is how the world views us), the prosecution of hate crimes-police brutality-white collar crime-abuse of power-and other attacks on hard working citizens (ala US Department of Justice) and simple governmental reform. The results of their power play was first and foremost, shielded and cloaked in secrecy by the utilization of diversionary tactics to draw our attention away from the manner in which they conducted governmental affairs as stewards of the people. The first and most effective diversionary tactic that was utilized was the creation of the first Homeland Security secretary Tom Ridge who Bush referred to as a "friend who he was appointing to the newly created post!" Of course there was no affirmative action or nepotism at work here! (wink, wink) The pick of his friend paid off tremendously when he devised a "Color Scheme" that would keep the public enthralled and shackled with fear, which subliminally gave them carte blanche to strip Americans of their civil rights, oppressing dissent, invading sovereign nations, writing blank checks to countries, torturing and murdering foreign leaders and its citizens for the sake of Democracy and the protection of our freedoms without ever having to explain their actions.

He trampled the U.S. Constitution while relegating it to "Charmin" bathroom tissue. This gangster move has caused our privacy and civil rights to be disregarded by one code-word, "Enemy Combatant." Imagine being arrested and surreptitiously detained in a jail for an indefinite period of time without having the opportunity to be told what you are being charged with, not being able to see your family, not being able to utilize the services of an attorney, not being able to confront your accusers, not being able to tell your side of the story to a jury of your peers, while you are transported to "secret jail cells and facilities," tortured, only to have the federal government "lie to" and tell the American people that these facilities do not even exist! Imagine all of this being done without any repercussions or legal jeopardy being imposed upon any of them. You may ask, "How is any of this being allowed?" Through the gift of complete power, given to them by "We the People," to exercise authority over our lives through the utilization of the politics of Fear, we have found ourselves and our country on the brink of destruction with no one suffering but "We the People."

HOW DID THIS PROCESS OCCUR

I could address this section for you, but I believe that our then Secretary of Homeland Security can speak for himself. Listen to him as he so eloquently lays the foundation for the covert intentions of this administration.

Remarks by Governor Ridge Announcing Homeland Security Advisory System Washington, D.C.

GOVERNOR RIDGE: "Thank you very much for that kind introduction. And, Mayor Williams, I know you had to accommodate a change in your schedule to be with us today. It's very important to have you join us, and I'm thankful for your participation, but your leadership -the challenges that confront this magnificent city are those that accompany metropolitan America generally. Your work is complicated by the fact that it is also the seat of national government. So having you here is very important to us, and we thank you for that.

Madam Secretary, I know you're going to speak in a few moments, but I'd be remiss if I didn't say that we devised the system we're going to announce today with the input of the Homeland Security Committee, and one of the most energetic -- in giving us some very specific direction during the meetings that we had happen to come from you and your department. So we thank you very much for that.

Dale Watson, our friend from the FBI, we're glad to have you participate because your team has been so involved, so very much involved in this. And, Mayor McCrory from Charlotte, a good friend, it's great to see you here, again along with your colleagues representing America's cities.

First of all, I want to publicly express my appreciation to Attorney General Ashcroft and his extraordinary team at the Department of Justice, as well as Bob Mueller and his team at the FBI, as well as my own Office of Homeland Security. The staffs of these respective agencies and organizations have been working for months; put long, long hours in to create this system. And their extraordinary effort should be acknowledged in a public way.

If you want an example of why collaboration and cooperation and partnerships are so important in our collective effort against terrorists and terrorism, look no further. This is a perfect example of what happens when we cooperate and collaborate and work together toward a common solution, once we have identified the problem. So I say to all of you, well done.

Sixty years ago, this building, Constitution Hall, was used by the American Red Cross to help the war effort. It was a time when the civilized world fought enemies bent on our destruction, when civilization itself hung in the balance, when Americans united to support the war effort and took new measures to guard ourselves from attack here at home. In short, times very much like our own.

We, too, must take new measures to protect our cities, our resources and people from the threat we face today, the threat of terrorism. That is why today we announce the Homeland Security Advisory System. The Homeland Security Advisory System is designed to measure and evaluate terrorist threats and communicate them to the public in a timely manner. It is a national framework; yet it is flexible to apply to threats made against a city, a state, a sector, or an industry. It provides a common vocabulary, so officials from all levels of government can communicate easily with one another and to the public. It provides clear, easy to understand factors which help measure threats.

INTRODUCTION OF THE THREAT AND FEAR LEVELS

And most importantly, it empowers government and citizens to take actions to address the threat. For every level of threat, there will be a level of preparedness. It is a system that is equal to the threat.

Here's how it works. The advisory system is based on five threat conditions or five different alerts: low, guarded, elevated, high and severe. They're going to be represented by five colors: green, blue, yellow, orange and red -- as you can see by the screen and the graphic to my right and to my left.

Now, the decision to name a threat condition will rest with the Attorney General, after consulting with members of the Homeland Security Council, after consulting with me. He will be responsible for communicating the threat to law enforcement, state and local officials, and the public.

Now, a number of factors will be used to analyze the threat information: Is it credible? Is it a credible source? Have we been able to corroborate this threat? Is It specific as to time or place or method of attack? What are the consequences if the attack is carried out? Can the attack be deterred? Many factors go into the value judgment; many factors go into the assessment of the intelligence.

Now, the American people want to know what is behind these alerts and, to them, perhaps even more importantly, what shall we do in response to them. I believe this system, when in full force and effect, will provide those answers. For the first time, threat conditions will be coupled with protective measures.

Now, for the moment, for the time being, as we are developing this system with our state and local partners, these protective measures will apply solely to the federal government. In time, they will apply to all levels of government, every community, and hopefully, with buy-in from the private sector, the companies in the private sector, as well.

Now, for example, under a guarded or blue condition -- that's a general risk of terrorist attack -- federal agencies may review and update their emergency response procedures. We want them to test their emergency communication systems. They may also share with the public any information that would strengthen our response.

The next threat condition is yellow or elevated, representing a significant risk of terrorist attacks. Agencies under yellow condition may increase their surveillance of critical locations, and implement contingency plans where appropriate. Again, we have a level of threat, a level of preparedness, and the recommendation that we give with regard to preparedness is a floor, it's not the ceiling. And this is the same procedure and the same process and engagement that we want the state and local communities to deal with. Take a look at a level of threat, and then assess where your level of preparedness should be.

Now, obviously, we are going to be working with the state and local communities in that assessment and in that effort, as well.

Now, presently, the nation currently stands in the yellow condition, in elevated risk. Perhaps the next administration will lay to rest this "fear scam."

SUBLIMINAL PERMISSION TO WAGE A LONG-TERM EXPENSIVE WAR

"Chances are we will not be able to lower the condition to green until, as the President said yesterday, the terror networks of global reach have been defeated and dismantled. And we are far from being able to predict that day.

And again, this is an information-based system. Based on the information we know -- there may be some information and some things going on in the world or in this country that we will know about. But when we get information, and it is credible information, and corroborated, this system will kick into effect.

The fourth is the orange condition, which indicates a very high, high risk of attack. And finally, the red condition, the highest or most severe risk of attack. Under red you might see actions similar to the ones taken on 9/11, when we basically grounded most or all of air traffic for an extended period of time.

We anticipate and hope that businesses and hospitals and schools, even individuals working with their community leaders to develop the local plan, will develop their own protective measures for each threat condition. This system is designed to encourage them to do just that.

The Homeland Security Advisory System also allows us to designate a threat condition for the entire nation or a portion of this country. If we received a credible (uncorroborated) threat at one of our national monuments, obviously, the Secretary would be very interested in that -- it could be designated orange, while the rest of the country remained at yellow. But that would simply mean that the Department of Interior, based on that assessment and the elevation of the risk, would have to elevate or extend the conditions that she had prepared in advance, in response to the higher risk. Again, level of risk, level of preparedness, and level of fear. Because the threat varies, our system must be versatile and flexible enough to meet it. Now, many states have told us that they are eager to go ahead with their own threat advisory system. States encouraged us to act. Now they have a template to guide their actions. Now, we will not mandate -- the federal government cannot mandate the use of this system. As the name implies, it is advisory.

If, for example, governors or mayors choose not to take extra protective measures in face of a credible and specific threat -- or conversely, take added measures for a threat that has passed -- that is their right. But we are hopeful that with a 45-day review period, when they can take a look at this advisory system and apply it to their communities and to their states, and begin working on the measures that they'll take to protect their communities and states, we will have a national system.

Finally, I think it is very important to underscore -- I think the Mayor did it and Jay Stevens did it, and others will -- the system will not eliminate risk; no system can. We face an enemy as ruthless and as cunning and as unpredictable as any we have ever faced. Our intelligence may not pick up every threat. And unlike natural disasters, as hurricanes, terrorists can change their patterns and their plans based on our response, based on what they see that we're doing. But the President has certainly pledged to bring every possible human and technological resource to the task of implementing this advisory system.

The Homeland Security Advisory System is designed to encourage partnerships. And this can't be emphasized and reiterated enough. The system is designed to encourage partnerships between the public and the private sectors, between all levels of law enforcement and public safety officials, and between -- and among all levels of government. Our emerging national homeland security strategy will rely on the anti-terrorism plans of all 50 states and the territories. But there are 3,300 counties and parishes, and there are about 18,000 cities. So we all need to work together to coordinate and collaborate our effort to be prepared. Working together is the only way this system will work. It's the only way we can have a national system.

The system is the end result of countless conversations with first responders, local and state officials, business leaders and concerned citizens. And I certainly express our appreciation for their input and their participation. And for the next 45 days, we're going to ask all Americans to comment on this system.

With a Homeland Security Advisory System, we hope to make America safer and more aware. But we also hope to make America better and stronger. Attorney General Ashcroft has said that information is the best friend of prevention. But not just prevention of terrorism, information is also the best friend of crime prevention, fire prevention and disease prevention. It often starts with one doctor, one police officer, and one eyewitness. They are America's eyes and ears. And we must work to get that information from the grass roots to government in as quick a time as possible.

Six months after September 11th, our resolve is stronger than ever. Our fight against terrorism is making real progress on both fronts, thanks to the leadership of our President, the strong bipartisan support of these initiatives in Congress, and the extraordinary work that our military has done overseas.

However, we should not expect a V-T day, a victory over terrorism day anytime soon. But that does not mean Americans are powerless against the threat. On the contrary, ladies and gentlemen, we are more powerful than the terrorists. We can fight them not just with conventional arms, but with information and expertise and common sense; with freedom and openness and truth; with partnerships born from our cooperation. If we do, then like the men and women who fought Nazism and Fascism 60 years ago, our outcome will be equally certain, victory for America, and safety for Americans.

But as I said before, we're asking all federal departments and agencies to make this system work immediately, integrate their plans into this advisory system, and work with us over the next 135 days to a final system.

It's certainly now my pleasure to introduce one of those members of our Homeland Security Council who had so much input in the advisory system, and who will help us make it happen, both nationally and within the federal agencies, Secretary Gayle Norton. Madam Secretary." (Tom Ridge, 2001)

THERE IS A SCIENCE TO FEAR AND INFLUENCING PUBLIC OPINION

Cultivation Theory and Media Effects

According to George Gerbner, in his work "A First Look at Communication theory," 3rd edition, McGraw-Hill, 1997. He argues that the "Cultivation analysis is the third part of a research strategy designed to examine the role of the media in society. The first component, "institutional process analysis," investigates how media messages are produced, managed, and distributed. The second component, "message system analysis," examines images in media content. The third component, "cultivation analysis," studies how exposure to the world of television contributes to conceptions that viewers have about <u>the real world</u>. In its simplest form, cultivation analysis tries to ascertain if those who watch more television, compared to those who watch less but are otherwise comparable, are more likely to perceive the real world in ways that reflect the most common and repetitive messages and lessons provided by <u>television programs</u> and the media." (Gerbner, 1997) However, for the sake of this discussion I will be addressing this theory from the second and third component perspectives.

Message system analysis is a system used to encode and quantify characters and their actions in prime time programming; it is a content analysis of television programming. Coders record information like the sex of the character, race, intellect, and height, level of aggressiveness, drug, alcohol, and tobacco use. For every conflict a prime time character may encounter, the coder records what the character does and how. For example, if the character got angry, how was the conflict resolved, was it violent? If the character was part of a violent act, was the character committing the act or a victim of the violence? Are realistic consequences of violence portrayed in the program? The results are then studied to find trends in the portrayal of the characters. For example, if white women seems to be the most recurring victims of violent crimes or if black males are most commonly portrayed as angry and get into trouble. If a demonstrator spits on a congressman, call our President a "socialist," or say "we want our Country back," it is not determined to be racist in intent.

When a Virginia governor designates a month to celebrate neo-colonialism yet entitling it "Confederate month" to instill pride in our heritage yet fails to mention the scars of slavery (wink, wink), his intent is seen as honorable with no racial motive. The "Message system analysis" is a tool for making systematic, reliable, and cumulative observations about television content. We use message system analysis not to determine what any individual viewer (or group of viewers) might see, but to assess the most representative, stable, and recurrent aggregate patterns of messages to which total communities are exposed over long periods of time" (Gerbner, Gross, Morgan, Signorielli, 1986).

Message system analysis looks for patterns in the way certain character types are portrayed in television, and how those patterns form the basis for shared meaning, assumptions, and definitions about the world and the people who live in it. These patterns form the basis for cultivation analysis and oftentimes form the agenda for the mainstream media, even during Political seasons.

"Cultivation theory" is not concerned with the "effect" of particular programs or with artistic quality. Rather, it looks at television as the nation's "credible storyteller," telling most of the stories to most of the people most of the time. While these stories present broad, underlying, global assumptions about the "facts" of life and of news personalities rather than specific attitudes and opinions, they are also market-and advertiser-driven. Television's stories and the reporting of news worthy items provide a "dominant" or mainstream set of cultural beliefs, values, ulterior motives, and practices. Heavy viewing may thus override differences in perspectives and behavior that ordinarily stem from other factors and influences. In other words, viewers with varied cultural, social, and political characteristics should give different answers to questions about values, beliefs, and practices. These differences, however, are diminished or even absent from the responses of those who watch a large amount of television, while they exist for viewers who watch small amounts of television. Thus, television cultivates common perspectives; it fosters similar views and perspectives among those who, on the surface, should be very different."

"The methods and assumptions behind cultivation analysis are different from those traditionally employed in mass communication research. Cultivation analysis begins with identifying and assessing the consistent system analysis or by examining existing content studies. These findings are then used to formulate questions about people's conceptions of social reality. The questions juxtapose answers reflecting the television world with those that are more in line with reality. Questionnaires and Polls also measure television viewing, typically by asking how much time the respondent watches television on an "average day," and assess demographic variables such as age, gender, race, education, occupation, social class, and political orientation."

The cultivation questions posed to respondents do not mention television, and the respondents' awareness of the source of their information is seen as irrelevant. The resulting relationships, if any, between the amount of television viewing and the tendency to respond to these questions in the terms of the dominant and repetitive facts, values, and ideologies of the world of television (other things held constant) illuminate television's contribution to viewers' conceptions of social reality.

For example, some of the most examined features of television is gender-role-racial stereotyping. Study after study has found that women and minorities are under-represented and that most television characters are race and gender-typed. Two cultivation analyses focusing on gender roles examined children's responses to questions that dealt with genderrole-racial attitudes and behaviors. The questions that were related to race and gender-role attitudes asked if certain chores (i.e., wash or dry the dishes, mow the lawn, take out the garbage, help with the cooking, clean <u>the house</u>, help with small repairs around the house, and make the bed) should be done by boys only, girls only, or either girls or boys. Responses to these questions were analyzed to indicate whether or not they reflected traditional gender-role divisions of labor. The children's gender-role behaviors were also determined by asking which of these seven chores they did. In these studies, the "television answer" was the response that only girls should do "girl chores" (i.e., wash or dry the dishes, help with the cooking, clean the house, and make the bed) and that only boys should do "boy chores"(i.e., mow the lawn, take out the garbage, and help with small repairs around the house). Other polls and studies have most recently been conducted asking Americans about the ability of minorities or a woman to be trusted to "have the experience" to lead a major nation. With regard to the children's own behaviors, the "television answer" was indicating that they did those chores that were consistent with their gender. These studies found that those who watched more television typically gave more gender-stereotyped views about which chores should be done by boys and which should be done by girls.

The most well-known area of cultivation analysis has focused on the manifestation of television violence through the "mean-world syndrome." These questions (with the television answers in italics) included the following:

1. Would you say that most of the time people try to be helpful, or that they are mostly just looking out for themselves?

2. Do you think that most people would try to take advantage of you if they got a chance, or would they try to be fair?

3. Generally speaking, would you say that most people can be trusted or that you cannot be too careful in dealing with people?

However, the influential aspect of Cultural analysis can even be addressed on the Political landscape. Consider the timely article by Dr. James Herndon, a media psychologist with Media Psychology Affiliates who argues in the following article about the often unnoticed influence of "Political polling and who benefits from it.

"It seems self-evident (at least to me) that voters are ill-served by the process of political polling. Yet, oddly, few political commentators seem interested in questioning the rationale behind this process, or, its fallout.

Perhaps no aspect of America's political landscape stands before us more starkly than the almost absurdly ubiquitous urge to "poll." On the surface, the process may seem harmless, and even, ultimately, meaningless.

But, a number of underlying objectives are achieved. And a number of powerful (or, power-hungry) constituencies are fed. The mainstream media, for one, feast on superficial conflict, controversy, and drama.

Polls, particularly political ones, help satisfy this craving. Polling results, always expressed in easy-tounderstand percentages, provide the "voting-class" (that is, the powerless) with a sports-like sideshow, in which members of society's "leader-class" vie for supremacy. Big-media's obsession with political polling is also a primary means through which the "common man" is conditioned to believe that he lives in a representative democracy. After all, if well-known politicians, newspapers, television networks, and websites are interested in my opinion, it must mean that I have a voice (however small) in determining my country's political and

social direction. It thus stands to reason that politicians, and their handlers, are especially enthralled with polling, which offers them the potential to provide "scientific" evidence of their "leadership" qualities to the voting public. But, for me, the reality is that virtually all traditional mainstream polling remains, and will always remain, in service to a perpetually re-elected incumbent: the status-quo. The proof? We only need take note of the embarrassing paucity of controversial mainstream polling data, not to mention controversial (that is, truly representative) mainstream politicians. The typical voter may be nodding at the wheel. But, I maintain, he is not yet totally asleep. But, based on the results of most national polls, you'd never know it. Which raises the questions: How truly "mainstream" is your typical voter? And, how truly believable are polling data?

It is both amusing and distressing to persistently hear the polling process referred to as "scientific," with the implication being that it is therefore immune to purposeful distortion. To which I would counter: Yes, and Bill Clinton was a Rhodes Scholar. Could such a person lie? But, some might additionally argue, national polling of the general public reveals them to hold, largely, the same mainstream views as their leaders, and is, therefore, validated as a meaningful process. To which I would respond: In fact, the general public is extremely hesitant to express its true feelings to total strangers over the telephone; and, that the majority of polling processes are rife with outright fraud. From my perspective, there is only a slender thread linking what we call "polling" with what we call "science." Simply, there are dozens of well-worn ways to deliberately skew polling results, all of them accepted as "scientific." And all of them brazenly deceptive. For example, few realize how easy it is to word-craft political survey questions to achieve a pre-determined outcome. Every sophisticated pollster knows how to tweak a question to provide maximum "value" for his client. And random sampling? Anyone who says that a random sample of less than 10,000 can statistically "represent" the entire population of American voters is either a liar or an idiot. What is a typical polling sample size? Almost always less than 1,000. Ridiculous.

Virtually every supposedly random sample we find in traditional survey research is fatally flawed, most often in ways that utterly strip the results of both validity and reliability.

And it is well to keep in mind that polls are designed to provide maximum convenience (and maximum profit) for polling organizations, with a minimum of effort. The result? A huge "scientific" compromise. And, really, can you imagine your typical robotic, sub-minimum-wage (often volunteer) telephone pollster getting a reliable answer from a construction worker who has to get up from the dinner table to answer the telephone? Come on. The bottom line? Traditional telephone surveys produce, at best, half-baked approximations of the truth, and, all too-often, serve an agenda with only a fleeting connection to objectivity.

And who is the typical client for such pseudo-scientific endeavors? Someone with money and power, or someone who wants it. And what "value" is provided? The "right" answer, through which to "train" a target "audience."

Whatever this process is, it is not my idea of science. And it's not my idea of politics. So, what does polling really accomplish for a voter? It can sometimes provide him with (insignificant) psychological confirmation of a choice he has already made. And it can make him feel part of a potentially "winning team." Most often, however, it is a mechanism in his disenfranchisement, the core message of which is: Don't waste your vote on a losing candidate. Better to vote for a "winner," even though he (or she) may be the proverbial "lesser evil." And don't bore me with the oft-heard claim that, by continually taking the public's "pulse," polling is somehow serving the public interest. This might sound impressive. But the reality tells a different tale. So, does political polling have any intrinsic value at all? It depends on which side of the poll you're on. Better to ask: Who benefits from political polling? My answer? It's usually everyone but the voter." (Dr. Herndon, 2007)

Again, the results of these studies indicate that those who spend more time watching television's mean and dangerous world tend to have conceptions that the world in which they live is a mean and dangerous place, but this influence can be found in other areas of concern.

As in most studies of media effects, the observable empirical evidence of cultivation tends to be modest in terms of its absolute size. In most national surveys a trivial, and demographically diverse, number of respondents (about 4% or less) say they do not watch television. Consequently, there are no real control groups. Even "light" viewers watch some television and live in the same cultural environment as "heavy" viewers. However, if one argues that the messages are stable, that the medium is virtually ubiquitous, and that it is accumulated exposure that counts, then it seems reasonable that almost everyone should be affected, regardless of how much television they watch. This means that the cards are stacked against finding evidence of cultivation. Therefore, the discovery of a systematic pattern of small but pervasive differences between light and heavy viewers may indicate farreaching consequences. Indeed, in study after study, the evidence continues to mount as to the viability of cultivation theory in explaining the cumulative, long-term effects of <u>watching television</u>." (Gerbner, 1997)

In summary, cultivation theory is an attempt to understand and explain the dynamics of television as a distinctive feature of the modern age. Cultivation analysis concentrates on the enduring and common consequences of growing up and living with television: the cultivation of stable, resistant, and widely shared assumptions, images, and conceptions that reflect the underlying dimensions, institutional characteristics, and interests of the medium itself. Cultivation analysis examines television as the common symbolic environment— the true "melting pot" of the twentieth and twenty-first centuries.

Mainstream media has a huge responsibility. A responsibility that is not formalized like it is in governmental power structures, and therefore the responsibility and requirements for selfjustice is actually greater. Therefore, it is sad to see that some journalists and pseudojournalists think that they are critical if only they manage to focus as negatively as possible on an issue. Moreover, the saddest thing is that it is almost never those with power and influence that are in the spotlight when they have been naughty. On the contrary, America has lowered the bar when it comes to press ethics; it is not like we have a free press, at least not in the sense that rich and poor guys get the same treatment.

About negative news: It is of course possible to be critical without being negative. But the fact is that main stream media is full of pointed negative news that has little or no bearing on our lives, that does not provide objective information which might be of use to make an informed opinion on an issue and that we have no possibility to do anything with anyway. We have the repeal of the fairness doctrine to thank for that. Negative news, perhaps particularly in the areas of terrorism and race, does nothing but generate fear, mistrust, anger, and the consequences for society and individuals are immense. Nevertheless, fear is a very useful tool for those who wish to manipulate the masses, shown blatantly in the last American oilwar, Desert Storm. Media, in this context runs the risk of being useful puppets for groups with their own agendas, agendas that they do not intend to share with the masses.

On a personal level, it is a fact that what you focus on has a tendency to occur more frequently. If you worry too much about terrorists, there is a significantly increased probability that you will become more paranoid towards your safety compared to someone with a more normal attitude towards safety. In addition, the same is actually the case for crime, and, surprise, surprise; I have heard that terrorist-paranoid U.S.A. experiences a lot more terrorism against Americans than before 9/11.

So what is positive news? Well, there is actually plenty, but they are not so easy to find as so much negativity inundates the airwaves. You have a graduate from school of outsourcing as a Presidential candidate, a man who has chosen the architect of big spending (Ryan) to be a vice-presidential candidate, Americans continue to get their intelligence insulted, Obama is a Muslim, Obama is inexperienced but Palin is experienced, Romney is a great businessman but he is only concerned with "his business", Obama wants to raise everyone's taxes, Obama is teaching our little children about sex, Obama takes money from lobbyists, Obama won't even take care of his own brother, Congressman Weiner had to resign for a shirtless photo and but Vitter remains in the Senate after being in the top ten of the high priced call girl Fleiss's black-book, Palin has met with heads of countries at the United Nations so she now has foreign policy experience, McCain is much smarter than Obama even though he finished almost last in his graduating class at the Naval academy while Obama graduated with honors from Harvard Law, Rush Limbaugh heads the Republican party with Michael Steele having been fired after they no longer needed colored political window dressing, and the mission in Iraq is accomplished. It could be fun to elaborate on the socio-psychological reasons for this, but well, perhaps some other time. So yes, main stream media carries a huge responsibility. I wonder whether they are really conscious about it. Because if they really are, we are all in big trouble but "we the people" can stop this game.

CHAPTER TWO

LEAVING THE PAST BEHIND

One of the tragedies of a professed Democratic nation is the inability for its people to leave their past behind. In this 200 plus year experiment in Democracy, we have been referred to in past glory days as the Great American Melting Pot! Without running the risk of dating myself, in the eighteenth and nineteenth century, the metaphor of a melting pot" was used to describe the fusion of different nationalities, ethnicities and cultures. It was used together with concepts of America as an ideal <u>republic</u> and a "<u>city upon a hill</u>" or new <u>promised land</u>. It was a metaphor for the idealized process of <u>immigration</u> and <u>colonization</u> by which different nationalities, cultures and "races" (a term that could encompass nationality, ethnicity and race) were to blend into a new, virtuous community, and it was connected to <u>utopian</u> visions of the emergence of an American "<u>new man</u>." This society was referred to as "One Nation under God" because God is with any nation that is on "One Accord," indivisible, and working as one color-blind unit. The exact term "melting pot" came into general usage in 1908, after the premiere of the play <u>The Melting Pot</u> by <u>Israel Zangwill</u>.

An early use in American literature of the concept of immigrants "melting" into the receiving culture may be found in the writings of <u>J. Hector St. John de Crevecoeur</u>. In his <u>Letters from an American Farmer</u> (1782) Crevecoeur writes, in response to his own question, "What then is the American, this new man?" That the American is one who "leaving behind him all his ancient prejudices and manners, receives new ones from the new mode of life he has embraced, the government he obeys, and the new rank he holds. He becomes an American by being received in the broad lap of our great <u>Alma Mater</u>. Here individuals of all nations are melted into a new race of men, whose labors and posterity will one day cause great changes in the world." Unfortunately, that was then, and this is NOW! Because realistically speaking, the dream for one America is under siege due to impediments in our society.

Impediment 1: Racism

"I am an invisible man. No, I am not a spook like those who haunted Edgar Allen Poe; nor am I one of your Hollywood-movie ectoplasms. I am a man of substance, of flesh and bone, fiber and liquids --and I might even be said to possess a mind.

I am invisible, understand simply because people refuse to see me. I, like the bodiless heads you see sometimes in circus sideshows, it is as though I have been surrounded by mirrors of hard, distorting glass. When they approach me they see only my surroundings, themselves, or figments of their imagination --indeed, everything and anything except me." - Ralph Ellison, The Invisible Man.

To my fellow brothers and sisters contending and struggling with the impediment of Racism; When you look at me, who do you see? Do you see a citizen of this country on whose backs, blood, sweat, and tears this country was built? Or do you see a criminal who is intellectually inferior, who is lazy, shiftless, untrustworthy, criminal, and irresponsible? Do you see someone who threatens you and incites your satanic hatred so much, that you have to go out cloaked in the dark of night and place hateful propaganda in your neighbor's mailboxes, and threatened to murder me if I ever rise to power? Did you know that I love like you, that I cry just as you do, that I like sunsets, that I am a fourth generation college graduate? How about the fact that I am not a rapper but I could be one, that I am not an athlete though I once was, I am a college professor, I am your neighbor, I am a father, I have a family that I love who depends on me to survive! Surprised? I know that you have heard it all before, and I hope that you do not have your mind made up. I hope that you collected your facts about me from interaction and relationship with me, instead of depending on prejudgments formed at subliminal supremacist political rallies; I even hope that you learn to form opinions about me based upon how God created me, because you know that I am made in his image! I can be black, Asian, Caucasian, Latino, Mexican, or Native American.

Therefore, when you attempt to judge me based upon my appearance, or mistrust me based upon false images that have been created by the media understand one thing, you are indicating with your actions that God made a mistake because he did not create me to look like you, and that I cannot help. Perhaps you should judge me on areas that I can control and can be measured, like my character, my integrity, my heart, and how I treat you, because at the end of the day, although my color is different than yours, our Paths are the same.

Impediment 2: Complacency

I am sure that we will all agree that we are a nation of Capitalistic and Hedonistic people whose philosophy is "Me First" and "Do You." So as we drive around in our idols, attend church where the rest of the people who are on our level attends, while we live in our lavish three-story idols, we have made more money than we have ever made, we have the right job, we got the right kind of friends, we belong to the right organizations, we command the respect of men, and if you ask many of us, we would acknowledge to you that we have made it! Right? I mean we have achieved the American Dream, so now we even, watch this; we now have to re-evaluate what political affiliation best serve our needs now. You have been a loyal member of the Democratic Party all of your life, but now that you have a little change in your pocket and a modest share of the trappings of wealth, you no longer feel as if your needs can be served by the Democratic Party. You feel as though your philosophy is more in line with the Republican Party. The same Party that does not acknowledge anyone who makes under $500,000.00 per year, but that is okay, I understand. You even seemed to have forgotten that you were once impoverished, living in the ghetto, had no goals, and was trying to make a dollar out of fifteen cents, but that was then, and this is now. So now, you feel as though "those people" need to get off of their butts, lift themselves up by their imaginary bootstraps, and make a life for themselves and stop depending on the Federal Government to bail them out, but you never mention the corporations, wall street, and the rich who are depending on the federal government to bail them out! I understand my friend, and I am not shocked either.

I understand that you and many like you are suffering from a condition commonly referred to as Complacency. Complacency defined is the state of being self-satisfied to the point of being unaware of possible dangers. This is a concern of mine, because I believe that this country is on the brink of destruction, because many of you are asleep and are complacent. I mean your response to the times is typical to your current state of denial, "Everything seems to be okay to me." "I just don't understand all of this demonstrating and calling for boycotts, you all are just a bunch of trouble-makers." "That comic strip by the N.Y. Post was just artistic expression, you are always trying to play the race card." "Rush Limbaugh is a true patriot who loves his country." "Fox News is a true and balanced news site and I don't understand why those people on Radio One continue to keep this entire racial division thing going, everything is not always about race, something should be done about these grass roots organizers too, because all they are doing is exploiting blacks and collecting money, Barack ain't gonna help no blacks it's just un-American." To you I say, look around you, while you are fronting about what you have, there are people like Warren Buffett who has 5 billion dollars that he just invested in a failing company (Goldman & Sachs). You have Wall Street tycoons that buy up failing banks for billions of dollars. You have the Bill Gates of this world who can vacation indefinitely, while living off the interest of their money and extending 10 billion dollar lines of credit to countries, and you say that you made it? Pluheeezzzeee. A house? McCain has twelve of them! A car or even cars? Warren Buffett can walk onto a car lot, and be given any car or cars of his choice based upon who he is and his net worth! Romney has elevators for his cars! My god, Oprah gave away cars to her entire audience! However, you are a baller and a shot caller? Sure you are. Tell me baller, when was the last time you made the cover of Fortune magazine? Are you able to sit around and do nothing on a daily basis because you live on the interest of your money or investments? Well until you are able financially, to accomplish any of the aforementioned feats, please wake up from your stupor and realize that many of you are not even a part of the economic infrastructure of this country, and it is rare to have an opportunity to vote for anyone who has your best interest at heart and is not a puppet being controlled by a capitalistic-minded "marionette manipulator". If you remain asleep, you too could become the next economic casualty of this country, for there is a movement towards a corporate controlled takeover of our economy where we will become a legislatively imposed third world country! There is a Republican party in this nation that is fighting President Obama every step of the way over his attempts to provide financial support for each of our families in the working class. They are excommunicating and turning their backs on every Republican that wants to help "all American people," from their party and talking about them like a dog with no show of loyalty to even those members of their party who served faithfully for over 20 years! Can you say Charlie Crist? Yet you want to be affiliated with their party, when the most that they will allow you to do is to serve drinks in a butler's suit! Oh sure they touted Arturo as the Democrat who defected from the Democratic Party, but his speech was aired during the network commercials! Why do you think that our former President Bush called for a World Economic summit? Although he ran out of time, ask yourself who will be completing former President Bush's mission at the expense of the American people, which will certainly cause a "class conflict." Think for yourself.

Impediment 3: High Tech Uncle Toms and Programmed Aunt Jemimas

I decided at the ninth hour to create this categorical impediment after I listened to the Al Sharpton show on WVON on March 17, 2009. His guests were a black professor from Northwestern, and a black female who tag teamed with each other to express their contempt for President Obama in his perceived refusal to help uplift the black race. I did not list their names because quite frankly they did not deem that much respect, as they did not give any respect to our President. The foundation of their argument was the drawing of inferences to President Obama and how he has failed to name to his cabinet or initiate any policies in the first 45 days that would position black America for future success. Therefore they could conclude that he will do nothing to uplift black America during his term as President. After I took a deep breath and visited my happy place, I decided to address these vile and meanspirited remarks that these two stooges made. First of all, let me begin my commentary by stating that I am not taken aback by these remarks at all. Why? Because my grandmother who ironed shirts for a living, told me a long time ago about the people within my race that I would encounter during my lifetime. She told me that they would be cut out of the same cloth as the black people that she studied as a younger woman during Jim Crow days. They were referred to as high tech uncle toms and programmed aunt jemimas.

Defined, a high tech Uncle Tom is a black man who has reached the pinnacle in the realm of academia or another noteworthy profession. Because they reached this pinnacle of achievement, they do not want you to refer to them as black men, but simply as a man. They will proclaim to the world that they have an education from this type of institution, having more degrees than a thermometer, and that they are a professor of business, etc. but they will never tell you what their true intentions are or what political affiliation they espouse to. But if you just listen to them when they are given a platform, they will enter into a vicious diatribe attacking a black man, namely our current President and make irresponsible, baseless comments and blanket statements concerning what the President will not do to further the black agenda. There is an old saying by the KKK that they no longer have to worry about attacking blacks anymore because their own race are doing a better job at it that they could ever do! If the professor was so concerned about blacks being uplifted then why does he not teach at a historically black college or university? If he is so interested in uplifting the black race then why is he not running for political office and positioning himself to complete the agenda that he is placing at the President's feet? It is easy to stand at his lectern at a predominantly white university and complain about what someone else is not doing for the black race, while he is continuously protecting his own interests. You see that is the problem with men such as himself, he will utilize his race to promote himself to his chosen places of success, and never reach down his hand to lift up his brother, yet he will critique what President Obama is not doing. His entire personality and presentation is frightfully similar to Clarence Thomas who rode the vehicle of affirmative action all the way to the hallowed walls of the Supreme Court, only to strike down the same programs after he benefitted from them. Such a shameless display of hypocrisy! But let us not forget about the programmed aunt Jemima, who defined is any black female who has fostered contempt and hatred for any black male who is just as successful as she is. Because she has become so successful, suddenly there are no good black men "on her level" available to date. Therefore she has to date outside of her race because most of the black men are trifling, irresponsible, underachieving, on drugs, blue collar workers, uneducated, in prison, not cultured enough, not smart enough, or simply does not measure up to the unrealistic expectations that she cannot even measure up to herself. Her image of black men is so jaded that she would be the first to tell you that if she would happen to run across a black man who is on her level, he would probably be in the Smithsonian Institute. Therefore, I am not surprised by her baseless attacks on our President. After all, he is a black man that is on her level educationally but transcends her professionally, and since Rev. Sharpton was gracious enough to give her a platform, she chose this time as her opportunity to impugn the image of our President who has only been in office for 45 days. Yet when a caller asked about President Bush's contribution to the black race, she became conspicuously silent. However, her seemingly schizophrenic behavior does not surprise me at all. Perhaps she can explain to the people why there is so much emphasis on the black agenda in the first 4 years although the last President had 8 years? Why did she not speak in a balanced manner on the President's body of work as a grass roots community organizer, as a brilliant and accomplished black lawyer who headed the Harvard Law review, who decided to forego the golden parachutes of Wall Street to help those persons who were less fortunate than he was? Why would she not speak about the Senator in Chicago and the disregarded black neighborhoods that his legislation gave a voice to? Because there was so much that they both could have spoken about, but chose not to. I cannot help but wonder if we had "two spooks that sat beside the door," and the puppets that did the bidding for the Republican Party who the black race has tuned out and rendered as a non-issue. My fellow Americans, if you do not do anything else in your lifetime, make sure that when you encounter these types of clandestine double-agents, that you make the conscious choice to give them the high-tech uncle tom and programmed aunt jemima test. Ask them, what is their political affiliation? Ask them what have they done to improve the state of black America. Ask them who did they vote for in the last election. Ask them who they work for. Ask them to talk about the positive contributions that President Obama has made in the black community. If they are unable to articulate these questions in a positive manner without becoming guarded, defensive, and territorial, then you probably have encountered a plant from the Republican Party who has been paid to create division in the black community. What am I asking you to do? It is simple. I am asking each one of you to think for yourselves, and to understand that the forces that seek to keep this nation divided along racial lines are not uni-racial in scope! On the contrary, as I articulated in the earlier chapters of this book, there are slaves who are hired by capitalist establishments to keep America divided along racial lines, and it is being done in a manner that subtlely releases subliminal messages over the airwaves that suggests to us that not only can we not trust our Presidential leader, but we cannot trust one another. Remember we have been deceived with this century old ploy of "divide and conquer long enough." We cannot afford to fall into this trap again less we will perish as a nation.

Impediment 4: Defining the Black Agenda

I suppose that somewhere between the expectations by Black America of our current President to rescue America from the precipice of financial oblivion; to preserve the homes of victims of mortgage fraud that caused record foreclosures with families becoming homeless with no options or credit; that somewhere between the creation of jobs to replace the millions that the Republican Party with their incompetent leader "Wubya" shipped out permanently to other countries through Fast-Track authority; somewhere between the imposition of regulations on a free-wheeling unregulated Wall Street; somewhere between the passing of a healthcare bill that will end the deaths of Americans at the hands of multimillion dollar conglomerates who choose to end American's coverage than save their lives; and while fighting to pass the necessary legislation that will move America forward and restore world-wide trust and respectability against the resistance and media lies of Senator(s) Brutus and Judas Iscariot, that there must be a Black agenda! I cannot help but wonder where this agenda was during the candidacies of President(s) George W. Bush Sr., William Jefferson Clinton, and George W. Bush Jr. Could it be that an unrealistic expectation by the learned and the unlearned alike has been placed on President Barack

Hussein Obama to complete such a daunting task of restoring America in 42 months and ignore the rest of America to concentrate solely on the Black agenda?

I pose this question in all sincerity as I speak candidly on this impediment on the eve of Tavis Smiley's call to rally and converge on Illinois, the hometown of President Obama in an effort to have a summit to define the, (wait for it) "Black Agenda." Is this the same Mr. Smiley who has been inviting the alleged "best and brightest" black talent in America, while ignoring the people in the trenches, to sit on the stage on national television like "actors on display" and postulate about the plethora of problems in Black America through at least three Presidential candidacies with no proposed solutions? Was this the same Mr. Smiley who created the "Contract with Black America" which remained on the New York Times best-seller list for months and made him a Fort Knox type of financial windfall? I actually thought that this "collaborative work" framed the black agenda! Pardon my hopefully misplaced cynicism, but it appears that education of our children still remains a problem; unemployment in the community still remains a problem, Courthouses that have to furlough attorneys due to State governments mismanaging money still remains a problem, teachers being fired and furloughed still remains a problem, Policemen and Firemen are still being laid off, banks continue to foreclose on homes, domestic terrorist cells continue to rise up in the backwoods of America, the media continues to spew hate over the airwaves unfettered, and corporate sponsored tea parties continue to incite violence against our Black President who only sin is "Governing while Black" and call it political speech and the democratic process.

But now that President Obama has been inaugurated, he is expected to bear the cross of over 200 years of hatred, disregard, functional illiteracy, negative stereotypes, second class citizenship, police brutality, Katrina-type incidents, ignored poverty, black bitterness and cynicism, black self-hatred, an utter disregard for education, media misinformation that contributes to black ignorance, indecision over black leadership due to bruised egos and jealousy, all while our chosen Representatives on the State and Federal level continue to vote pay raises for themselves and leverage the taxpayers money to place themselves, their friends, and their associates in positions of financial comfort and solvency. It is simply unconscionable, yet we are continuing to struggle to define the black agenda! As I indicated earlier in my book, supremacy or its appearance "in any form" is counterproductive and does absolutely nothing to create cohesiveness among all Americans, to promote good will among all Americans, that will be necessary to promote a country that will work together to solve the plethora of problems that this country faces to survive. Do not get me wrong, I as an academic and black male understand the unique challenges that our race face on a daily basis, and I understand that there are some challenges that are unique to our race alone, just like there are definitive issues that are unique to the Asian, Latino, Caucasian, and Mexican communities, and it would have served Mr. Smiley's interest and the broader interest of America to invite more than his "circle of contacts" and those that he deemed as competent to sit on the stage to discuss these issues, if the objective were to resolve these issues. Definitively, is there an Asian agenda? Is there a Latino agenda? Is there a Caucasian agenda? Is there a Mexican agenda? No! There is an American agenda! Everyone is out of work! Everyone needs healthcare! Everyone wants a quality education for their children! Everyone is an American and President Obama is attempting to be the leader for all of the people, and any attempt to do anything less by imposing a race specific agenda on to the people who have the same needs would be political suicide, divisive, and separate America by making the job easier for the "racial dividers" who are attempting to keep our country distracted and traveling down the road of destruction. Let me be very clear, pushing an agenda of Supremacy in "any form" is wrong and should never be supported, but I will address that subject in my next section. If we are to speak competently about the "State of the Black Union," I need to hear from Pookie and Ray-Ray from the hood who can speak about the realities of growing up poor and struggling to survive, what it means to be hungry, what it means to not be able to go to school today because I have to take care of my siblings because momma is on crack, what it means to be sleepy and inattentive in class because they were kept awake all night by gunfire, and what it truly means to be "left behind" and not be a "priority" to their representative until it is time to vote. That is the reality that we continue to miss in our discourse! However, when one considers the "State of the American Union," we need the ideas of all races, civil rights leaders, pastors, social justice representatives, hood kings and queens, activists, and academics from all schools, at the table for discussion and planning. But at this juncture of our discourse, that is irrelevant, and there are far more pressing issues to discuss that I believe undermines the very spirit of President Obama's candidacy. For when I look at the progress that he has made in a 42 month period, when I consider the fact of how long it took for this country's infrastructure to be dismantled, and when I think about the reality that Mr. Obama will be President for 4 years, my question is "Why won't we give him time to do his job?" Or in clearer terms, "Is there some reason why we have failed to give our current President at least half the amount of time that it took our last President, Vice-President, and his cronies to dismantle our country? After all the spirit of attempting to divide and conquer our race by leaders of this country is not unique among our community, but I believe that when the attempt to be divisive is attempted by leaders who "look like us," and whom we have entrusted with a platform to speak into our lives, and have entrusted with a modicum of power within our race and communities, then there is an expected responsibility that these same leaders who have reaped the benefits derived from addressing our interests would support our chosen black leaders with the same amount of time that it took for them to develop their social consciousness.

Impediment 5: Knee-Gros

Katrina hit and tens of thousands of our people died as Bush did a drive by in his plane but never landed, you never said a word; You celebrate rapper's exploitation of our women but attack the activists who speak up against the behavior; Wall Street was bailed out and you continue to be foreclosed on, you never say a word; You want to throw the gays out of the church but your Pastor has his wife on one side of the church and his girlfriend on the other side while preaching holiness, but you look the other way; you are never respected, the police beat you up, shoot you in the back and lie under oath, but you rely on Al Sharpton to stand for you while you hide behind his coat tail in fear of offending the white establishment, sound familiar? Some of us may find my ebonic description of this impediment a bit offensive, but if the shoe fits wear it. Because I make no excuse for my indignation and disappointment of how our leaders, especially our current President has been defamed, debased, and dehumanized by knee-gros in the media and who call into our shows. You may wonder what a Knee-gro is and I am glad that you asked. Based upon my ebonic definition, a knee-gro is any person of color who spends time on their <u>knees</u> allegedly praying to God while displaying a form of Godliness on Sundays, but after church and on any other day, they never <u>grow</u> spiritually or morally thus <u>knee-gro</u>. Now many of them are not really hard to identify, because you can find them calling in to the media talk shows talking about how bad President Obama is, how he cares about all other races but the blacks, he should have gotten to us by now, he should have taken care of his own before he addressed any of these other problems! Maybe some of you are drinking that "Obama kool-aid" but not me because I know what he is about. He is just one of these uppity negroes who is trying to fit into the white man's world and appease them at our expense. The knee-gro is one who makes all of these baseless accusations while they never get off of their butts and change their lives or the lives of others. It is Obama and "the man's" fault that they cannot succeed or move forward with their lives, no its because you are lazy, angry, hateful, vindictive, bitter, and make excuses for why you cannot succeed in life. Is it Mr. President's fault that he decided to have dreams for a better life? Is it the President's fault that he decided to attend school, keep up his grades, stay out of the clubs, and keep good grades so that he can graduate from an Ivy league school? Is it his fault that America has embraced him, and is it his fault that his optimistic message of hope and unity is contagious? One thing I will not do, and no one else should ever do, Never dim your light so that someone else can shine because they are angry at your success. The same God that I serve, you say you serve, why don't you stop faking and start believing that all things are possible because all of us who are trying to effectuate change do not attend pity parties, and we definitely do not accommodate haters and their messages. Get over it or step to the left there is too much work to do. Do not ever bring me a problem without a proposed solution, because if you do, you transform yourself into the problem and impediment and lay the foundation for impediment number 6.

Impediment 6: Armchair Quarterbacking

Defined, an Armchair Quarterback is a person who offers advice or an opinion on something in which they have no expertise or involvement. You know, maybe it's just me but as I continue to view media programs and the responses and self-serving, uninformed commentaries that are made by the guests of the show, the private citizens who call in to the shows discussing what our President is doing that is wrong, and how they would address terror, the economy, immigration reform, jobs, wall street reform, peace in the middle east, wars, crime, hate, terror, and the black agenda, I am reminded of the saying that if one is ignorant then remain silent, instead of speaking and settling all doubt. From my vantage point, I realize that everyone has an opinion and are entitled to it. But I also know that it is easy to sit on the sidelines and complain about what is wrong with our Country, what is wrong with the President and agenda, what he is doing that is wrong, how incompetent his administration is, and it has become an impediment with the message of unity that we are attempting to convey in this nation. I expect it from those persons who hate our President, but on behalf of those persons who are suffering financially, who are discriminated against on a daily basis, who cannot feed their families, who are unemployed, who have no healthcare, who are victimized by the abuse of corporations, I find it utterly shocking to hear it coming from you! There is an old saying, that if you are not part of the solution, then you are part of the problem. That's right! In other words, what are you doing in your community to address the problems? Or is it more convenient for you to talk about what is wrong and complain? These are the persons who do not vote and always sit back and judge others based upon their standards. But the word for the day to you is if you are not helping, get out of the way but most of all, "Shut Up" so that we can keep it moving.

Impediment 7: Supremacy and the Republican Party

When one looks at this terminology, the first inclination is to think about adjoining the word "White" to this term, but I would argue that in this context you would be doing so in error. Because I would argue, that Supremacy entails a position of superiority or authority exercised over all others, which could be said about all races. Supremacy is derived from ones' belief that they are superior and everyone else is inferior to them, based upon data that they have used to make this conclusion. This data includes but is not limited to, socioeconomic status, being above the law, enjoying a minimal amount of success in life, and relationships that one may have formed with the societal elite. That is why many persons who have been friends since middle school sometimes part ways, because one of them has determined that they have progressed to another level socio-economically and they now need to have a circle of friends who are "On their level." This impediment is commonly referred to as an attitude of Supremacy! What you just witnessed was supremacy on a primary level; however, supremacy can get so divisive that class systems are set up in churches, in families, in races, and in countries! Once this system is in place, it can determine how the poor are treated (Katrina); how minorities are treated (U.S.A.); how agents of the criminal justice system treats its offenders and suspects (Sean Bell, Troy Davis, Ariston Waiters, Travon Martin and Police Brutality); how monies are allocated in our educational system; how capitalists are treated (the Wall Street bail-out); how the middle class and working poor are treated when our federal government decides to intervene; how the poor and women continue to be exploited in our churches; how families treat their light and dark skinned members; how hate groups interact with minorities; how some political candidates' conversations develop at political rallies; and how some American media personalities exercises double-standards towards its public servants. That being said, the secondary level of Impediment 4 deserves special mention and attention because over the last ten years the Republican Party and its leadership has become a destructive and divisive force in the political landscape and has seemingly escaped detection. So much so, that through their selfish, self-serving, political decisions and legislation, where they spent taxpayers' money like drunken sailors on furlough and created millionaires amongst their party members and friends with everyone else suffering to the point that it has placed our economy on life-support. Yet they hypocritically call for fiscal conservatism after their fearless leader (Bush) exits out of the back door of the White House. I have always argued that a group of millionaires with supremacist views will never serve the interests of the working and middle class. Yet the middle and working class have voted them back into office on a consistent basis with many of their lives never being improved. I have never professed to be a financial wizard, but when one continues to spend money in Iraq and other countries through a self-absorbed war and never re-invest money during those periods of time into the American economy, then the economic infrastructure of America collapses. Now there are conflicting and incendiary dialogues by the GOP concerning the destruction of America led by the drug abusing, draft dodging, unpatriotic, college academic failure Rush Limbaugh. Because the GOP wants to rewrite history and attempt to sit this "economic destruction" at President Obama's feet. That is why I will enumerate for the readers, how we got here.

HOW WE GOT IN THIS PREDICAMENT OF ECONOMIC DECIMATION

In a very insightful and honest article entitled, "Who's Counting Bush's mistakes," Steven Pizzo published on Alternet on February 20, 2006, and the record is set straight once and for all. Please read carefully and allow the facts to debunk the innuendoes of the capitalists cloaked as pseudo-financial and political talk show hosts blaming President Obama for the stock market crash and the financial ruin of this country. We hear it every day. We are going to get penalized for being rich. We must run the government from the pages of a 1929 book called the "Great Crash." He is just unstable and not experienced enough to run this country. He is giving money to working class citizens, which amount to socialism. Yet the greedy, selfserving capitalists of the GOP lead by Rush Limbaugh will continue to leave untreated, the political amnesia that they seem to develop when it comes to how we arrived at this abyss of economic destruction. Therefore, due to their untreated condition, I will choose not to impose upon them the burden of revealing the truth and trigger a relapse; instead I will take it upon myself to discuss the hidden truth.

In his timely and insightful article entitled, "Who's Counting Bush's Mistakes?" **Stephen Pizzo** writing in **News for Real** and posted **February 20, 2006**, states the following.

Given how ambitious and wide-ranging the incompetence of this administration has been, it is high time we started keeping track of its many failures.

Ralph Waldo Emerson said it best, "The louder he spoke of his honor, the faster we counted our spoons." And no administration in U.S. history has spoken louder, or as often, of its honor.

So let us count our spoons

Emergency Management: They completely failed to manage the first large-scale emergency since 9/11. Despite all their big talk and hundreds of billions of dollars spent on homeland security over the past four years, this administration proved itself stunningly incompetent when faced with an actual emergency. (Katrina Relief Funds Squandered)

Fiscal Management: America is broke. No wait, we're worse than broke. In less than five years these borrow and spend-thrifts have nearly doubled our national debt, to a stunning $8.2 trillion. These are not your father's Republicans who treated public dollars as though they were an endangered species. These Republicans waste money in ways and in quantities that make those old tax and spend liberals of yore look like tight-fisted Scots. This administration is so incompetent that you can just throw a dart at the front page of your morning paper and whatever story of importance it hits will prove my point.

Katrina relief: Eleven thousand spanking new mobile homes sinking into the Arkansas mud. President Bush taking five days to arrive in New Orleans. Seems no one in the administration knew there were federal and state laws prohibiting trailers in flood zones. Oops. That little mistake cost you $850 million -- and counting. Important to note, to date, Bush and his republican cohorts blatantly disregarded the poor in the 9th ward to date, and has the unmitigated gall to blame everyone else for their failures but the "cowards in the mirror." Yet the Governor of Louisiana, yet another Republican who refused to take any money from a "black man" in the form of our President has realized the predicament that his racist doctrine placed the people that he swore to protect and serve, and now he wants to run for President. That's just what the people need, incompetence, selfishness, and a disregard for the poor on a National scale.

Medicare Drug Program: This $50 billion white elephant debuted by trampling many of those it was supposed to save. The mess <u>forced states to step in</u> and try to save its own citizens from being killed by the administration's poorly planned and executed attempt to privatize huge hunks of the federal health safety net.

Afghanistan: Good managers know that in order to pocket the gains of a project, you have to finish it. This administration started out fine in Afghanistan. They had the Taliban and al Qaeda on the run and Osama bin Laden trapped in a box canyon. Then they were distracted by a nearby shiny object -- Iraq. We are now $75 billion out of pocket in Afghanistan and its sitting president still rules only within the confines of the nation's capital. Tribal warlords, the growing remnants of the Taliban and al Qaeda call the shots in the rest of the county. And, its easy to identify an election year for the Republicans, because these same miscreants inundate the airwaves with FEAR (false evidence appearing real) tactics. Bomb threats here, Bin Ladin tapes surfacing, a terrorist threat on the front pages, yet we ignore the state-wide terrorist militias who threaten our President daily. Are we fighting terrorism or simply distorting the reality of what we know. That is about scaring Americans into voting Republican so that we can end up sleeping under bridges if they gain control again, while they laugh all the way to the bank. You want proof of their selfishness and scamming, just ask for tax return reviews, you will see where the money went.

Iraq: This ill-begotten war was supposed to only cost us $65 billion. It has now cost us <u>over $300 billion</u> and continues to suck $6 billion a month out of our children's futures. Meanwhile the three warring tribes Bush "liberated" are using our money and soldiers' lives to partition the country. The Shiites and Kurds are carving out the prime cuts while treating the oncedominant Sunnis the same way the Israelis treat the Palestinians, forcing them onto Iraq's version of Death Valley. Meanwhile Iran is increasingly calling the shots in the Shiite region as mullahs loyal to Iran take charge.

Iran: The administration not only jinxed its Afghanistan operations by attacking Iraq, but also provided Iran both the rationale for and time to move toward nuclear weapons. The Bush administration's neocons' threats to attack Syria next only provided more support for religious conservatives within Iran who argued U.S. intentions in the Middle East were clear, and that only the deterrent that comes with nuclear weapons could protect them.

North Korea: Ditto. Also add to all the above the example North Korea set for Iran. Clearly once a country possesses nukes, the U.S., Bush, and the GOP who bullied everyone else drops the veiled threats and wants to talk.

Social Programs: It's easier to get affordable -- even free -- American-style medical care, paid for with American dollars, if you are injured in Iraq, Afghanistan or are victims of a Pakistani earthquake, than if you live and pay taxes in the good old U.S.A. Nearly 50 million Americans can't afford medical insurance. Nevertheless the administration has proposed a budget that will cut $40 billion from domestic social programs, including health care for the working poor. The administration is quick to say that those services will be replaced by its "faith-based" programs. Not so fast...

"Despite the Bush administration's rhetorical support for religious charities, the amount of direct federal grants to faith-based organizations declined from 2002 to 2004, according to a major new study released yesterday. The study released yesterday "is confirmation of the suspicion I've had all along, that what the faith-based initiative is really all about is defunding social programs and dumping responsibility for the poor on the charitable sector," said Kay Guinane, director of the nonprofit advocacy program at OMB Watch."

The Military: Overused and over-deployed. Former Defense Secretary William Perry and former Secretary of State Madeleine Albright warned in a 15-page report that the Army and Marine Corps cannot sustain the current operational tempo without "doing real damage to their forces." ... Speaking at a news conference to release the study, Albright said she is "very troubled" the military will not be able to meet demands abroad. Perry warned that the strain, "if not relieved, can have highly corrosive and long-term effects on the military.

With military budgets gutted by the spiraling costs of operations in Iraq and Afghanistan, the Bush administration has requested funding for fewer National Guard troops in fiscal 2007 -17,000 fewer. Which boggles the sane mind since, if it weren't for reserve/National Guard, the administration would not have had enough troops to rotate forces in and out of Iraq and Afghanistan. Nearly 40 percent of the troops sent to those two countries were from the reserve and National Guard.

The Environment: Here's a little pop quiz: What happens if all the coral in the world's oceans dies? Answer: Coral is the first rung on the food-chain ladder; so when it goes, everything else in the ocean dies. And if the oceans die, we die.

The coral in the world's oceans are dying (called "bleaching") at an alarming and accelerating rate. Global warming is the culprit. Nevertheless, this administration continues as the world's leading global warming denier. Why? Because they seem to feel it's more cost effective to be dead than to force reductions in greenhouse gas emissions. How stupid is that? And time is running out.

Trade: We are approaching a $1 trillion annual trade deficit, most of it with Asia, $220 billion with just China -- just last year.

Energy: Record high energy prices. Record energy company profits. Dick Cheney's energy task force meetings remain secret and protected by his friends on the Supreme Court. Need I say more?

Consumers: Americans finally did it last year -- they achieved a negative savings rate. (Folks in China save 10 percent, for contrast.) If the government can spend more than it makes and just say "charge it" when it runs out, so can we. The average American now owes $9,000 to unregulated credit card companies. Imagine that!

Cheney, Human Rights, National Security, and Valerie Plame: As America viewed disturbing photographs of tortured Guantanamo Bay detainees, and listened to Bush administration officials wanting us to believe that "Private First classes" orchestrated such atrocities and acted outside of the scope of their "chain of command, it defied logic. Mostly due to the fact, that during my stay at Fort Lee, Va., where I received my training as a soldier in the military; I was adamantly told by my trainers, non-commissioned officers (NCOs), Drill Sergeants, and Company Commanders alike, that the United States (U.S.) unequivocally does not torture prisoners of war! It was further explained to me that under the war governing rules of the Geneva Convention; that if a prisoner is captured by the U.S. military, they were to "treat that captured soldier as if they were one of our own." Failure to do so would result in the prosecution of anyone found to be in violation of these orders. The setting was clear, and everyone abided by the law until the Cowboys from the GOP and their President and Vice-President took office after the September 11 attacks on American soil. I am not sure if these rules only applied to actual "military personnel," and not to persons who either dodged the draft through deferments or just chose to not serve their country and destroyed their military records to avoid detection.

Nevertheless, this category deserves special attention as I have listened to our "media touring" former Vice President Cheney, as he attempts to "dumb down" Americans concerning Torture and our National Security. He argues that in cases of protecting our country from the threat of "potential and perceived terrorists" that have never been identified, torture is justified. Think about what Cheney's argument is. He believes that it is okay to violate the "International Human Rights" laws, and "torture" alleged "enemy combatants" who by all intents and purposes are in America's care during "war time!" This is where we will deconstruct Cheney's arguments as he fails to address the issue of human rights as it relates to U.S. prisoners during war time. His logic is that since the Bush administration passed the "Patriot Act," and these prisoners were subsequently labeled as "enemy combatants," they could be imprisoned indefinitely and without being able to see their family, their friends, or their attorney! He also believed that the legal technicality of this title somehow exempted their administration from adhering to International Law concerning how "war prisoners" were to be treated under the rules of the Geneva Convention. After all, if we are torturing "enemy combatants" and not "Prisoners of War," then we are not bound by international law. Be that as it may, Mr. Cheney, at the end of the day, when it is all said and done, perhaps the foundation of this discussion should not be about torture, but rather about "human rights violations."

Defined, Human Rights are

Rights inherent to all human beings, whatever our nationality, place of residence, sex, national or ethnic origin, color, religion, language, or any other status. We are all equally entitled to our human rights without discrimination. These rights are all interrelated, interdependent and indivisible. Our Constitution refers to these rights as "inalienable." Contextually, and in this case, Universal human rights which are often expressed and guaranteed by law, in the forms of treaties, customary international law, general principles and other sources of international law are at the forefront of this "political debate."

International human rights law lays down obligations of Governments to act in certain ways or to refrain from certain acts, in order to promote and protect human rights and fundamental freedoms of individuals or groups. This aspiration has been enshrined in various declarations and legal conventions issued during the past fifty years, initiated by the Universal Declaration of Human Rights (1948) and perpetuated by, most importantly, the European Convention on Human Rights (1954) and the International Covenant on Civil and Economic Rights (1966). Together these three documents form the centerpiece of a moral doctrine that many consider to be capable of providing the contemporary geo-political order with what amounts to an international bill of rights. While the practical efficacy of promoting and protecting human rights is significantly aided by individual nation-states', in this context, the United Nations; legally recognizing the doctrine, the ultimate validity of human rights is characteristically thought of as not conditional upon such recognition. The moral justification of human rights is thought to precede considerations of strict national sovereignty. An underlying aspiration of the doctrine of human rights is to provide a set of legitimate criteria to which all nationstates should adhere. Appeals to national sovereignty should not provide a legitimate means for nation-states to permanently opt out of their fundamental human rights-based commitments. "Opt out" meaning any nation that is a member of a democratic international governing body such as the United Nations (U.N.), does not have the right to say that "You are either for the United States or against the United States," if you do not agree with U.N. policy allowing the Weapons Inspectors to do their job and look for "weapons of mass destruction" in Iraq, before you invade the "sovereign nation." "Opt out" meaning that you disregard governing policy and walk away from the ruling body of the U.N., to form a "stand alone" policy against the World as it relates to invading Iraq, which creates an atmosphere of "lawlessness" in the U.S. government, that had a "trickle down" effect that created a lawless and secret subculture that recklessly and systemically violated human rights. Thus, the doctrine of human rights is ideally placed to provide individuals with a powerful means for morally auditing the legitimacy of those contemporary national and international forms of political and economic authority which confront us and which claim jurisdiction over us.

To that end, the United States government in general, and the Obama administration in particular, made the decision to "morally audit" the Bush administration's position on human rights by declassifying memos authorizing "torture" of prison detainees by water boarding, keeping detainees naked, in painful standing positions and in cold cells for long periods of time. With the exposure of other techniques that included depriving them of solid food, slapping them, depriving them of sleep, defacing the Holy Quran, prolonged shackling and threats to a detainee's family. These are clear violations of international and national law, yet former Vice-President Cheney and other officials want to argue semantics, technicalities, gray areas, and accuse the Obama administration of somehow making "Americans less safe" by making public to the enemy our techniques of interrogation! Certainly, Mr. Cheney and this administration had no such concerns when they "made public" the identity of C.I.A. operative, Valerie Plame with no consequences. Did her exposure compromise the government's mission against terrorism then, or is the media allowing Cheney to "cherrypick" his issues with this current administration? I believe that that the "ultimate question is," does 8 years of covert, lawless behavior that has violated human rights, international law, and created enemies of the U.S. both foreign and domestic, warrant a "free pass" by the Justice department and the International Courts or is part of restoring the international image of this country contingent upon prosecuting these miscreants?

I could go on for another 1,000 words listing the stunning incompetence of the Bush administration and its GOP sycophants in Congress. But what's the use? No one seems to give a fig. The sun continues to shine in this fool's paradise, even with George gone and a minority in the House and Senate continuing this madness! Looks like the American people will have to save them from themselves.

But don't bother George W. Bush with any of this. While seldom right, he is never in doubt. Doubt is Bush's enemy. Worry? How can he worry when he has no doubts?

Me? Well, I worry about all the above, all the time. But in particular, I worry about coral. (Pizzo, 2006)

Let's talk budgets, where Congressman Ryan gave his President a blanket "yes" vote :

The Bush and Republican backed budgets: On Monday February 6, 2006 President George Bush presented his $2.77 trillion fiscal year (FY) 2007 budget to Congress. This proposal came only days after Congress passed a budget reconciliation bill for FY 2006, in which $40 billion was cut from entitlement programs, programs that were governed by legislation in a way that legally obligates the federal government to make specific payments to qualified recipients, over five years which include programs such as Medicaid, welfare, child support and student lending. President Bush's budget for FY 2007 included reductions in non-security discretionary spending and the termination or reduction of 141 federal programs. Discretionary spending is spending made through appropriations bills which includes Agriculture, Commerce, Defense, the District of Columbia, Energy and Water, Foreign Operations, Interior, Labor, Health and Human Services, Education, Legislative, Military Construction, Transportation, Treasury and Postal, Veterans Affairs and Housing and Urban Development. The budget for FY 2007 focused on military spending, homeland security, energy research, and global competitiveness through improved math and science education and research. The biggest spending increase would be for the Department of Defense with a total budget of "$439 billion for 2007, an increase of $29 billion, or 6.9 percent over 2006.

This figure does not include the projected expenditures for military operations in Afghanistan and Iraq. $120 billion was appropriated for Iraq and Afghanistan in 2006 through emergency supplemental bills, emergency funding requests made outside of the federal budget. The White House also made an additional $50 billion emergency supplemental request for part of 2007. Remember how Senator McCain complained about the prices of President Obama's helicopters? Well, a portion of the Bush budget for The Department of Defense went toward continuing conventional weapons systems, which included $15 billion for new helicopters and fighter jets, and $11.2 billion for two new Navy destroyers, one submarine and two combat ships. Pentagon spending on weapons procurements doubled in current dollars from $42 billion in 1996 to $84 billion in 2007. The cost of research and development also grew, reaching $73.2 billion in the 2007 budget." The proposal does include $21 billion for the Defense Health Program in 2007 to continue providing troops and their families with health care and a 2.2 percent increase in basic military pay. The President's second major area of focus in his budget was homeland security. The President proposes a $58.3 billion budget for homeland security activities of 32 government agencies, a $3.4 billion or 6 percent increase over 2006. While the proposal increases funding for homeland security activities for federal government agencies, "the budget would cut homeland assistance to state and local governments by $602 million." Included in the President's proposal was "over $3 billion for the Border Patrol the mobile uniformed law enforcement arm of the Department of Homeland Security responsible for patrolling U.S. borders with Mexico and Canada, and coastal waters surrounding the Florida Peninsula and the island of Puerto Rico, an increase of 29 percent over 2006, providing funding for 1,500 new agents. This includes $100 million for new technology at [U.S.] borders. $2.1 billion allocated to support detention and removal of illegal aliens including a $387 million increase for more than 6,000 new detention beds, staff, removal, and transportation costs."

Wow, after all of the President's proposed "big spending and pork," he needed to reduce the budget and free up more money for his priorities, therefore he recommended "a reduction of $2.2 billion in government operations that were unrelated to the nation's security.

Consequently, eleven agencies would receive less money than they did in 2006, with the deepest cuts to the Transportation, Justice and Agriculture departments." "Additionally under the President's budget, appropriations for non-defense programs remained at a virtual freeze through 2011." Cuts were made to programs such as "education programs, environmental programs, and numerous programs across to assist low-income families, children, and elderly and disabled people, and research related to cancer, heart disease, and other medical conditions. What a compassionate group of neocons, but they were not finished.

The budget also eliminated $65 billion in spending over the next five years, including a $36 billion reduction in Medicare. Wonder how Medicare lost money? There was also a proposal to reduce spending for Medicaid by $12 billion over five years. "The Centers for Disease Control (CDC) and Prevention" would see a $367 million reduction, to $5.8 billion (this is significant, because by cutting CDC's funding so significantly, their research and development department will suffer. Suffer because they cannot conduct the necessary research to identify new health threats, and take the necessary steps to develop new vaccines that could counteract these new threats that would be discovered, all because the Bush administration and the GOP voted to cut $367 million dollars from their budget. I hope that no Americans die due to this administration's negligence) According to a February 5, 2005 New York Times report by Robert Pear, President Bush's budget for 2006 cuts spending for a wide range of public health programs, including several to protect the nation against bioterrorist attacks and to respond to medical emergencies, budget documents show.

Faced with constraints on spending caused by record budget deficits and the demands of the war in Iraq, administration officials said on Friday that they had increased the budget for some health programs but cut many others, including some that address urgent health care needs.

The documents show, for example, that Mr. Bush would cut spending for several programs that deal with epidemics, chronic diseases and obesity. His plan would also cut the budget of the Centers for Disease

Control and Prevention by 9 percent, to $6.9 billion, the documents show.

Additional funding for the Health Resources and Services Administration would drop $252 million, to $6.3 billion." Before FY 2007's reductions were completed, 42 programs were cut from the Education Department, including arts education, Budget by Spending Categories vocational education, parent resource centers, the drug-free schools program and Functional Category education technology grants. Discretionary spending on education would drop $3.1 billion, or 5.5 percent from a year ago. Money budgeted for the Department of Education was used to fund elementary and secondary schools and programs; special education programs; rehabilitative services; vocational and adult education programs; student financial assistance; higher education programs; and institute of education sciences programs. However, the budget did propose $380 million for math and science education.

Other program terminations included; the Commodity Supplemental Food Program which provides nutritional food packages to more than 400,000 low-income elderly people; the Preventative Care Block Grant which provided grants to states for preventive health services for underserved populations; and the Community Services Block grant which provides funding for a rage of social services and other types of assistance to low-income and poor families, with elderly and disabled individuals as well. The budget also included deep budget cuts in programs serving low-income families and the poor. Child Care funding cuts would total $1 billion over the next five years according to the proposal. Also agreed upon by President Bush and the Republican party were cuts of 26 percent for housing for the low-income elderly; a 50 percent cut in housing funds for low-income people with disabilities; a 30 percent cut to the Community Development Block Grant program; and a 79 percent cut to the Community Oriented Policing Services (COPS), which promotes community policing primarily by putting police on the streets.

However, the FY 2008 budget was "one for the ages." Because while President George W. Bush has called for bipartisan compromise on key economic issues and has finally recognized growing economic inequality as a problem, unlike President Obama, his proposed budget reflected none of this. Specifically his budget preserved expensive tax cuts for the wealthy and boosted military spending dramatically, while cutting crucial programs for the most vulnerable Americans: children, the elderly, the poor and the sick. The president even proposed major cuts in domestic programs over the next five years, starting with $13 billion in cuts for FY 2008, rising each year until FY 2012, when cuts in domestic programs would reach $34 billion. Even more telling is this administration often talking of preparing America's workers to meet the challenges of competing in the global economy, but his proposed budget contained more than $1 billion in cuts for job training and employment security programs. At a time when America's workers face the loss of millions of good-paying jobs to flawed trade policies and off shoring, the Bush administration with the Republican party's backing renewed Fast Track authority, the president's budget proposed cuts to $102.9 million from the Trade Adjustment Assistance program, which provides income support and training to workers who lose their jobs due to trade. I need to be more specific about this "targeted GOP attack on the American people, so read carefully.

You know the true measure of a Real Man who has character and integrity admits when they have done wrong. That said, there is a group of politicians, citizens, liars, cheats, who are greedy, selfish, racist, and uninformed, who want to conveniently place this mess that we call the United States at the feet of our current President, Mr. Obama. It is likened to setting a group of fires, and waiting on the fire department to arrive, and claim to have no knowledge as to how the fires were started, but at the same time, they secretly cut off the water supply so that the firemen are unable to put out the fires. Such as it is in the case with President Obama, he took office about a 16 months ago, and has had to contend with racism, bigotry, hate, people plotting his demise, a powerful media machine of racists and slaves (black people who attack him) intent on destroying his image, when all his goal was to attempt to pull America from the brink of destruction that resulted from Republican policies led by Bush laws. You are welcomed to read the following information below which will enlighten Americans as to how we got into this mess before you try to blame our current President.

Mr. Senator: What Happened to America's Jobs?
Fast Track/Presidential Trade Promotion Authority:
Is This Democracy? No. 379, Adopted 2007

"Fast Track" or "Presidential Trade Promotion Authority" is a mechanism by which Congress gives the executive branch the right to dictate trade policy and formulate trade agreements. Under Fast Track, the president and the USTR (United States Trade Representative) have the power to select our trading partner nation(s), negotiate a trade agreement, and then submit the agreement to Congress for a simple 'up' or 'down' vote. Discussion time is limited to 60 days. No amendments are permitted. Therefore, under Fast Track, our representatives in Congress have virtually no say concerning trade policy and the contents or language of trade agreements.

Fast Track was introduced by the Nixon administration in 1974. President Clinton used Fast Track to speed NAFTA (North American Free Trade Agreement) through Congress in 1993.

The process was re-christened "Presidential Trade Promotion Authority" by the George W. Bush administration. Through a process of misrepresentation of consequences and unconscionable railroading through Congress, the Bush Administration succeeded in having Fast Track renewed in 2001. George W. Bush used it to pass CAFTA (Central America Free Trade Agreement) in 2005, as well as several other less contentious deals.

Global trade agreements do not simply regulate the exchange of goods; they increasingly facilitate international corporate investment. Agreements like NAFTA and CAFTA have functioned to increase the power and profits of corporations, to the detriment of workers' livelihood and environmental sustainability. Trade agreements negotiated during the past two decades include control over services (such as provision of natural resources), over laws passed at the local and state levels (such as living wage laws, or environmental protections) and over intellectual property rights (including distribution of generic pharmaceuticals). Simply stated: trade agreements reach into all aspects of our lives and those of the populations of our trading partner nations.

Trade agreements can be written and negotiated to raise living standards for workers and to enforce environmental protections vital to survival of the planet. The evidence is clear that, acting on its own, the administration will continue to craft trade agreements that benefit corporate investors instead.

(see ADA Resolutions #350, #371 & #378 for further details on global trade)

Fast Track will expire at the end of June, 2007, and Congress again will be asked to authorize the Bush administration to choose our trading partners, negotiate the agreements without transparency, then present them to Congress for a 'yes' or 'no' vote. It is the position of ADA that it is inappropriate for any president to request or be granted Fast Track authority. The process constitutes an abrogation of power and responsibility by the people's elected representatives in Congress. Democracy requires checks and balances by the branches of government. Fast Track is not democracy.

Globalization Viva La Fast Track!
by Kelly Cogswell, April 24, 2001

The Americas free trade train left the station on Sunday in Quebec when Western Hemisphere leaders signed an agreement to open their markets by December 2005.

Only countries with democratic governments, however papery, can be a part of the 800 million-people common market known as the Free Trade Area of the Americas (FTAA). But if George W. Bush gets the fast-track negotiating power that Congress denied Bill Clinton, the train itself may steamroll fragile Latin American democracies into oblivion.

SETTING THE TONE

The deal was forged behind closed doors in North America's only walled city. Legislators and environmental and human rights groups from the 34 American countries in attendance were shut out, though trade bureaucrats and un-elected corporations were well represented.

While the FTAA's organizing body has agreed to publicly release a 'blueprint' for the agreement, it is no substitute for the real thing, particularly when thirteen years after the North American Free Trade Agreement (NAFTA) was approved, the actual details of that deal are still unknown. The whole FTAA deal will be even further removed from the realm of the lowly U.S. citizenry if Bush gets fast-track authority. Congress will only be able to approve or reject, not amend any FTAA-related trade treaty Bush brings it. In other words, our duly elected officials will be circumvented, left only with veto power.

Trade: The New Gunboat Diplomacy

But the chief problem of an Americas open market is the current gargantuan economic gap between the U.S. and the 33 other participating American countries. The fast-tracked FTAA will likely be dominated by the United States, and, for the foreseeable future, the very corporate-friendly, and labor and environmentally-challenged George W. Bush. This sets the stage for stepped-up bullying of poorer countries by the United States.

Just last week the U.S. indulged in a good, old-fashioned display of arm-twisting and veiled threats to win a rebuke of Cuba at the U.N. Human Rights Commission in Geneva. Most Latin American governments think that both Cuba and the U.S. should be censored— the former for human rights violations, the latter for the punitive 41-year economic embargo it has inflicted on the island.

Uruguay's Foreign Affairs Minister reportedly got an eleventh hour phone call from Colin Powell himself, linking a bilateral trade agreement to Uruguay's vote. "The only things that Uruguay can bring to the table are political concessions... What else can Uruguay offer [the U.S.]?" an unidentified diplomatic source told the Montevideo daily La República.

Uruguay caved, even when it had officially condemned the U.S. embargo on Cuba. Before the vote, thousands of people took to the streets in Montevideo denouncing the expected Uruguayan flip-flop and the U.S.'s "pathological inability to accept Cuba as an independent nation."

Also voting with the U.S. were Guatemala, Costa Rica, and Argentina, which is once more on the brink of financial meltdown—a condition probably requiring Washington's bailout largesse in the near future. Cuba and Venezuela voted against. Mexico, Brazil, Colombia, Ecuador, and Peru abstained. Not because of lack of concern over Cuba's human rights violations, but, as Mexico's Foreign Ministry spokeswoman Liliana Ferrer put it, because the U.S.-backed motion was too "unilateral, selective, and politicized." This kind of big stick politics in the FTAA will erode Latin America's struggling democracies, and destabilize the region if, as in the past, the regular humiliations of weaker nations by the voraciously self-interested U.S. fuels a new round of nationalist movements. In other words, a U.S.-controlled FTAA handing down unfair, non-negotiable regulations forged in secrecy could spur violence instead of development and democracy.

NAFTA-ize Me, Please!

Despite all the perils, demonizing globalization and the trade bloc frenzy it has spawned remains far more popular in the U.S. and Canada than south of the border, where small, economically struggling countries face astronomical unemployment rates. It's not that the prospect of globalization doesn't stir up a myriad of anxieties; it's that, with the socialist utopia dead, and state economic intervention discredited, there's no other game in town.

The only way to square the circle, improving trade without crushing democracies, is to follow the relatively successful lead of the European Union, which addressed many of the problems by establishing an elected governing body, commissions for the environment and human rights, and a judiciary. The EU, insofar as is possible in any union, also tries to respect each nation's sovereignty and culture.

The first step in the U.S. is to pressure Congress to deny Bush what it denied Clinton, the fast-track negotiating powers, and to demand for the FTAA what any real democracy requires: transparency, representation, accountability, equality, participation.

The Often Not Discussed Bush Record:

President Bush has led the country for over three years, ample time to establish a record on issues that affect working Americans.

During that time, workers have found themselves fighting to protect principles like the eight hour day, the basic health of the Medicare system and prevailing wage laws, all while enduring high unemployment and reduced prospects for finding work.

The following is a compilation of article links posted on the (International Brotherhood of Electrical Workers) IBEW web site throughout the Bush presidency that lend credence to this discussion.

COLLECTIVE BARGAINING

The Bush administration has used the war on terror and national security to curtail the bargaining rights of thousands of federal employees while allowing private employers to run roughshod over the rights of workers.

- IBEW, Unions Fight New Defense Rules - 4/16/04
- December 10 Events Highlight Worker Rights - 12/5/03
- Employee Free Choice Act Seeks New Deal for Organizing - 11/13/03
- The Union Busting Business is Booming - 11/7/03
- IBEW Members Face Loss of Protections - 6/5/03

TRADE:

A decade after NAFTA finds the United States industrial sector further losing out to overseas competitors like China, where labor comes cheap and laws and regulations to protect workers are almost nonexistent. Congress in 2002 restored the so-called "fast track" authority that gives the president even more flexibility to negotiate trade pacts. The widespread corporate practice of off shoring American jobs to places like India will likely be an issue in this year's election.

- U.S. Majority Disapproves of Government's Trade Approach -4/13/04
- Bush's Pick for Manufacturing Czar Withdraws - 3/15/04
- IBEW Members Face Shutdown at Thomson Inc. Plants - 3/22/04
- Administration Finds Good News in Job Flight Overseas - 2/12/04
- Industrial Trade Workers Mobilize on Capitol Hill - 2/9/04
- Trade Imbalance Likely to Worsen With New Agreements - 3/7/03
- Industrial Unions Demand Results from Congress - 2/6/03
- Industrial Council Aims to Reverse Manufacturing's Decline - 1/31/03
- Tale of the Tape: So Much for Made in America - 1/23/03
- Bush Signs Fast Track; Trade Bill Now Law - 8/6/02
- Senate Takes Wheel on Fast Track: Runs Over Workers - 5/30/02
- Bush Administration Moves on Fast Track - 11/1/01
- House Opponents Unlikely to Derail Fast Track - 7/6/01
- Bush Wants to Expand NAFTA - 4/17/01

OVERTIME:

A full year of lobbying by workers could not sway the administration from its goal of stiffing hundreds of thousands of workers of their hard-earned overtime pay. The labor department issued its final rules for new overtime regulations in April, 2004.

- Overtime Pay in Jeopardy for Millions of Americans - IBEW Journal, 4/04
- 150 Creative Ways to Cheat Workers Out of Pay, by the U.S. Labor Department 1/12/04
- Democrats Launch Last-Ditch Attempt to Thwart Damaging Regulation - 11/25/03

- Bill Would Nix Overtime Regulations - 7/14/03
- Hundreds Rally to Protect Overtime Pay - 7/1/03
- DOL Targets Overtime Pay - 6/26/03
- Overtime Rules Menace Workers Nationwide - 5/30/03 Bush Proposes Changing Overtime Rules - 4/2/03

MEDICARE:

Late last year, President Bush signed into law the most sweeping changes to Medicare since the retiree health program was created in 1965. Most of its changes will not occur until 2006, when many retirees are likely to be the losers.

- Medicare Drug Proposal Bad Deal for Seniors - 11/24/03

HEALTH CARE:

Health care costs have continued unchecked over the past several years as drug companies rack up bigger profits. The rising cost of medical insurance has emerged as one of the most contentious issues in contract negotiations but the Bush administration and Congress have done nothing to address necessary health care reform.

- What the Drug Companies Don't Want you to Know - 5/8/03
- Number of Uninsured Rising - 3/7/03

Yet now that the historical healthcare reform bill has been signed into law on 3/23/10 by our President, Mr. Obama, the Republicans have yet made another commitment to the corporations and against the people of America as they have vowed and I quote, "To do everything in their power to make sure that this law does not stand." In other words, I am in support of depriving the American people who are suffering physically and economically with a law that will instantly give them relief and serve their interests."

IN CONGRESS:

A Republican-controlled Congress has acted more on the interests of their corporate contributors than middle class America.

- Railroad Labor: Bill Passed Gives No Relief for Asbestos Victims - 4/13/04
- Labor Prevails to Defeat Comp Time Legislation - 6/11/03
- Republican House Majority Leader Calls Unions Unpatriotic - 2/10/03
- Republican Party Uses India Call Center to Raise Funds - 8/5/03

JOBS:

Despite tax cuts and other economic policies supposed to create jobs and jump-start a faltering economy, chronic unemployment continues. Millions of Americans are out of work, job prospects appear bleak and wage levels remain stagnant. Each day unemployment benefits expire for more Americans, Republicans fight to not renew them. All this is happening at a time of increased productivity, a measure that is supposed to bring good times.

- Congress Gives Jobless Unwelcome Holiday Gift: An End to Employment Benefits 1/2/04
- Republican House to Jobless: Let Them Eat Cake - 10/21/02
- House Republicans Delay Action While Unemployed Exhaust Benefits - 2/22/02
- Manufacturing Job Loss Undermines Union Gains - IBEW Journal, April 2001

WORKING FAMILIES:

The richest Americans have reaped the benefits of Bush's lopsided tax cuts at the expense of the middle and lower classes. Average Americans are concerned about the economy, less secure in their jobs and fearful about the escalating costs cost of health care.

- AFL-CIO Report: Working Families Hurt by Bush Policies - 1/29/03
- Top Dems Push for Worker Relief - 10/17/02
- Working Families Agenda Top Priority for Americans - 10/2/02
- U.S. Labor Laws Need Teeth, Workers Tell Congress - 6/21/02
- Bush Cuts Worker Training Programs - 2/6/02
- Unwilling to Freeze Taxes for Rich, Bush Puts U.S. in Red Ink - 1/14/02
- Judge: Bush Anti-Worker Order is Unlawful - 1/9/02
- Workers Lose to Corporations as Congress Passes Stimulus Bill - 10/25/01
- How Do We Pay for Bush's Tax Cut? - 4/18/01

LABOR DEPARTMENT:

The federal department charged with protecting workers has under President Bush turned on America's workforce, advocating for pro-employer policies while removing labor rights and safety measures for workers.

- Judge Puts One-Year Hold on New Labor Reporting Requirements - 1/6/04
- 50 Creative Ways to Cheat Workers Out of Pay, by the U.S. Labor Department 1/12/04
- Bush Deals Union A Compliance Nightmare - 10/20/03
- Bush Takes Don't Ask, Don't Tell Approach to Repetitive Motion Injuries - 7/1/03
- Bush Attempts to Bog Unions Down in Red Tape - 2/28/03
- Labor Department Layoff Report Terminated - 1/6/03

- Bush Ergonomics Rules: Compliance Optional - 4/10/02
- Bush's OSHA to Cut Jobs - 3/5/02
- Ergonomics Assault: DOL Strikes a Blow to Worker Safety - IBEW Journal, April 2001

Yes it is all related! So not only did former President Bush and the Republican Party callously take jobs away from Americans and their families, they also took the steps to ensure that these same displaced unemployed American families were unable to receive much needed job training and income support from their Republican controlled government. Yet we complain about President Obama!

On health care, the Bush budget also went precisely in the wrong direction. At a time when nearly 45 million Americans are without coverage and millions more struggle to meet rising costs, the Bush tax proposal would actually make those who had coverage pay more and provided no real help for the uninsured. Unconscionably, it also cut more than $100 billion over five years from Medicare and Medicaid, shifted more costs to the states and limited eligibility for children now receiving coverage under the State Children's Health Insurance Program (SCHIP).

In the important area of occupational safety and health, the Bush budget increased funding in nominal terms. An increase in funding was appropriated for Mine Safety and Health Administration (MSHA), particularly the coal enforcement program. However, when inflation was factored in, the FY 2008 budget in fact represented a cut in funding compared to FY 2006. The Bush budget also cut in the National Institute for Occupational Safety and Health (NIOSH) budget, reducing the nation's commitment to researching and preventing workplace injuries, diseases and deaths. With a combined budget request of $1.056 million for the federal job safety agencies, in FY 2008, the Bush administration spent $7.32 per worker to protect America's workers from job injuries, illnesses and death.

As further proof that the Republican controlled White House did not listen to, or was ever concerned about, working families who voted for them, the Bush budget retained the proposal to privatize Social

Security, despite its overwhelming rejection by all Americans. The budget included a placeholder of $29 billion in 2012 as the first year cost of setting up individual accounts and a total cost of $637 billion over the first six years for a proposal that must once again be rejected.

President Bush should have put our nation's exchequer into building a better future for America's working families instead of forcing more cuts in much-needed programs in health care, worker training and health and safety. His 2008 budget simply did not work for America's working men and women.

The following sections address the effects of the Bush FY 2008 budget on a range of programs vitally important to workers and their families.

Estimated receipts for fiscal year 2008 were $2.66 trillion.

- $1.25 trillion - Individual income tax
- $927.2 billion - Social Security and other payroll tax
- $314.9 billion - Corporate income tax
- $68.1 billion - Excise tax
- $29.2 billion - Customs duties
- $25.7 billion - Estate and gift taxes
- $50.7 billion - Other

Yes the President's budget for 2008 totaled $2.9 trillion. Percentages in parentheses indicated percentage change compared to 2007. This budget request is broken down by the following expenditures:

Mandatory spending: $1.788 trillion (+4.2%)

- $608 billion (+4.5%) - Social Security
- $386 billion (+5.2%) - Medicare
- $209 billion (+5.6%) - Medicaid and the State Children's Health Insurance Program (SCHIP)

- $324 billion (+1.8%) - Unemployment/Welfare/Other mandatory spending
- $261 billion (+9.2%) - Interest on National Debt

Discretionary spending: $1.114 trillion (+3.1%)

- $481.4 billion (+12.1%) - <u>Department of Defense</u>
- $145.2 billion (+45.8%) - <u>Global War on Terror</u>
- $69.3 billion (+0.3%) - <u>Department of Health and Human Services</u>
- $56.0 billion (+0.0%) - <u>Department of Education</u>
- $39.4 billion (+18.7%) - <u>Department of Veterans Affairs</u>
- $35.2 billion (+1.4%) - <u>Department of Housing and Urban Development</u>
- $35.0 billion (+22.0%) - <u>Department of State</u> and Other International Programs
- $34.3 billion (+7.2%) - <u>Department of Homeland Security</u>
- $24.3 billion (+6.6%) - <u>Department of Energy</u>
- $20.2 billion (+4.1%) - <u>Department of Justice</u>
- $20.2 billion (+3.1%) - <u>Department of Agriculture</u>
- $17.3 billion (+6.8%) - <u>National Aeronautics and Space Administration</u>
- $12.1 billion (+13.1%) - <u>Department of Transportation</u>
- $12.1 billion (+6.1%) - <u>Department of the Treasury</u>
- $10.6 billion (+2.9%) - <u>Department of the Interior</u>
- $10.6 billion (-9.4%) - <u>Department of Labor</u>
- $51.8 billion (+9.7%) - Other On-budget Discretionary Spending
- $39.0 billion - Other Off-budget Discretionary Spending

The Iraq War and the War in Afghanistan are not included in the regular budget. Instead, they are funded through special appropriations.

With projected receipts significantly less than projected outlays, the budget proposed by President Bush predicts a net deficit of approximately 240 billion dollars, adding to a United States governmental debt of about $10.8 trillion.

LEFT OUT IN THE COLD
(the following is a summary of the GOP's list of nonpriorities)

On Jan. 31, President Bush headed to Wall Street and acknowledged for the first time that income inequality exists in America: "The fact is that income inequality is real. It has been rising for more than 25 years."

But apparently, he's not quite ready to do anything about it. Bush's 2008 budget cuts crucial aid for America's middle class:

— "$77 billion in funding cuts for Medicare and Medicaid over the next five years, and $280 billion over the next 10."

— $223 million in funding cuts (4 percent decrease from this year's levels) to the Children's Health Insurance Program.

— "$4.9 billion, or 8 percent, cut in education, training, employment and social services" grants.

— $100 million cut for Head Start, which provides child development services to economically disadvantaged children and families.

— "$2.4 billion cut in community and regional development grants — which often provide funding for low- and middle-income communities — to $16.5 billion from $18.9 billion.

— $400 million — 18 percent — cut in the Low-Income Home Energy Assistance Program, "which provides $2.2 billion to help people pay heating bills this year while his corporate friends are becoming wealthier."

— $172 million — nearly 25 percent — cut in funding for housing for low-income seniors. While Bush forgot about the middle class in the new budget, he made sure to look out for the wealthy. As the Tax Policy Center notes, "People with incomes of more than $1 million would get tax cuts averaging $162,000 a year (in 2012 dollars) in perpetuity."

The debate over Iraq diverted attention and overshadowed an important, and bitter, budget fight between Congress and the president, who has threatened to veto a host of modest, responsible congressional spending proposals. With the battle lines drawn, Republican controlled Congress made it clear with whom they supported: an out-of-touch president and a bankrupt ideology, but not the best interests of the American public. Yet President Obama, for the sake of the American people, continues to reach out for bipartisan support. What a concept! Guess this information debunks the Republican's contention of the Democrats not including them in any discussions on policy and how this is a first-time occurrence.

Moreover, President Bush and the Republican opposition party had no fiscal responsibility credentials. His policies racked up $3 trillion in new debt. His annual budget projections significantly overestimated the deficit at the beginning of the year, which allowed him to claim his policies have decreased the deficit at year's end. Despite the president's fiscal shortcomings, 147 House Republicans pledged to sustain his vetoes of appropriations bills, almost three-fourths of the Republican caucus, including its leadership. They chose loyalty to the president and a failed ideology over the American people. Yet the GOP wants secretly sponsor tea parties as an affront on the President? Wow?

Why should anyone believe his budget requests are responsible? But not only that, why would anyone vote for any of them again in the midterm elections? And now my fellow Americans, for the denouement of this countries' economy at the hand of a Republican controlled White House; the "housing meltdown."

The Housing Meltdown: I remember within the same year of President Bush taking office after the Supreme Court elected him to office, coupled with the GOP gaining complete power in the House and Senate; the President began to encourage any American that listened to him to become a "home owner" with the GOP following their

President's lead! Now one might say that this was a noble gesture by our President and his GOP legislative support system. After all, they are encouraging Americans to seize their part of the American dream while they worked toward financial independence. What a concept! Right? Wrong! You see, what our then President and the current minority GOP "Grand Ole Obstructionists" did not tell you and perhaps did not anticipate, was the fact that this one simple gesture would be the catalyst that brought our economy in America to a screeching halt. Be that as it may, I must ask the same question of the readers that the Republicans and media miscreants are asking of our current President; why did the Bush administration's economic advisors not anticipate this current meltdown. Or did they simply not care? Now in the past few weeks (2009) following the Inauguration of President Barack Obama as the first black President of the United States, there has been conflicting accounts of how our economy reached the point of being near insolvency. The Republicans, as I have indicated to you before, have committed themselves to the cause of destroying the reputation and credibility of the President while accepting no responsibility for this economic crisis in America. Therefore, it has become imperative for me to continue my synopsis for the reader concerning "how we reached economic critical mass."

In a March 4, 2009, report by "Wall Street Watch" entitled, "Sold Out: How Wall Street and Washington Betrayed America," the process was outlined. They began by arguing that the financial sector invested more than $5 billion in political influence purchasing in Washington over the past decade, with as many as 3,000 lobbyists winning deregulation and other policy decisions that led directly to the current financial collapse. They stated that the report shows that from 1998-2008, Wall Street investment firms, commercial banks, hedge funds, real estate companies and insurance conglomerates made $1.725 billion in political contributions and spent another $3.4 billion on lobbyists, a financial juggernaut aimed at undercutting federal regulation. Nearly 3,000 officially registered federal lobbyists worked for the industry in 2007 alone. The report documents a dozen distinct deregulatory moves that, together, led to the financial meltdown. These include prohibitions on regulating financial derivatives; the repeal of regulatory barriers between commercial banks and investment banks;

a voluntary regulation scheme for big investment banks; and federal regulatory agencies' refusal to act to stop predatory subprime lending.

"The report further details, step-by-step, how Washington systematically sold out to Wall Street," says Harvey Rosenfield, president of the Consumer Education Foundation, a California-based non-profit organization. "Depression-era programs that would have prevented the financial meltdown that began last year were dismantled, and the warnings of those who foresaw disaster were drowned in an ocean of political money and we are paying a high price in the amounts of trillions of dollars for that betrayal."

"Congress and the Executive Branch," says Robert Weissman of Essential Information and the lead author of the report, "responded to the legal bribes from the financial sector, rolling back common-sense standards, barring honest regulators from issuing rules to address emerging problems and trashing enforcement efforts. The progressive erosion of regulatory restraining walls led to a flood of bad loans, and a tsunami of bad bets based on those bad loans. Now, there is wreckage across the financial landscape."

12 Key Policy Decisions Led to Cataclysm:

Financial deregulation led directly to the current economic meltdown. For the last three decades, government regulators, Congress and the executive branch, on a bipartisan basis, steadily eroded the regulatory system that restrained the financial sector from acting on its own worst tendencies. "Sold Out" details a dozen key steps to financial meltdown, revealing how industry pressure led to these deregulatory moves and their consequences:

1. In 1999, Congress repealed the Glass-Steagall Act, which had prohibited the merger of commercial banking and investment banking.

2. Regulatory rules permitted off-balance sheet accounting, tricks that enabled banks to hide their liabilities.

3. The Clinton administration blocked the Commodity Futures Trading Commission from regulating financial derivatives which became the basis for massive speculation.

4. Congress in 2000 prohibited regulation of financial derivatives when it passed the Commodity Futures Modernization Act.

5. The Bush Securities and Exchange Commission in 2004 adopted a voluntary regulation scheme for investment banks that enabled them to incur much higher levels of debt.

6. Rules adopted by global regulators at the behest of the financial industry would enable commercial banks to determine their own capital reserve requirements, based on their internal "risk-assessment models."

7. Federal regulators refused to block widespread predatory lending practices earlier in this decade, failing to either issue appropriate regulations or even enforce existing ones.

8. Federal bank regulators claimed the power to supersede state consumer protection laws that could have diminished predatory lending and other abusive practices.

9. Federal rules prevented victims of abusive loans from suing firms that bought their loans from the banks that issued the original loan.

10. Fannie Mae and Freddie Mac expanded beyond their traditional scope of business and entered the subprime market, ultimately costing taxpayers hundreds of billions of dollars.

11. The abandonment of antitrust and related regulatory principles enabled the creation of too-big-to-fail megabanks, which engaged in much riskier practices than smaller banks.

12. Beset by conflicts of interest, private credit rating companies incorrectly assessed the quality of mortgage-backed securities; a 2006 law handcuffed the SEC from properly regulating the firms.

When one considers any financial organization that was forearmed with such knowledge. Specifically, if an institution understood the process to be as follows:

a.) President Bush pushing home ownership as a means to acquire wealth.

b.) Mortgage brokers seizing the opportunity to offer mortgages for Main Street.

c.) These same Mortgage brokers who are in positions of trust by being privy to the amount of a home the average consumer could afford. For example, after your credit reports were run, after your debt ratio was determined, your income was verified, and it was determined that you could only afford a $140,000 home, but a house of that meager of means financially could never bolster your commission!

d.) Therefore, due to greed, promises were made and deceptions were engaged upon by our mortgage brokers who guaranteed that they could move the typical consumer into more expensive homes for teaser rates, interest only loans, but these mortgages had to be guaranteed. In comes Goldman Sachs, who understood several realities.

1. These loans that were made would provide the brokers with windfall profits at the closing of each of these homes.

2. That these mortgages of teaser rates and interest only loans were never addressing the "principle balances." Therefore once the principle becomes due, the mortgages of the average person on Main Street would balloon from $800.00 to $1,600.00 which is foundational catalyst concerning why the mortgage balloon burst. It is plain old American Capitalism which functions only when an exploitation of the taxpayer takes place. Realistically, these mortgage brokers and mortgage security firms were in positions of trust, as the American people "trusted" the professionals to inform

them of the house that they could afford, and to write them a fair and just mortgage contractual agreement. So again I ask, "How is it the people's fault."

3. Now if one was actually forearmed with such knowledge due to being one of the financial backers of these mortgage holders, and possessed insider information on the state of these mortgages, and began to invest against the success of these mortgages, when the balloon burst they would become billionaires by betting against the success of the mortgage industry, yet the GOP is battling financial industry reform in this nation. Consider how we arrived to this point and think about it.

Bring back the Sheriff of Wall Street

Although many of you cannot remember the time when we actually had true Wall Street regulation, so let me assist you. It was during the time when Wall Street had a Sheriff in the form of Attorney General Eliot Spitzer who understood the complicated web of deception that Wall Street entails. During his days as N.Y. Attorney General, he policed Wall Street with honor, vigor and tenacity that is unmatched to date as many financial titans met their waterloo. No he did not make deals, he prosecuted corruption and he was resented for it. So much so, that when the opportunity presented itself, he was exposed as governor for his sexual proclivities, in his exploits with prostitutes. Now before you take the moral high ground, let me remind you of Governor Mark Sanford and his jaunts to Rio de Janeiro as he left South Carolina without a governor and his family without a father, yet he remains in office. Did I mention ole Rudy and his many exploits that would make a pimp blush? How about Vitter in Louisiana? Who loves prostitutes but continues to be a presence in politics. I could go on with sexual trysts of McCain, Gingrich, Edwards, the list goes on so do not judge. On the contrary, if you look at the events that led up to Mr. Spitzer's resignation, I would argue that if any laws were broken why was he not prosecuted? Because the turn of events were not about the shaming of his office as Governor, the act was all about neutralizing a despised adversary of Wall Street who stood for regulation and accountability. It is for these reasons that if the White House and our Representatives are genuinely interested in Wall Street regulation and reform then "bring back the Sheriff" and appoint Eliot Spitzer as the economic czar of Wall Street.

Financial Sector Political Money and 3000 Lobbyists Dictated Washington Policy During the period 1998-2008 (Before Obama):

- Commercial banks spent more than $154 million on campaign contributions, while investing $363 million in officially registered lobbying.

- Accounting firms spent $68 million on campaign contributions and $115 million on lobbying.

- Insurance companies donated more than $218 million and spent more than $1.1 billion on lobbying.

- Securities firms invested more than $504 million in campaign contributions, and an additional $576 million in lobbying. Included in this total: private equity firms contributed $56 million to federal candidates and spent $33 million on lobbying; and hedge funds spent $32 million on campaign contributions (about half in the 2008 election cycle).

The betrayal was bipartisan: about 55 percent of the political donations went to Republicans and 45 percent to Democrats, primarily reflecting the balance of power over the decade. Democrats took just more than half of the financial sector's 2008 election cycle contributions. The financial sector buttressed its political strength by placing Wall Street expatriates in top regulatory positions, including the post of Treasury Secretary held by two former Goldman Sachs chairs, Robert Rubin and Henry Paulson.

Financial firms employed a legion of lobbyists, maintaining nearly 3,000 separate lobbyists in 2007 alone.

These companies drew heavily from government in choosing their lobbyists. Surveying 20 leading financial firms, "Sold Out" finds 142 of the lobbyists they employed from 1998-2008 were previously high-ranking officials or employees in the Executive Branch or Congress.

Now our President has submitted his legislation that would arguably move in the direction of correcting the economic destruction at the hands of our GOP and former President Bush. The utter audacity of these current republican and conservative democratic minorities, in attempting to make an argument about wasteful spending; especially when each and every one of them "cashed in" at the expense of the American people in this housing crisis. How do you engage in destroying a country, and selfishly attempt to prevent our current leader from correcting your deliberate clandestine and destructive behavior? It reminds me of the mafia who murders someone, only to return to the funeral to pay their respects, talking to the family members and telling them "how deeply sorry they are for their loss," when they caused it. After all, when these groups of miscreants vote against President Obama's stimulus package and budget, we must realize that they are protecting their selfish special interests, and sending we the people the message that it has never been about us and it has always been about them.

However, the most telling characteristic of this party is not in their disinterest in helping nonmillionaires to become self-sufficient, it is not in this party's hypocrisy in spending the taxpayer's money to improve the lives of their secret society while everyone else should stop asking for hand-outs, it is not even in this party's ability to still argue that no regulations in a free market economy is the way to go because they are already rich, it is not even in their "political amnesia" and conspicuous refusal to accept any responsibility for the dire straits that their "complete power" has placed on our economy, No! The most telling characteristic of this party is in their commitment to become an impediment to the Obama administration's attempt to resuscitate this oppressive economic system that helps the working class, the middle class, conservatives, democrats, independents alike and to restore America to the bastion of integrity and character that the world once used as an example on how to conduct themselves as nations.

On the contrary, because of the selfish, heartless, arrogant supremacy that defines their Party, they have made a decision on the night that then Senator Obama overwhelmingly defeated Senator McCain for the nomination of President of the United States, to do whatever it took to make sure that Mr. President does not enjoy any success, and that he does not end this Conservative induced oppressive economic system during his stay in the White House. The "Oxycontin warrior" of the Republican Party Rush Limbaugh has thrown down the gauntlet on this administration and has revealed the "Opposition Party's" plan to restore the image and trust of their beleaguered party in the eyes of the American people, so that is why I am exposing the plan of this Party so the people cannot be deceived again. It is as follows:

1)   Oppose and Blame:

Plan one by this party is to oppose and filibuster any significant bills that would impact, assist, and improve the lives of the American people for the next two years when the midterm elections take place. The platform that the Republicans will use is that President Obama's administration, the Democrats, Independents, and even some Republican traitors have not made any progress to improve the lives of Americans and therefore should lose their seats. What they will not tell you is that in spite of the President's attempts to reach across the aisle and have a bipartisan effort in rescuing America from destruction, and allowing these miscreants the opportunity to perform community service and restorative justice for their destruction of America, they have consistently slapped his hand and clenched their fists while opposing change in America. Just look at the current stimulus legislation that the President has presented and who voted for it, only 3 Republicans joined the President and voted to help the American people. The remainder of the GOP basically said with their actions that the American people in their districts could "die" as far as they were concerned.

Thank God that we have a current President who has the courage, unselfishness, and love for the American people (even the ones who hate him and plot his demise), to endure all of the hate, all of the mean-spirited attempts to undermine him, all of the threats on his life, all of the questions to his intelligence by mental pygmies, all of the attacks on his character by certain media factions who swear that he is not helping blacks, all of the race baiting and attempts to splinter our country, and yes all of the treasonous "name calling" at the hand of the domestic terrorist cells in our country. In spite of the entire plethora of obstacles, President Obama continues to be productive! Surprised? You should very well be, since many have done everything in their power to ensure his failure. But in spite of the Rights' "Ides of March" plot of failure according to Dr. Robert P. Watson, coordinator of American studies at Lynn University, he states:

"I am always being asked to grade Obama's presidency. In place of offering him a grade, I put together a list of his accomplishments thus far. I think you would agree that it is very impressive. His first six months have been even more active than FDRs or LBJs the two standards for such assessments. Yet, there is little media attention given to much of what he has done. Of late, the media is focusing almost exclusively on Obama's critics, without holding them responsible for the uncivil, unconstructive tone of their disagreements or without holding the previous administration responsible for getting us in such a deep hole. The misinformation and venom that now passes for political reporting and civic debate is beyond description.

As such, there is a need to set the record straight. What most impresses me is the fact that Obama has accomplished so much not from a heavy-handed or top-down approach but from a style that has institutionalized efforts to reach across the aisle, encourage vigorous debate, and utilize town halls and panels of experts in the policy-making process. Beyond the accomplishments, the process is good for democracy and our democratic processes have been battered and bruised in recent years." Listed below is Dr. Watson's account, along with my research and compilation of a few of President Obama's accomplishments:

1. Ordered all federal agencies to undertake a study and make recommendations for ways to cut spending.

2. Ordered a review of all federal operations to identify and cut wasteful spending and practices.

3. Instituted enforcement for equal pay for women.

4. Beginning the withdrawal of US troops from Iraq.

5. Families of fallen soldiers have expenses covered to be on hand when the body arrives at Dover AFB.

6. Ended media blackout on war casualties; reporting full information.

7. Ended media blackout on covering the return of fallen soldiers to Dover AFB; the media is now permitted to do so pending adherence to respectful rules and approval of fallen soldier's family.

8. The White House and federal government are respecting the Freedom of Information Act.

9. Instructed all federal agencies to promote openness and transparency as much as possible in government.

10. Placed limits on lobbyist's access to the White House.

11. Placed limits on White House aides working for lobbyists after their tenure in the administration.

12. Ended the previous stop-loss policy that kept soldiers in Iraq/Afghanistan longer than their enlistment date.

13. Is phasing out the expensive F-22 war plane and other outdated weapons systems, which weren't even used or needed in Iraq/Afghanistan.

14. Removed restrictions on embryonic stem-cell research.

15. Federal support for stem-cell and new biomedical research.

16. Increased new federal funding for science and research labs.

17. States are permitted to enact federal fuel efficiency standards above federal standards.18. Increased infrastructure spending (roads, bridges, power plants) after years of neglect and bridges collapsing.

18. Instituted funds for high-speed, broadband Internet access to K-12 schools.

19. Initiated new funds for school construction.

20. The prison at Guantanamo Bay is being phased out.

21. Initiated U.S. Auto industry rescue plan that is flourishing.

22. Initiated and continues a Housing rescue plan.

23. Initiated a $789 billion economic stimulus plan that is slowly turning the economy around.25. The public can meet with federal housing insurers to refinance (the new plan can be completed in one day) a mortgage if they are having trouble paying.

24. The U.S. financial and banking rescue plan is working with the stock market experiencing increasing trends.

25. The secret detention facilities in Eastern Europe and elsewhere, that the Bush and Republican administration denied existing are being closed.

26. He ended the previous policy; the US now has a no torture policy and is in compliance with the Geneva Convention standards.

27. Due to new legislation, better body armor is now being provided to our troops.

28. The missile defense program is being cut by $1.4 billion in 2010.

29. He restarted the nuclear nonproliferation talks and building back up the nuclear inspection infrastructure/protocols.

30. He has reengaged in the treaties/agreements to protect the Antarctic.

31. He has reengaged in the agreements/talks on global warming and greenhouse gas emissions.

32. He has visited more countries and met with more world leaders than any president in his first six months in office.

33. He successfully released a U.S. captain held by Somali pirates; and authorized the SEALS to do their job.

34. The U.S. Navy has been authorized by our Commander in Chief to increase patrols off Somali coast.

35. He initiated attractive tax write-offs for those who buy hybrid automobiles.

36. His cash for clunkers program offered vouchers to trade in fuel inefficient, polluting old cars for new cars stimulated auto sales.

37. He announced plans to purchase fuel efficient American-made fleet for the federal government.

38. He expanded the SCHIP program to cover health care for 4 million more children.

39. He signed national service legislation; expanded national youth service program.

40. He instituted a new policy on Cuba, allowing Cuban families to return home to visit loved ones.

41. He ended the previous policy of not regulating and labeling carbon dioxide emissions.

42. He expanded vaccination programs.

43. He had an immediate and efficient response to the floods in North Dakota and other natural disasters, unlike the Katrina debacle.

44. He closed offshore tax safe havens.

45. He negotiated deals with Swiss banks to permit U.S. government to gain access to records of tax evaders and criminals, and negotiated the payments of hundreds of millions of dollars back to the U.S. government.

46. He ended the previous policy of offering tax benefits to corporations who outsource American jobs; the new policy is to promote in-sourcing to bring jobs back.

47. He ended the previous practice of protecting credit card companies; in place of it are new consumer protections from credit card industry's predatory practices.

48. The energy producing plants must begin preparing to produce 15% of their energy from renewable sources.

49. His policies have lowered drug costs for seniors.

50. He ended the previous practice of forbidding Medicare from negotiating with drug manufacturers for cheaper drugs; the federal government is now realizing hundreds of millions in savings.

51. He increased pay and benefits for military personnel.

52. He improved housing for military personnel.

53. He initiated a new policy to promote federal hiring of military spouses.

54. He improved conditions at Walter Reed Military Hospital and other military hospitals.

55. He has increased student loans and the amount of Pell Grants.

56. He has increased more opportunities in the AmeriCorps program.

57. He has sent envoys to the Middle East and other parts of the world that had been neglected for years; thus reengaging in multilateral and bilateral talks and diplomacy.

58. He is establishing a new cyber security office.

59. He is beginning the process of reforming and restructuring the military 20 years after the Cold War to a more modern fighting force; this includes new procurement policies, increasing size of military, new technology and cyber units and operations, etc.

60. He ended the previous policy of awarding no-bid defense contracts. Sorry Halliburton!

61. He has ordered a review of hurricane and natural disaster preparedness.

62. He established a National Performance Officer charged with saving the federal government money and making federal operations more efficient.

63. He signed legislation to assist students struggling to make college loan payments, by having their loans refinanced.

64. He has improved benefits for veterans.

65. He has increased press conferences and town halls and much more media access than the previous administration.

66. He has instituted a new focus on mortgage fraud with new Wall Street regulations and oversight.

67. The FDA is now regulating tobacco.

68. He has ended the previous policy of cutting the FDA and circumventing FDA rules.

69. He has ended the previous practice of having White House aides rewrite scientific and environmental rules, regulations, and reports.

70. He has authorized discussions with North Korea and initiated a private mission by former President Bill Clinton to secure the release of two Americans held in prisons.

71. He has authorized discussions with Myanmar and mission by Sen. Jim Web to secure the release of an American held captive.

72. He is making more loans available to small businesses.

73. He has established an independent commission to make recommendations on slowing the costs of Medicare.

74. He appointed the first Latina woman to the Supreme Court.

75. He has authorized the construction/opening of additional health centers to care for veterans.

76. He limited the salaries of senior White House aides to the sum of $100,000.

77. He renewed loan guarantees for Israel.

78. He changed the failing/status quo military command in Afghanistan.

79. He deployed additional troops to Afghanistan.

80. He initiated a new Afghan War policy that limits aerial bombing and prioritized aid, development of infrastructure, diplomacy, and good government practices by Afghans.

81. He announced the long-term development of a national energy grid with renewable sources and cleaner, efficient energy production.

82. He returned money authorized for refurbishment of White House offices and private living quarters.

83. He paid for the redecoration of White House living quarters out of his own pocket.

84. He held the first Seder in White House.

85. He has reformed the nation's healthcare system which is the most expensive in the world and has a way for almost 50 million without health insurance and millions more under insured to enter the system.

86. He has put the ball in play for comprehensive immigration reform.

87. He has announced his intention to push for energy reform.

88. He has announced his intention to push for education reform.

And Now for Presidential Candidate Mitt Romney's plan for America: ???????????????

HE KILLED OSAMA BIN LADEN, THE #1 TERRORIST IN THE WORLD WHILE DISRUPTING THE AL QUAEDA NETWORK BY KILLING THEIR TOP OFFICIALS!

Oh, and he built a swing set for the girls outside the Oval Office.

What manner of man is this I ask? From my vantage point, it appears that the Right is going to have to choose another strategy because the "cat is out of the bag." Oops!

When one considers the accomplishments of this man in his first 3 years in office, I have to ask you in the manner of which Matthew

McConaughey asked an all-white jury in "A Time to Kill"; "Close your eyes, imagine that this was your child that these men raped, now imagine that the defendant were white"! That's right America, imagine if the 44th President of the United States were a blue blood white male with a Republican pedigree? He would win by a landslide!

Biggest Scam in America

Now one could make the argument that if we had a President who was trying to help Americans on Main Street, then he would receive the support of the Americans on Main Street. But that is not the case! On the contrary, there are unprecedented signs and symbols that the President is not being supported at all by all of the people! On the contrary, there is a hate and deeply embedded racism that is manifesting itself through the demonstration of a genre of unenlightened puppets that refer to themselves as "Tea baggers." I refer to them as unenlightened because they are being used for political purposes and do not even know it! You may say, "How is that Possible?" Simple! If I am a Politician who hates being in the minority party, and I harbor resentment towards the President whose only sin is "governing while black," and for helping the poor and the middle class, and if I understood that if I publicly displayed that racial hatred towards this man who is trying to restore America, that I would lose my seat in the district that I represent, then I would enlist others who are just as hateful and racist to express my disdain. The result would be an organization who will carry picket signs for me, who would have public displays of hate cloaked under the veneer of demonstrations nation-wide to do my cowardly work for me. Ask yourselves how can organizations of uneducated, poor, racist, angry, bitter, and ignorant people fund trips around America to set up these demonstrations? They cannot fund these racist escapades! However, those power-brokers who belong to certain political parties, who own companies, who head corporations, who own media conglomerates, whose husbands sit on the highest court, are able to fund these hate-fests that are destroying the very fabric of our society and should be held accountable for their clandestine and treasonous actions. It is unfortunate and saddens me to see these demonstrators who need healthcare, who need jobs, who are unable to feed their families, and who are being exploited by these wealthy sponsors, choose racial hatred of our black President over their best interests and the best interests of their families. Hate is a powerful thing but it should not be surprising that a small percentage of Americans HATE our President with the $25 million dollar woman leading the charge in Sarah Palin! What a strange dichotomy of special interest. If tea bagger Palin and other representatives who throw rocks and hide their hands, were so passionate about this movement that complain about "out of control" spending that will economically cripple their children, then why don't they attend these rallies and speak for free? I mean, if they are so invested in the future of their children, and since they refuse to mention how much money Mr. Obama's predecessor spent with the G.O.P.'s blessing, then why charge tens of thousands of dollars to speak at the rallies? So it makes me ask, "What is this movement all about again?

2)   Smoke and mirrors to create an illusion of inclusivity:

Due to the GOP's missteps, they earned the dubious distinction of being a party of exclusivity as it related to the issues of minorities and women in key leadership positions in the party and in this country. Refusing to accept responsibility for the "good ole boyish" type of Party that they had created, and how it has undermined the support that they have received each election year by working class, middle class and the rich respectively, they realized from the overwhelming defeat of their candidate that they needed to join the rest of Americans in the 21st century. Unfortunately, the party decided to engage in the gimmick politics of the past, so they tried to dupe America while taking advantage of a hard fought democratic nomination for President. A presidential race that appointed a black male over a woman, which prompted the GOP to appoint the unvetted, ditsy darling of the Presidential election as the vice-presidential candidate in Sarah Palin, a woman who was supposed to create the image of sensitivity towards women and get their candidate elected at the same time. However, on behalf of all of the many accomplished, outstanding, and capable women in America, to present such a candidate for the second top executive position in America was insulting to the women of America nation-wide and the party paid dearly for it.

Not learning from their mistakes, lacking any shred of wisdom, and believing that Americans are gullible, the party has again decided to utilize smoke and mirrors to distract "we the people" once again; this time with the nomination of Michael Steele, an accomplished black man in his own right, to become the 63rd Chairman of the Republican National Committee (RNC)! Let us recap. First, a woman was chosen by the GOP to become the vice-presidential candidate, who did not yield the results that the party anticipated, and now they elected a black male to become their national chairperson, who they elected after six rounds of votes by a narrow margin. Does this election have anything to do with the fact that Americans elected a black male as the U.S. President? Always remember that with this party, things are not always the way they seem and there are usually ulterior motives attached. Let us look closer. The representatives of the GOP would now like for the American people to believe that since 1856 and the choosing of 62 white male republican national chairmen that they now had an epiphany! On the contrary, these are the same party members that have committed to the demise of one black male, in President Obama by not supporting any of his legislation, but now they are suddenly committed to supporting the platform of another black male in Michael Steele? Do not be deceived, once again this is merely "black faced" politics at is best. To further insult the intelligence of the American people, the GOP then introduced to you on 2/24/09, the new improved and younger version of their party; an Indian who is just as selfish, heartless, deceptive, greedy and amnesiac as the old rich fogies and federal felons in his Party. He and not their newly elected Chair, was tasked with the responsibility of conducting the GOP's response to Mr. President's State of the Union address to we the people. First, this party has deceptively set the goal of conducting damage control by using Governor Bobby Jindal as the GOP poster boy for the perceived change that has never defined this party. Secondly, they hope to neutralize any momentum that the President may have built during his address that garners support from the American people. If they talk loud enough, if they complain about the administration's wasteful spending, if they inundate the airwaves with the same old lies, if they continue to attempt to shift the blame for this mess to the new administration, if they talk loudly enough about fiscal conservatism while they accept absolutely

We The People

no responsibility for their free spending for eight years, then they can perhaps damage Mr. President's popularity and wane his support. Remember, the definition of insanity is to do the same things over and over again, tax cuts for the rich, and expect a different result. Do not be fooled by the smoke and mirrors of these political Archie Bunkers, who draw you in with gimmicks like the affirmative action Indian and the token Negro, who provide the "window dressing" for their party, while they maintain and follow the principles of Rush Limbaugh and former imperial wizard of the Ku Klux Klan David Dukes; principles exercised by many Southern Governors who would rather starve and keep their constituents without employment benefits than take money from a black man. Once again we have come too far to turn back now.

3)   Utilizing the media to Neutralize Opposition and Dissent:

I must admit that before I began to study the political landscape of this country, I oftentimes trusted and believed that the news that was reported to the public was true and above reproach and patterned my belief system accordingly. However, after I began to study this election cycle and the manner in which there was an all-out media blitz on President Obama to the point of impugning his character and placing him under a cloud of suspicion in hopes of derailing his re-election for President, my unswerving devotion was met with a harsh reality. That reality was the understanding that the secret society of racist Capitalists in this country were committed to furthering their oppressive agenda against the middle class, the working class, republicans, democrats, independents, male, female, young, and old alike without being held responsible and while they retained their seats of power in Washington, DC. Just ask yourselves how in the world can a representative of the people continue to pass legislation that incarcerates, bankrupts, forecloses, probes vaginas, evicts, starves, lays off, and otherwise destroys the lives of their constituencies nation-wide and they never are voted out of office. It's simple! The secret society of the super-pacs, the billionaires, the Karl Roves, and the Koch Brothers provides for these lawmakers a public relations vehicle to keep the taxpayers and voters from gaining a clear understanding of the character and nature of their representatives. That vehicle is called the media, whose

242

purpose is to control the conversation, the thought, and to influence the opinion of the voters and in return neutralize any opposition and dissent to their oppressive laws that negatively impact Americans like you and I. Issues such as drugs laws, stimulus plans for the working class, abortion bans, voting rights legislation, affordable healthcare for families, unemployment funding, educational institutional funding, HBCU college funding, student loan legislation, balanced and fair tax codes, credit card regulations, fair housing laws, equal employment opportunities, civil rights laws that protect the average American, and voting rights laws that will ensure that "we the people" will never rise up and elect another Barack Hussein Obama as the U.S. President or any leader who represents all people.

Do they not realize that God made everyone in His Own Image and placed all of us in this country with the command to love one another and treat everyone with common decency? If it just were not for your money, socioeconomic status, appearance, and job title that create the illusion that you are better than those who are less fortunate than you are. So much so, that you will not even reach down and try to lift your fellow man up to a position of self sufficiency. But you, through the Christian Right will quote bible verses like the Lord said, "the poor will always be with us." Look at our government who are the stewards that God has placed over the taxpayers money and entrusted with the laws of the land, and how do they allocate the funding? How do they prosecute crime? How do they make and pass laws? Who or what special interest groups influence the passage of those laws. Do you not know that God owns everything? Do you not know that God loves everyone that he created and that he is no respecter of persons? So why are certain legislators fighting the President from extending a rescue package to the middle class or the working poor?

Our call as a nation is to be the light in darkness that God has designated to be an example to the World. In order for us to realize our divine purpose as a Nation, we must eliminate ourselves from all remnants of white supremacy, black supremacy, racial supremacy, economic supremacy, political supremacy, anger, bitterness, selfishness, strife, division, imperialism, and a lack of good will. We must also pray for and as a nation, distance ourselves from all persons who join forces in this country and form an "Axis of Evil" in the United States of America. Logically, if God dwells in a country that is on one accord, then it can be logically deduced that he is absent from a country that is divided against itself. America we have a choice that is before us to progress as a Human Race of citizens in this country, or perish as a stubborn, arrogant, immoral, racist, divisive country of fools. The choice is ours, but whatever you do, Think For Yourself, and be real about your beliefs. Do not tell me that you love God and country while you treat your brother and neighbor with disrespect, disgust, disregard, and disdain. This will be our last and greatest opportunity as a nation to determine our moral fiber and how we want to be viewed. How America determines its future on November 4, 2008 and beyond will determine how we will be defined as a nation. Yes, the world is watching, but most of all, God is watching and this time, we will be recompensed for our decision. Let the Sleeping Giant awaken.

THE SLEEPING GIANT

My fellow Americans, there is no reason for any of you to be angry, oppressed, or treated as second class citizens. Because in your hands lies the answer to you and your loved ones' future, and America whether you like it or not, has forced us to live in two distinctly different societies, and the potential that we possess as ONE NATION frightens the Capitalist establishment. Now even if you do not understand it, believe it or not, there is a power-base neutralizer in this country that is referred to as, "One Man, One Vote," and it remains the most powerful force in the United States of America! Why do you think that so much care goes into the passage of new voting rights laws, paying shock jocks millions of dollars to engage in divisive politics, using the U.S. Supreme Court to steal elections, not counting votes at all, the media creating fake polls of who is leading in the election to discourage voters from voting, Secretary of various States checking identifications and citizenships that rivals poll taxes, all of the Republican celebrities converging on Georgia to motivate the base to re-elect Saxby Chambliss with downright intimidation at the polls on voting day? Because when "We the People" stand up as one, with similar goals, with settled differences, and with love one for another and vote Our Interest, we can take our country back. Because "We the People" are the Sleeping

Giant and this is our country, with each person and citizen serving a purpose in this democracy, as we fit together like a "perfect union." However, this task will not be an easy endeavor due to a group of persons who have resigned themselves to stunt the growth of this great country by keeping it divided along racial lines and fear. Although I have identified these persons, you may wonder who these people really are and why do they seem to want to attack any candidate who aspires to use their influence to uplift and transform the masses economically, physically, and spiritually. The answer is a simple premise, these are people who simply cannot move forward, and do not want "We the People" to move forward. However, there is a method to their madness.

WHY SOME CITIZENS CANNOT MOVE FORWARD

My fellow citizens, make no mistake, there will always be that genre of persons in our society who will always remain hateful, divisive, angry, selfish, and mean-spirited. This subculture of people will not only always be among us, but they are not an isolated faction! They can be heard on our media stations worldwide, they occupy high political office seats, they are in our courtrooms, they prosecute our citizens, they are our law enforcement officers, they are in our classrooms and colleges, they are heading our corporations, and they are heading our churches, and are raising our children. By now, you have read most of this book, and have become knowledgeable of the blatant attempts by these persons to keep America divided, in fear, as angry and frustrated as they are, while their capitalist bosses continue to pilfer America of its resources. Unfortunately their shenanigans of labeling candidates, lying, oppressing dissent, creating fear, legislating incompetence, undermining voting rights, and spewing racist epithets did not work and America elected a black male President of this country! Yes this time, love overcame hate, and this time, perfect love casted out fear, but do not think for one moment that these miscreants of division are finished with their shameless attacks. Yes even though the majority of this country have spoken and have given President Obama a "mandate" for taking this country in a fundamentally new direction, this pack of degenerates will ignore this mandate, deny their obvious defeat, and will continue with their racist agenda simply because their psyche is one-dimensional which begs the question, Are they unable to move forward with America's mandate because they are mentally defected? Before you answer my question consider the following empirical data and scientific study

FEBRUARY 18, 2009 NEW YORK POST CARTOON

WHY DO RACISTS HAVE LOW IQs?

As I view the picture from the previous page, I am reminded of an undergraduate college field visit to Augusta Evans Middle school. I was astonished with the fact that all of the students at the school were drawing pictures in partial fulfillment of their school assignments. As I reflected back on the foundation of a normal academic environment, I am reminded of the various forms of communication that are embraced and utilized; forms such as learning words, writing sentences, paragraphs, papers, and yes drawing as well. So here I was, suspended in time and observing a dichotomy of two academic environments and philosophies, yet it became difficult to embrace any academic environment that communicated through the drawing of pictures only. This caused me to voice my concerns to the teacher of the special needs students, and how she replied to me transformed my unanswered questions into an educational experience. For she so eloquently stated that, for people in general, and her students in particular who have low IQs and are mentally challenged, they find it extremely difficult to communicate in conventional ways. Consequently, their only means of communication was through the drawing of pictures. Moreover, when we continuously witness mean-spirited, cowardly, and racist acts such as these with no visible culpability, it challenges us to ask the bigger question, do racists have low IQs? Studies going back over 50 years have repeatedly arrived at the same conclusion -racists have lower IQs than non-racists. The average intelligence quotient (IQ) of all members of the human race is 100 on the Stanford-Binet scale, as illustrated in the bell curves in the figure below. The average IQ of racists is up to 4 IQ points less than this (Montagu 1952 & 1988, Allport 1946, Frenkel-Brunswick and Sanford 1945). The reasons this is true are not entirely clear. Does racism attract the unintelligent or do the unintelligent default into racist mentalities?

An exploration of this phenomenon can be most informative.

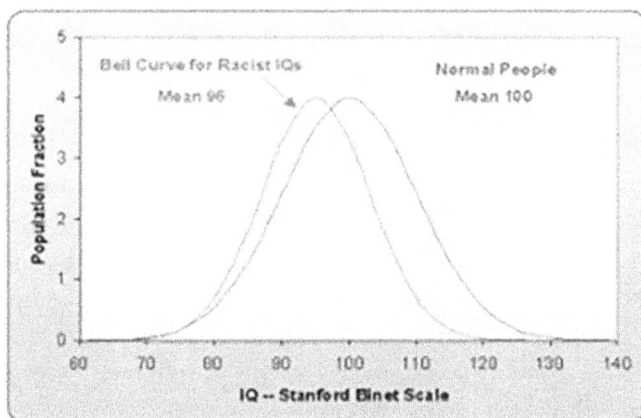

Since the average IQ of a racist is less than the average, racists have two-digit IQs, while normal people have three-digit IQs, on the average. This applies to Nazi skinheads, media cartoonists, media personalities, capitalist sponsors, politicians, tea baggers (the new KKK), the new G.O.P., American Nazis, private citizens, law enforcement miscreants, the oxymoronic Aryan supremacists, Christian Identity fanatics, anti-Semites, non-denominational bigots, and other such social atavistic rejects. The figure above is based on a standard deviation of 10, and is normalized for matching populations. Many studies have explored the psychology of racism and the familial and social backgrounds of racists. Some interesting generalities can be extracted from these studies, including the fact that racists tend to be conservatives, conformists, Republicans, and hypochondriacs. The high incidence of conservatism, conformism, and Republicanism are all related phenomena. That is, one would expect a conformist to be a conservative, and a conservative to be a Republican, and a Republican to be a conformist, etc. But why would they tend to be hypochondriacs? Perhaps they blame their body parts for imaginary illnesses in the same way they blame parts of society for imaginary social illnesses. (Allport, 1946)

The arguments of racism have been demonstrated repeatedly to be illogical and irrational. For example, racists claim that so-called white people are "superior" to so-called black people. Ignoring for the moment the inability of science to draw a sharp line between those who are subjectively considered to be white and those who are subjectively considered to be black, let's consider the claims of superiority by racist supremacists. As we look around us in America, today we see a country full of diversity in which American blacks and other citizens of non-European descent excel in all the arts and sciences, in all aspects of business, in engineering, in medicine, in law, in academia, in all political arenas, and in all athletics, coaching, other social activities, and yes even the Oval office. From our military commanders, to engineering, to education, to our religious and political leaders, to our star athletes both Olympic and professional, to our fastest-growing independent businesses, and in all genres of the entertainments fields -- art, music, acting, directing, film-making, etc. -- we witness a growing disproportionate dominance of non-whites, and this in spite of centuries of oppression and the continued denial of equal opportunities. Their successes are undeniable and ubiquitous, and yet the racists of our times act as if they are completely blind to this manifest proof that the superiority of whites is a dying mirage, and cannot conclude that in this country, color is a subjective term, and talent is the catalyst that will return this country to its greatness. The failure of these culprits to acknowledge this obvious reality that is supported with empirical data, exacerbates this country's divisions, and further corroborates this writer's conclusions of this subcultures' low level of intelligence that may require professional intervention. Let us continue by considering figure 2.

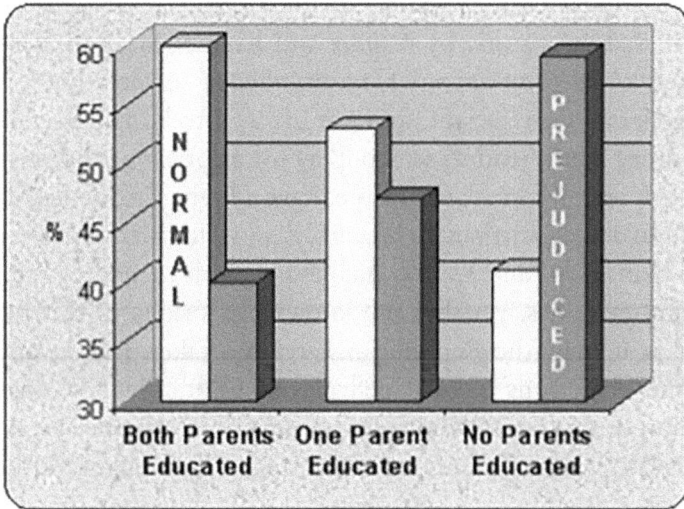

Figure 2: Tendency to be Prejudiced as a Function of Parents' College Education. (Allport 1946)

Figure 2 shows how prejudice tends to be a function of parents' college education. Obviously the more educated the parents are, the less likely their children are to become prejudiced. Again, we see a correlation of both intelligence and education with normality, while the lack of education and intelligence is associated with bigotry.

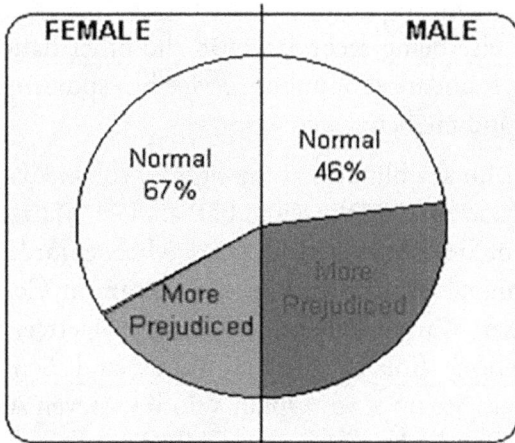

Figure 1: Tendency to be Prejudiced by Sex. Based on data from Allport (1946).

Figure 1 shows the percentage of each gender that tends towards racism, based on a study by Allport and Kramer in 1946. This chart is unlikely to surprise anyone for a number of reasons. First, women are, in general, more sociable and not inclined to be aggressive. Males, on the other hand, tend to seek outlets for aggression, and racism is a convenient one. Males, furthermore, have a higher incidence of idiocy and mental deficiency than do females. That is, females tend to be more normal than males and are less inclined to both mental extremes and behavioral extremes, yet they are known exceptions to this position. Be that as it may, the Republican Party has taken full advantage of this genre of persons' mental deficiencies by inciting the anger and frustration of this group who continue to struggle financially. A group who this Party has no intentions of assisting in their plight, through the passage of legislation to relieve them and all while they spend tens of thousands of dollars receiving lap dances at gentlemen's clubs like "the Voyeur" in West Hollywood with the after party held at the Beverly Hills hotel, charting private jets, renting stretch limousines, wining and dining at the Four Seasons Los Angeles, the Venetian in Las Vegas, holding their winter meeting in Hawaii running up a $43,000.00 tab all while their faithful political support group of the tea baggers are carrying their picket signs by day, and unable to feed their families by night. You are simply like every other Republican, as you profess to be a common man while espousing a doctrine of "Take Care of me first" with everyone else being secondary. On the other hand, Altruism is the underlying foundation of public service by espousing a doctrine of "Others First, and me being secondary.

Racists wear horse's blinders at the sight of the media heroes of our age -- Muhammad Ali, Charlie King, Barbara Lee, Martin Luther King Jr., Al Sharpton, Steve Harvey, T.D. Jakes, Michael Jordan, Debra Lee, Bishop Noel Jones, Derrick Boazman, Don Lemmon, Condoleeza Rice, Michael Baisden, Warren Ballentine, Charles Ogletree, Joe Madison, Andre Eggelletion, Roland Martin, Venus and Serena Williams, Soledad O'Brien, Stuart Scott, Oprah Winfrey, Steven A. Smith, Tiger Woods, Barry Bonds, Henry Aaron, Colin Powell Jr., Janet Jackson, Sidney Poitier, Bill Cosby, Dr. Cornel West, Tavis Smiley, Tom Joyner, Samuel Jackson, Sammy Sosa, Michael Johnson, Frank Ski, Wanda Smith, Andrew Young, Joseph Lowery, Michael Steele, Tony Brown,

Judge Greg Mathis, Armstrong Williams, Bev Smith, Judge Joe Brown, Dr. Boyce Watkins, Jeff Johnson, Clarence Page, Keith Olbermann, Rachel Maddow, Halle Berry, Will Smith, Bill Maher, Larry King, President Barack Obama, the list goes on endlessly. They are deaf to the sound of world records regularly being shattered. They write off eloquent, inspiring speeches that mobilizes the masses as mere rhetoric. They are dumb in their speech when asked to explain such obvious contradictions. Are racists deaf, dumb, and blind, or are they simply of such limited intelligence that they cannot recognize the truth when it is placed in bright lights before them?

That is why media tabloid comedic personalities like Sean Hannity, Glen Beck, Republican racist media strumpet(s) Anne Coulter & Tammy Bruce, Jerome Corsi, Dick Morris, Lou Dobbs, Paul Broun, Michelle Bachman, bigot extraordinaire Rush Limbaugh, R.N.C. chair candidate loser Chip Saltsman and Bill O'Reilly can relentlessly attack President Barack Obama and his administration with racial epithets and diatribes on moot and insignificant issues, and attempt to utilize the "guilt by association" ploy in an effort to impeach their credibility. Thus ignoring we the people, after we have issued a clear "mandate" concerning the direction that we want this country to go in, and who we want to lead us at this time. Because of these miscreants' deeply seeded psychological bigotry and racism towards certain groups and genres of people, and if we are not careful not to listen to their divisive rhetoric, we will find ourselves moving backwards towards more years of the despair, mediocrity, war, poverty, and denial of responsibility that the Republican Party imposed upon us while the aforementioned personalities and Fox News hirelings remain wealthy by earning their salaries from their pimps for a job well done.

Let us consider some examples of what passes for intelligence in the sub-society of what is truly an oxymoron, Aryan supremacy. Even the word "Aryan" is itself a mockery of the truth. The Aryan race doesn't exist, was merely a Nazi ideology, and has never existed. It is a myth invented by the Nazis to promote politically expedient propaganda. Hitler himself admitted that he knew there never were any Aryans, and that the notion merely served Nazi purposes, no more. All Aryan supremacists stand naked in the light of truth, but are unable to comprehend the fact that they have no clothes. Is it due to mental deficiency, or are they aware of this false myth? It is hard to say for sure, but their limited intelligence is certainly a factor in their confusion.

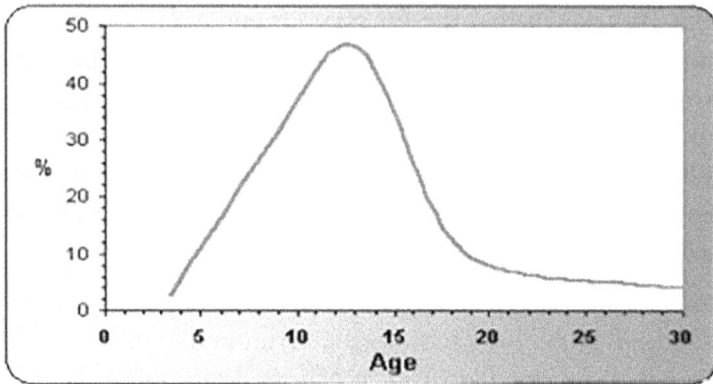

Figure 4: Age at First Onset of Prejudice. Average of anti-semitic and anti-black attitudes (Allport 1946).

Figure 4 illustrates the fact that prejudice is acquired at a young age. The mean age for the onset of prejudice is about 12. This is a most impressionable age and is the appropriate time to educate the young and immunize them against hatred for life. They should be told everything science knows about race and everything history tells us about racism. (Allport, 1946)

In America's war against terrorism, we should not forget about the domestic terrorist cells that have sprouted up in our own backyard. Nazis, skinheads, succession seeking governors, and other bigots are anti-American by their very nature. If America is a nation of all races, religions, and cultures, then the Enemies of any of those races, religions, and cultures are enemies of America. (Allport, 1946) The attempts on the part of a secret society, Nazi skinheads, media cartoonists, media personalities, political candidates, private citizens, and the new KKK, the tea baggers, to intimidate or encourage acts of violence against innocent people because of their race or creed is terrorism by definition. Once al Qaeda has been shut down, it would be prudent to focus America's attention on cleaning up all the nests of racist extremists that are festering inside our own borders. They are all just terrorists who have committed, and are waiting to commit an act against good natured, hardworking public servants and Americans such as ourselves that borderline on treason since we are at war.

"We the People" disagree that violence is a proper response to what is essentially a mental disease. We believe that education is the key to erasing racism; we believe that love can combat hate; we believe that unity as one nation can transcend division, and that this could be accomplished within the space of a single generation if we simply show our neighbors and our children the light of truth, and dispel the darkness of ignorance. We also believe that hateful and divisive techniques can be limited with the passage of the proper legislation that will neutralize this doctrine! A repeal of the "Fairness doctrine" is a positive step towards ending this racist, cowardly one-sided conversation by the media that oppresses dissent and promotes the potential for racially motivated criminality, while it ignores every Americans right in this country to be free of hate, to love without reservation, to understand the issues, to make an intelligent decision, and to support every doctrine that promotes a unified front.

CHAPTER THREE

WE THE PEOPLE

W hite people, they are here; Black people, they are here; Bigots, they are here; The greedy and the selfish, they are here; Racists, they are here; Media Icons, they are here; The Bitter, here they are; Agape love, it is here; People who hate God, here they are; People who love the Lord, right here; People who do not even know God and only belong to Christian Political organizations, over here; Teachers, over here; Civil Rights activists, they are here; Drunks, over here; Junkies, here they are; Hillbillies, right here; the Corporation Executives, here they are; Mothers, yes; Fathers, of course; People who abuse their power, you bet; Divisive forces in the media, right here; Liars, they just left the White House; Grass Roots community demonstrators/organizers, look around you, they are in the trenches and will soon be in the White House; Capitalists who care about the poor and capitalists who feel like the poor should help themselves, they are here; Businessmen who mismanage money and collapse countries, check the news, they are here; Engineers, here they are; Bank Executives, they are here; Criminologists, here we are; Families in jeopardy of foreclosure, although forgotten about, they are here; female Vice-Presidential candidates, we have been wanting to talk to you but can't find you because you quit on the people, but I know that you are here; Jim Crow's children who create mean-spirited laws, they live here; Racist prosecutors who enforce these laws, they are in our court rooms; Those who wear their expensive boardroom suits, they are here; Those who wear their pants sagging, yes they are here; Those saying, "Yes we can," over here; and Others who call your "audacity to hope" a fallacy, and declare, "No you will not," they are here as well.

Yes, we are ALL HERE in America. ALL races, ALL genders, ALL attitudes, ALL genetic makeups, from every walk of life, and from ALL NATIONS, for We Are the People. A country, whose humble beginnings began and was founded upon the principles of dissent. When during America's first 150 years, most of the settlers came from Great Britain. Along America's Atlantic coast, these colonists built settlements that became what is commonly called the "Original Thirteen Colonies."

A country of British settlers, who lived under the rule of the King of England; Citizens, who worked hard to build homes, farms and towns, even though they did not own these places. Settlers who worked so hard, that they wanted to be involved in making decisions about their lives and property.

And yes, the British, much like our government, knew that the colonists/our citizens wanted their independence. But the British, like our government, instead, tried to take more control of the colonists/our citizens. By the mid-1770s, King George III and the British government taxed everyday goods, such as tea. The deal breaker occurred when the first direct tax was imposed upon the colonists in the form of the Stamp Act of 1765. This required stamps to be purchased or included on many different items and documents such as playing cards, legal papers, newspapers, and more. The money from it was to be used for military defense, sound <u>familiar</u>? In response to this, the Stamp Act, Congress met in New York City. <u>Twenty seven</u> delegates from nine colonies met and wrote a statement of rights and grievances against Great Britain thus their written dissent was the beginning of the creation of what will be referred to as the Declaration of Independence which was a "Dear John" letter that was written to King George III effectively ending their relationship with Britain. America at its inception, formed because the people worked together to free themselves from an oppressive and intrusive government that took advantage of its citizens.

We now have come full circle as all of these people past and present, despite their differences, despite their devilish characteristics, their love, their hate, their attitudes of supremacy, their lies, their trickery, their condescending attitudes, their accomplishments, their failures, their fears, and despite their divisive deeds, share what I call the common denominator of their humanity. We are ALL Americans FIRST. The beauty of this two hundred year experiment in democracy is that in spite of our differences, we have always found a way to co-exist. We the people are like a family who at times appear to be dysfunctional, but must never forget that we share more in common than we have differences. We all want our children to have affordable educations, we all want to be able to work for competitive wages so that we can feed our families, we all want to feel safe within the boundaries of our country, we all want representatives and leaders who tell the truth, display integrity and character to run our country and protect our interests, we all want our government to treat us like they treat the rich, we all want affordable healthcare, we all want educational loans without loan shark rates to repay, we all want to live in houses without the threat of foreclosure, we all want our kids/adults to be safe without being murdered by Police Officers, we all want our kids to attend schools that will not label them as unable to be educated due to disciplinary or mental health reasons, we never want innocent citizens to be incarcerated or executed in our United States court system, and we want our fellow man to embrace our racial, ethnic, and intellectual differences without rejecting or undermining us as we are ALL AMERICANS FIRST and we all have a right to be here. The White has a right to be here, the Black has a right to be here, the Asian has a right to be here, the Mexican has a right to be here, the Latino has a right to be here, the Indian has a right to be here, the Jew has a right to be here, the Greek has a right to be here, the Buddhist has a right to be here, the Christian has a right to be here, the Muslim has a right to be here, the Atheist has a right to here, the Klansman has a right to be here, the Athlete has a right to be here, the Pimp has a right to be here, the Immigrant has a right to be here, the Prostitute has a right to be here, the Homosexual has a right to be here, the fiery Pastor has a right to be here, the hated has a right to be here, the beloved has a right to be here, the Lesbian has a right to be here, the Alcoholic has a right to be here, the Addict has a right to be here, the bishop has a right to be here, the President has a right to be here, the Learned has a right to be here, the Unlearned has the right to be here, the lying Media personality has a right to be here, and yes the Truth-fighters in the media have a right to be here. They have a right to be here because God has endowed us and has given to all of us the inalienable right to life, liberty, and the pursuit of happiness. The problem with the country lies in our inability to grasp the Godly concepts of unselfishness, working as One Color-blind Nation, exercising agape love, caring for our fellowman, caring for the poor, loving justice, exercising patience, temperance, honesty, integrity, with the abandonment of the satanic concepts of selfishness, superiority complexes, prejudice, ulterior motives, capitalist mindsets, lying, tearing down one's character, greed, hatred, bitterness, racism, holding grudges, perpetual double-standards, the murdering of the innocent, disrespect for God's clergy, not accepting responsibility for our actions, and our hiding of the truth. For here lies our ability to be the Great Nation that God intended for us to be. However there is much work to do as a nation, and We The People have the challenge of becoming educated to the issues, forming one unit, and determining what legislator(s) and leader(s) are actually protecting our interests and those who are taking advantage of their office and abusing their power. After all, our leaders have been entrusted with the passage of legislation and the making of decisions that determine our futures and the futures of our families, and it is through our trust in designating them as the stewards of our lives that they have been able to live in the lap of luxury, send their children to the finest of schools, have the best healthcare for their families, and position themselves and their families for future financial success after their careers in Washington D.C. have passed. It is disingenuous of them to insult the intelligence of their constituencies by revealing to us in word and legislation that they are protecting our best interests when they are not. That is why we as a people and nation must become wiser, and conduct our own research. What legislation affects me and my community? How did my representative vote on that issue? What did he/she promise me during his/her campaign? What decision did he/she make when it was time to vote?

Once we gather this information and have read it for content, we must then create a voting bloc that will fire those leaders who care nothing about us, and hire those leaders who we know from our research is protecting our best interests and positioning us for success. Unfortunately, the very possibility of our success in becoming "one nation under God" continues to be threatened by an established and covert society of greed, hate, and hypocrisy that continues to render the middle and working class segments of our society helpless as an entity, and whose sole purpose is to exploit and undermine this segment of the electorate for a profit.

A BLUEPRINT OF FAILURE FOR OUR NATION TO OBSERVE

This fact has rung no truer than with the Georgia re-election bid of Senator Saxby Chambliss.

He defeated Candidate Jim Martin by mobilizing the "smear and fear" political machine of the Right who has enjoyed complete political power in the State of Georgia. Therefore the same party of power must accept responsibility for the current failures of Georgia. Sadly enough, the good people of Georgia believed the ads that sought to tear down the character of Mr. Martin by running smear and fear ads on him on a daily basis. I am presenting this information to the nation as a "tool of learning" that must be understood if we are to ever move beyond our petty differences.

1.) Fear and Smear tactics have a purpose:

When you witness fear and smear antics of any political organization and candidate, ask yourself the question, why are the issues not being discussed? In this case, the Saxby campaign, like in the Presidential election, chose not to discuss the issues because the people who voted for him were not important to him. In the midst of a 10.4% unemployment rate, record foreclosures, high lay-offs, schools and universities being closed, professors being laid off, extreme poverty, overcrowded prisons, no business being brought to the state, gas prices that are going up again, high health care prices, uninsured children and families with no healthcare coverage, double-standards for the rich and the working class, it is no wonder the issues were never discussed. These tactics simply were utilized to divert the people's attention away from the issues that affect them on a daily basis, and by the time the smoke cleared, he had won another term. I hope that Georgians realized what they just did, or they will be duped again in the midterm elections.

2.) Georgia has two legal systems and separate standards of justice for many offenders:

Let us consider the dichotomy of the cases of Michael Vick (a black male athlete) and Stewart Parnell (a white male CEO) of the South Georgia Peanut Company respectively. As I argued in the section entitled "America's unreported illness," Virginia and Georgia were instrumental in passing laws that were inherently racist towards minorities and the poor, but lenient towards members of this countries' "power base," even to date! Before I discuss in detail the criminal justice double standards of these cases, I would argue that these two cases represent two separate societies in Georgia and lay the backdrop of the attitude of our American system as it relates to meting out justice.

The similarities of these cases: They involve the State of Georgia representing the locations of each person's place of employment, Mr. Vick, at the time with the Atlanta Falcons, and Mr. Parnell, as the head and chief decision-maker of the South Georgia Peanut Company, with Virginia being the places of potential court cases. Lynchburg, Virginia represents the location of the headquarters of the Peanut Corporation of America, with the South Georgia Peanut Company being one the corporations' plants and distributors. Virginia also represents the location for Mr. Vick's bankruptcy hearings. Hearings where he does not have the luxury of "waiving his appearance," because the "confederacy-minded" Judge wants to look at Michael to see if "he is believable!" What is the believability of nine people murdered?

The charges: Michael Vick being convicted of conspiring and funding the dog fighting venture of Bad Newz Kennels. He also was said to have been responsible for the deaths of 6-8 dogs as well. Consequently and due to "good ole boy" U.S. District Judge Henry E. Hudson in Virginia, not believing that "Michael was remorseful enough" and despite the early surrender, the loss of millions, the public humiliation, the racist attacks by PETA, unyielding attacks from the Atlanta and national media, the suspension from the NFL, a public apology and participation in an animal sensitivity training course, Vick was denied an "acceptance of responsibility" credit that would have reduced his sentence. Of course, federal prosecutors opposed awarding Vick the credit. Therefore, he was given the maximum sentence range of 23 months in federal prison.

Prosecutorial double-standards: Interesting enough, this same US Attorney's office and prosecutor Michael Gill who adamantly stated "He did more than fund it," referring to the "Bad Newz Kennels" dog fighting operation. "He was in this thing up to his neck with the other defendants." The judge agreed.

"You were instrumental in promoting, funding and facilitating this cruel and inhumane sporting activity," he said. However, this same attorney's office and "law-abiding" bench is conspicuously silent as it relates to Stewart Parnell and the Peanut Corporation of America's indictable "willful and wanton conduct" concerning a fatal nationwide salmonella outbreak that has yet to be moved upon. He even had the audacity to "refuse to testify" before Congress, without any repercussions! Notwithstanding these diligent officers of the court ignoring the "murders of nine people;" if by some act of God Parnell was charged, these would be the facts surrounding the case.

On or about January, 2009 a salmonella outbreak occurred in 43 states and has been blamed for at least nine deaths and 575 illnesses. More than 1,550 products have been recalled. According to the FDA, the outbreak was traced back to the South Georgia Peanut Corporation that is owned by Stewart Parnell. Specifically, investigations revealed that as far back as 2007, salmonella-laced products were shipped by a Georgia Peanut company that knew the peanuts probably were tainted and sometimes after tests confirmed that contamination, inspection records show. Some of the problems the FDA discovered at the plant in 2001 are similar to those found in 2007, when federal inspectors returned to the plant after nearly eight years. The 2001 inspection found dead insects near peanuts and holes in the plant big enough for rodents to enter. Those inspectors also discovered that workers at the plant used an insecticide fogger in food-processing areas and didn't wash the exposed equipment. They also found dirty duct tape wrapped on broken equipment.

Federal law forbids producing or shipping foods under conditions that could make it harmful to consumers' health. Parnell promised that he would correct the problems because he "wanted to assure us that he wanted his firm to be in compliance," FDA inspectors wrote. Parnell told inspectors that the insecticide's "labeling had been changed and they had not been aware of the change," according to the FDA report.

But further investigations would suggest that Parnell did not fix the problems, but lied instead. Because on February 11, 2009 at a U.S. Congressional oversight and investigation subcommittee hearing where Peanut Corp. of America President Stewart Parnell was forced to appear, he invoked the Fifth Amendment and refused to testify. These revelations depict a company focused on profits rather than food safety.

In addition, e-mails between Parnell and Sammy Lightsey, manager of the company's Blakely plant, were released as part of a congressional hearing that started at 10 a.m. Wednesday.

- In one e-mail, Lightsey wrote Parnell discussing positive salmonella tests on its products, but Parnell gave instructions to nonetheless "turn them loose" after getting a negative test result from another testing company.

- In another e-mail, Parnell expressed his concerns over the losing of money due to delays in shipment and costs of testing.

- Parnell in another company-wide e-mail told employees there was no salmonella in its plants, instead accusing the news media of "looking for a news story where there currently isn't one."

On Jan. 19, Parnell sent an e-mail to the U.S. Food and Drug Administration, pleading with the agency to let it stay in business.

He wrote that company executives "desperately at least need to turn the raw peanuts on our floor into money."

Other revelations underpinning the Salmonella outbreak:

- The Georgia Department of Agriculture conducted two inspections of the company's Blakely, Ga. plant in 2008, but did not test for salmonella on its own on either occasion despite an internal agency goal to conduct such tests once a year.

- The company's largest customers, including Kellogg, engaged contractors to conduct audits, but they did not conduct their own salmonella tests.

- The FDA did not test for salmonella at the plant, despite the 2007 salmonella outbreak traced to the Con-Agra plant about 70 miles from Peanut Corp. of America's Blakely plant.

Food and Drug Administration officials earlier had said Peanut Corp. of America waited for a second test to clear peanut butter and peanuts that initially were positive for salmonella. But the agency amended its report Friday, saying that the Blakely, Ga., plant actually shipped some products before receiving the second test and sold others after confirming salmonella.

In 2007, the company shipped chopped peanuts on July 18 and 24 after salmonella was confirmed by private lab tests, the FDA report said. Peanut Corp. sold products "on or after the positive salmonella results were obtained."

In other cases, the company did not wait for a second round of salmonella tests.

Since the US Attorney's office and I am aware of the nature of human beings in not accepting responsibility for their actions, I would argue that at best, there should be indictments passed down for Involuntary Manslaughter. For those who do not agree, consider the legal definition, it is the act of unlawfully killing another human being unintentionally.

Most unintentional killings are not murder but involuntary manslaughter. The absence of the element of intent is the key distinguishing factor between voluntary and involuntary manslaughter. In most states, involuntary manslaughter results from an improper use of reasonable care or skill while performing a legal act, or while committing an act that is unlawful but not felonious.

Many states do not define involuntary manslaughter, or define it vaguely in common-law terms. Some jurisdictions describe the amount of Negligence necessary to constitute manslaughter with terms such as criminal negligence, gross negligence, and culpable negligence. The only certainty that can be attached to these terms is that they require more than the ordinary negligence standard in a civil case. With this approach, the state does not have to prove that the defendant was aware of the risk.

Other jurisdictions apply more subjective tests, such as "reckless" or "wanton," to describe the amount of negligence needed to constitute involuntary manslaughter. In this approach the defendant must have personally appreciated a risk and then chosen to take it anyway.

For all intents and purposes, that is exactly what South Georgia Peanut Company and Stewart Parnell did and I quote again, "turn them loose."

So that we are clear in this analysis, the federal government did nothing to prosecute Stewart Parnell and the corporation for causing the deaths of at least nine human beings, yet Michael Vick is, by all practical purposes bankrupt, and remains in prison for killing dogs. In addition, there remains the matter of the filing of bankruptcy by both parties in the State of Virginia. According to my investigations, the Vick case's bankruptcy filing was due to his inability to pay his accumulated debts due in part to his incarceration and his inability to earn a living. To exacerbate his financial situation, many debtors have come forward alleging that he breached contractual agreements with their companies and were awarded millions of dollars in damages. However, despite the Court's foreknowledge of the negligence of the Virginia based Peanut Corporation of America, the filing by attorney Andrew S. Goldstein who lists 14 lawsuits against the company related to the outbreak, the 475 businesses with claims against the company, and the fact that the Hartford Casualty Insurance Company, who insures the corporation, sued to protect themselves from backing the company financially, they allowed the Lynchburg-based Peanut Corporation to file for Chapter 7 bankruptcy as the fallout from the outbreak grew. This Judicial decision was allowed by the Virginia Federal Courts in spite of the fact that the company's plant in Blakely, Ga., was identified as the sole source of the salmonella outbreak that sickened more than 550 people, nine of whom died. Can someone tell me, where is the outrage over the lack of prosecution, the court-imposed liability, or even the media's demand for justice over the loss of lives at the hand of this Corporation? But you probably do not know about this case or many of the decisions that your Georgian leaders have made over the past several years and you have **Bill Number:** HB218, **Sponsor:** Georgia Rep. Ron Stephens in **Legislative Session:** 2006 to thank for it. Rep. Ron Stephens, of the ironically-named Garden City, has offered this measure that would make meetings and records of any public agency engaged in economic development activities exempt from open meetings and open records laws. An amendment added by the House Economic Development Committee includes such agencies as local industrial development authorities to those which will be shrouded in secrecy, despite the almost criminal record of some of these appointed bodies in Georgia at trying to recruit obnoxious operations such as landfills, sewage sludge disposal plants, medical waste incinerators, power plants and the like to poor rural counties. Citizens' efforts, as well as those of government officials and members of the press, should be at improving access to government-held information, not limiting it. Each closure of a public meeting or loss of availability of public records is an erosion of our ability to be a knowledgeable participant in our governance.

Each year, dozens of bills are introduced in the Georgia Legislature that tries to do just that.

Too often, those bills sail easily through legislative committees. One current bill before the General Assembly, HB218, is doing just that. Because of intense competition among communities for economic development, legislation is being considered to close out any public knowledge of government negotiations with companies until after crucial decisions are made. That is why Georgia has been decimated with no explanations from our current leaders as to how we arrived at this bad place. How we arrived at economic disparity, how we are losing all of our teachers, how we experiencing a constitution crisis in our court systems, how employees are losing their jobs and are forced to take furloughs with no signs of recovery in sight! And it was all done by the republicans in the secrecy and sanctity of their legislative chambers. You have a Governor in Sonny Perdue, who as most republican leaders do in times of crisis; accept no responsibility for the dilemmas in Georgia or remain conspicuously absent so they cannot answer any questions or be held accountable. Yet, he wishes to "use the legal system as a weapon" as he attempts to recall our Attorney General (Baker) for refusing to protect the healthcare corporations, by exercising fiscal responsibility, or waste the <u>tax payers</u>' money in a fight with our President over a healthcare law that will provide access to a multi-billion dollar industry for the middle class and the poor. Two different legal systems Georgia, what do you think?

Then to add insult to injury, they want to keep their seats and serve the people of Georgia! God Bless America!

Truly, we are living in two separate and unequal systems of justice in Georgia generally, but in this country specifically. This is but a few examples of the utter disregard for the law on a federal and local level, and as I think of all of the Genarlow Wilsons, the Troy Davises, the Matthew Shepards, the Plexico Burrises, who are way laided and encumbered in our court systems and jails, it can be argued that it is attributed to the fact that politicians with ulterior motives are allowed to write crime policy and not criminologists. After all, we trust medical problems with doctors and other medical practitioners, we trust engineering problems with engineers, we trust legal problems with lawyers, we trust spiritual problems with clergy, yet we fail to trust crime problems with degreed criminologists and other criminal justice practitioners, which is disrespectful to our discipline. This is important because like our other professional counterparts, we have received specialized training that is unique to the subject matter and concerns that we as Americans face on a daily basis. That is why it is my hope that the Obama administration will be mindful of these realities when it is time to write corrective crime policy that may prevent prisoner abuse that may alleviate police brutality, that may decrease our crime problem as the presence of more police officers on the street will only serve to incapacitate criminals. If they are released back into an environment that is conducive to continuous criminality, then they will recidivate. Another issue in our system is with gun control or the lack thereof; many people argue that increased gun control is not the problem and that guns do not kill people, people kill people. Tell that to the widows of our fallen police officers; tell that to the families of the Columbine victims, and tell that to the grandmothers and mothers who outlived their murdered children. Although this is a common gun lobbyist's argument and although it is cliché, it rings with a modicum of truth. However, my argument is with the obvious loopholes that are currently in the legal codes of our nation concerning gun purchases, that I believe are negligent and without merit, and are not discontinued due to what I commonly refer to as the covert unwritten "two for one" rule in our system. Imagine if you will a case of "John Q Citizen" from New York who purchased a gun through the normal channels. He submitted to the three-day check, and subsequently passed the background check and made his purchase in Atlanta, Georgia. He then travels to the New York inner city and meets up with a little black gang member or terrorist whom he sells the gun to! I know what you are thinking, but no, the seller does not have to conduct a "background check" on any potential purchaser of a gun in a private sell! Notwithstanding the "moral responsibility" that Mr. Citizen has, he is under no obligation to stop his purchase, even if he assumes that the gang member is going to use the weapon to terrorize and murder another black teen. However, after the murder occurs, we now have the police intervene and arrest the perpetrator. The perpetrator subsequently is sentenced to "25 to Life" imprisonment in the Department of Corrections. Now you have one of our black kids dead, and the other black kid is in prison for life. Therefore, the system has successfully effectuated a "two for one," as one child is dead and the other one will never be free. Is there an insidious desire for this type of policy that watches our black teens die and have their freedom taken away simultaneously, the reason why we never change our gun laws? To the high priced lobbyists, why can we not even close our loopholes? This is but another example of a politician with ulterior motives writing crime policy. This practice must stop or we will lose a generation of our children.

3) We are all in the same boat and have been disregarded from day one:

What is so disheartening is the fact that Georgians foolishly believe that their interests can only be served by a Conservative ideology, when what they fail to realize is that this mentality and ideology is the foundational cause of their poverty, incarceration, unemployment, and inability to provide for their families. Specifically, what Georgians need to realize is that the Republican Party is reserved for people who make $250,000.00 or more per year. Their interest is to continue to make their voters feel as if they matter, when all they desire from them is their vote so that they can continue on their quest for "State Imperialism."

Since I believe in letting the facts speak for themselves, tell me, over the past six years, how have you or your family benefitted from a Conservative Georgia? Has your income increased or decreased? Every one of your Republican representatives are rich, can you still pay your bills? Do you still have your home? You are being furloughed, why does everyone have to take a furlough but our republican representatives? Do you still have health insurance? Are you still employed? When the Governor turns down stimulus money that could help you, what will you do to survive? I can assure you that the upper level wage earners in this state are not hurting financially, yet you struggle. If I never get an opportunity to speak with you again remember this, that struggle and poverty has no color or political affiliation. To become a progressive state once again, all of our residents need to realize that United We Stand, and divided We Fall. It has never been about color, like America, it has always been about "socioeconomic status" and adhering to the special interests of the class and money system of the State of Georgia, which is making it look like the exclusive country in which we live. When the Governor and the Republican controlled legislature took office several years ago, they passed legislation that gave them the ability to meet secretly and not let the residents of this State know about the "secret deals" that they make behind closed doors. So now, we are bearing witness to the carnage of their selfish decisions. A cut in the Education budget, that forced teachers to be laid off with plans to eliminate the community college system in Georgia. Important to note is that the intrinsic value of State community colleges became prominent over the past few months when Martha Kanter, chancellor of the Foothill De Anza Community College District, was nominated by the Obama administration to the government's top postsecondary-education position. Now this Party wants to add insult to injury, and elect for Governor, a woman in Karen Handel who does not even have a college degree, yet this same Republican Party who supports her candidacy without the requirement of a higher education are setting the tone for the State to phase out Adjunct Professors with a plethora of experience in their respective fields from the Georgian University system classrooms without possessing a Doctorate degree! What hypocrisy and anti-progressive thinking, as seemingly, Georgia's Republican legislators seem to be the only lawmakers in America who are committed to State Party illiteracy as they choose a candidate who barely has the credentials and education of a Jethro Bodine! I make this statement humbly as I argue that if any State Government is facing historical budget shortfalls, one of the manners in which one could save money is by utilizing the services of Adjunct Professors! Why? Because Adjunct Professors teach on a part-time basis for menial compensation which eliminates the fiscal drain of high salaries paid during a recession, health, dental, and vision insurance requirements. Utilizing their services for evening and weekend classes will lend the academic freedom to the full-time tenure track Assistant Professors to perform their research and writing which should be part of their job description. This impractical process is unprecedented and is prehistoric in many other States, but the Republicans are "in charge of the State" and dictate the tenor of the imposed policy in most areas and as they sit on their golden perches, passing down judgments and decrees, they could care less who their draconian policies impact.

In addition, there are cuts to counties which will make us less safe, as many counties have been forced to lay off firefighters and police officers; cuts to the justice system, so many prosecutors and public defenders have either lost their jobs or are being furloughed every month, therefore the rights of the accused have been unconstitutionally compromised; due to secret legislation, Georgia has become number 40th nationwide in unemployment yet the wealthy representatives of the Republican party do not want any of you to receive unemployment benefits from our President, that will enable you to feed your families! In addition, the Republican lawmakers have set their sights on the destruction of Fulton County, Georgia as they have passed legislation and pushed for the succession of counties from Fulton to set up their own cities and municipalities. This is significant because if they successfully succeed in the succession of a few more counties, they will inevitably ensure the unemployment of thousands of employees that comprise of at least 85% minorities. This will no doubt move Georgia's unemployment percentage to perhaps number one in our nation. However, it does not have to be this way, and there was a time when it was not that way. What opportunities will you and your children have after the Georgia Republican lawmakers are finished? Will we continue to allow mediocrity to lead us? Will we ever demand accountability from our state Government? Will this State ever look beyond the "God given characteristic" of color, and choose leaders with the "character and integrity" to help "all Georgians succeed," or will we perish as fools?

Will Georgia move beyond its "generational curse of racism and classism" or will the State destroy itself? Important to note, is that if Georgians, like Americans ever decide to move beyond their differences with one another, and decided to work together in electing officials with integrity and character, Governor Sonny Perdue and the Republicans are prepared for you! For at the writing of this section on 4/30/09, he appeared before the U.S. Supreme Court to argue for the repeal of a key section in the Voting Rights Act (Section 5) that has prevented discrimination and racism at the election polls and precincts. In other words, Governor Perdue who was conspicuously absent during Georgia's gas crisis due to being "on vacation," and who indicated to the State's citizens that there was nothing that he could do as the "head of our State" to lower gas prices! Teachers are getting laid-off, Sonny where are you? Furloughs for the State of Georgia, Sonny where are you? Our State Constitution is in a crisis state due to lack of legal representation for the poor, and you've got it Georgia. Again I ask, Sonny where are you? However, he can be "present and accounted for," and travel cross-country to the U.S. Supreme Court, when it is time to ratify legislation on Section 5 that will disenfranchise minorities, enlightened whites, Asians, Latinos, and the poor alike. His reasoning, well you know there is no discrimination in the State of Georgia, since America elected a black for President, suddenly everything in Georgia is fair again! Therefore, I tell you what. When Sonny returns from Fantasy Island and finishes filing his lawsuit to prevent the poor and working class from receiving quality healthcare, perhaps he can be "man enough" to hold a "State of the State" address and tell Georgians what his real motives are. To maintain a G.O.P. stranglehold on the State where "clandestine" Republican decision making has brought this State to the precipice of economic destruction. Because it was not enough that Obama was defeated in Georgia, but he wants to ensure that no other blacks or progressive minded individuals get any bright ideas about running for political office, and have a "fair and democratic" opportunity to win another office in the State of Georgia. His presence before the U.S. Supreme Court is a gleaming example that discrimination still exists as there is an attempt by our governor to "suppress progressive Georgians and minorities' right to vote," through the drawing of voting districts that will dilute the strength of our votes, through a ninth hour change in voting times and locations to disenfranchise voters and escape legal challenges, and to blatantly disregard the right to vote for the Georgia elderly, Hispanic, African Americans, Asians, Latinos, and Whites who historically vote democrat and independent. The Secretary of the State Karen Handel, Perdue's choice for Governor, has already used the Court to disenfranchise voters in the State with one of the most restrictive "voter ID" laws in the nation, but apparently that is "not enough," they want to silence the dissent of any "non-Republican voter" which undermines the spirit of the law in the U.S. Constitution which affords to every citizen the "right to vote." He is a shining example of a member of the "Christian Right" who claim to "know God" but does the works of the devil. Maybe he can tell us why this issue is of so much importance to him when he took an oath to be the Governor for "All Georgians?" The next couple of years will tell whether this state will fall or rise again, for the head of the State has clearly made his position known.

COUNTRY FIRST?

As I watched the Republican National convention in Minneapolis, Minnesota, and now a repeat performance at the Obama hate-fest in Tampa, Florida, I could not avoid seeing this banner draped behind the stage of all white, older, rich, men that provided the platform for which they would launch their campaign and endorse their choice for President of the United States of America; it read, "Country First." So I accepted this premise, if only for a moment as I understood that either it would be proven or disproven by their actions during this election cycle. Not that it has not already been proven by the collapse of the economy, the bail out of Wall Street financiers absent any regulatory oversight, a war that contributed to America's demise, and a culture of criminality, greed and free-wheeling lobbying that would seek to maintain the status quo. The problem with the Bush administration, his G.O.P. cabinet, and even the Republican contrfamily-ownedment of Georgia is that they are operating the people's government like a family-owned business. The first rule of thumb for any Federal or state government or municipality is the reality and adherence to the principles of a government "Of the people, for the people, and by the people." Yes, they were hired (voted for) by the people to work in "The People's Government." To that end, there should never be an attitude by any hired leader that conveys a message that I am not going to cooperate with those people across the aisle, instead I will filibuster any legislation that I do not agree with, even if it will help the people that trusted me enough to vote for me. Because while you continue to filibuster, people are being foreclosed on and removed from their homes; while you continue to filibuster, prisoners continue to be tortured and murdered with no sanctions; while you continue to filibuster, our privacy has been compromised and our phones are being tapped; while you continue to filibuster, millions of Americans are losing their jobs and many businesses are closing; while you continue to filibuster, Katrina remains the symbol of shame and governmental neglect in our rich Country; and while you continue to filibuster, this Country has entered into a recession and is teetering on a depression.

These counterproductive strategies of the Republican Party cannot be allowed to continue, while this Nation is fighting for its very existence and identity. On the contrary, Americans will have the rare opportunity in the coming months to determine which one of their party's representatives will protect their interests as we strive to become a Perfected Union of One Nation. While you are making your decision, I would like for you to look at your representative, observe their actions towards our President as it relates to their support of the "People's agenda," consider the leaders who are leading the insurrection and attacks against our President and consider their state's unemployment rates as President Obama entered office which is as follows:

STATE	NATIONAL RANK	UNEMPLOYMENT PERCENTAGE
Georgia	36th	10.4%
Mississippi	37th	10.9%
Tennessee	37th	10.7%
Ohio	40th	10.8%
Alabama	42nd	11.1%
South Carolina	48th	12.6%

STATE	NATIONAL RANK	UNEMPLOYMENT PERCENTAGE
Georgia	36th	9.2%
Mississippi	37th	9.1%
Tennessee	37th	8.5%
Ohio	40th	7.2%
Alabama	42nd	8.5%
South Carolina	48th	9.6%

****After at least 36 months under President Obama's leadership.

If you would observe, many of the States with the highest unemployment rates either has Republican Senators, and Governors, or both, who voted "no" for President Obama's budget, stimulus package, healthcare law, and refused to accept unemployment compensation for their States. With the exception of Republican turned Independent Governor Charlie Crist in Florida who was excommunicated from his party (G.O.P.) for choosing to accept the money from the Obama administration, display true courage, conviction, and leadership, by addressing the economic suffering of the Florida people. Consequently, it saddens me to say that we are not off to a good start as we are still operating as two societies with no interest in placing the citizens of our country first. Just look at the carnage of each State's budgets with their leaders accepting "no responsibility" and taking no action to resolve these crisis situations that is ruining their citizens collectively.

TWO SEPARATE SOCIETIES AGAIN

The passage of bail-outs for certain typologies of corporations has begun to reveal our Senate leaders priorities and determination in maintaining the status quo of creating "two separate societies" again. In my analysis of these bail-outs, I can determine that there are two separate and unequal types of corporations that they are assisting! Corporation One is our Capitalist corporations that consists of rich, greedy capitalists (banks financial institutions, and Wall Street) who exploit their customers with arbitrary ever changing high interest rate credit cards, lines of credit, student loans and mortgages with high interest imposed upon them even when they pay on time. In this business model, these same institutions have decided to stop lending money, and to stop extending lines of credit that has virtually frozen our economy, business, and mortgage industry. Yet they need a $70 billion dollar bail-out without any oversight, regulations, or governmental requirements? Corporation Two is our Working/Middle class corporations that consist of the automobile industry that employs millions of people from our Senate leader's constituencies who depend upon these corporations to feed their families, to contribute to the economy, and to have shelter and clothing.

Now corporation one has been given the first installment of the $70 billion dollars at 0% interest without any restrictions or oversight and they have proceeded to behave as follows:

1. AIG spent $440,000.00 of our taxpayers' money on a spa get-away. I guess their arms were sore lifting all of those money bags.

2. The banks remain inflexible and stoic while they do not extend any lines of credit to businesses or consumers. So in essence, they are contributing to the demise of the economy. One bank official from Bank of America stated after they arbitrarily canceled the line of credit of the Republic Windows and Doors plants that "The bank is not responsible for Republican's financial obligation to its employees."

3. A friend of mine stated that this same Bank of America arbitrarily raised her interest rate in spite of the fact that she never was late on a payment. She is contemplating drawing money from her 401K just to settle her debt.

4. Another man in Georgia sold one of his cars to pay his debt to Bank of America after they raised his interest rate and imposed arbitrary penalties upon him after he paid his bill on-line and was 30 minutes late. He had a ten year relationship with them, but again our leaders and representatives do not provide oversight over this industry!

5. The Cash room of the Federal Reserve still had their lavish Christmas party no doubt with the taxpayer's money.

6. Citigroup using the proceeds from the bail-out to purchase a $50 million luxury jet. I guess the bank executives needed to fleece the taxpayers in style.

7. Students continue to be charged over 21% interest on their student loans from Sallie Mae while they receive billions of dollars in financial subsidies from the Bush White house annually. They are still charging me for a student loan without allowing me to verify my debt.

Now corporation two is undergoing unmerciful scrutiny at the hands of these same Senate leaders and representatives of the people, as they fight to keep the few American companies that we have remaining from closing its doors and placing an estimated over 3 million plus families in the unemployment line. Yet they are receiving resistance from some of our Senators who have been less than forthcoming concerning the steps that they took over the past eight years to ensure that companies like General Motors did not become viable! Specifically, and important to note is the fact that as I was viewing a March 29, 2006 60 minutes documentary on Brazil, who was experiencing a similar energy crisis based upon their dependence on foreign oil. However, Eduardo Cavallo and the energy officials addressed this problem by investing in an alternative source of fuel that was created from Sugar cane. The fuel was "sugar ethanol" and it now accounts for one fourth of the energy source of Brazil! However, what is more telling is the fact that the cars that they are driving to date are "flex vehicles," that are built by the Ford and General Motors car companies! These are the same companies that the Government is accusing of not being viable companies, so they want to bankrupt them instead of investing in them. Think about this statement by the Brazil government, when they were asked why the American government had not commissioned these American car companies to create a similar type of vehicle in their own country. I mean cars like the Ford Flex automobile is in the American market, but it has a gasoline engine in most cases, and not a flex engine that would enable it to operate on alternative fuel sources. It was said, "Because many American Senators had voted down, filibustered, or destroyed any legislation that would cut into the oil companies' profits and help the American people!" These Senators are Republican representatives Mitch McConnell (KY), Jon Kyl (AZ), Richard Shelby (AL), Jeff Sessions (AL), Spencer Bacchus (AL) and Roger Wicker (MS). Their statements include the attitude that is very telling as it disregards the desires of the people that they represent in our nation and I quote. "Even though all Americans want this industry to succeed, I cannot support a plan to spend taxpayer money to bail them out. Sacrifices are required." (Rep. Bacchus) Important to note, is that Alabama boasts three automotive assembly plants: One owned by Korea's Hyundai Motor Co., one owned by Japan's Honda Motor Co., and a Mercedes-Benz plant owned by German owned Daimler. Alabama and its leaders who oppose this automotive bail-out paid these companies $175,000.00 per employee to create those jobs there. In 1993, it provided $258 million in incentives and tax breaks to land its first foreign automaker, Mercedes. The state has spent hundreds of millions since to attract the Honda, Hyundai and Toyota plants. Among the companies adding jobs, no company is courted more than Toyota, the world's richest car company, which is gaining strength even as G.M. falters. Beyond expanding its engine plant here, where its ultimate investment will be $450 million, Toyota has opened a $1 billion factory in San Antonio with 4,000 workers. And company officials are looking at even more places, including Arkansas, to build additional factories. Nissan has constructed a new North American headquarters in Tennessee with a new plant in Canton, Mississippi. Kentuckians are proud of Toyota because they are in Lexington, and South Carolinians are equally proud of their BMW plant. What do all of these companies have in common? They are all foreign owned and un-American companies that have been invested in by our Senators who oppose the automotive bail-outs. Simply put, they are willing to invest in non-American companies, while they allow American companies to die with millions of hard working Americans becoming unemployed. It begs the question whose interests are these Senators representing? However, there is a far more insidious plan at work here. This plan was corroborated by the message that was conveyed by Senator Jeff Sessions on Bloomberg Television as he spoke about the crisis facing the U.S. auto industry. "We have a very large and vibrant sector in Alabama and I don't feel like this is the end of the world." What a cold, calculating statement from someone who is supposed to have a genuine concern for one of America's largest employers as a United States Senator who represents America. Why would he make such a statement? Even more, why would this coalition of Senators be so adamant about destroying the Big Three? Well if you remember, in the beginning of my book I spoke about the principles of the Republican Party that were adopted during the Reagan administration and one of those principles was "union busting." That is correct, the glaring difference between the American and foreign automakers hinges upon their affiliation with unions. These Senators interests and plots can be tied to their desire to destroy the union. Why? Because unions ensure that our American corporations do not outsource our jobs to foreign owned companies; and unions afford representation for their workers who are victims of unsafe working conditions, workplace harassment, and being paid fair wages, healthcare, dental, overtime, and life insurance. However, life without the United Autoworkers Union (UAW) will drive wages down with the potential for no benefits or cost of living increases, violate ethical standards, violate environmental laws, create unsafe working conditions, allow workplace harassment, allow for U.S. labor overtime law violations, and allow for job outsourcing, which negatively impacts the people of these Senators' constituency and places them without any recourse for improved working conditions except through the benevolence of their bosses. Be that as it may, these States and their representatives are consistently working hard to replace union jobs at American automakers in the northern states in a longer-term effort to ultimately defeat unions, and engaging in ultimately self-defeating tax giveaway competitions with other states to lure these companies to their States at the expense of the American people. My guess is that if this auto bail-out bill comes before the Senate, the G.O.P. will attempt to kill the bill in spite of the fact that millions of AMERICAN PEOPLE are depending on this bill to feed their families. How Un-American and Unpatriotic is that? Now I do not have a problem with Capitalism and earning money, but I do have a problem with selfishness, exploitation, and serving the special interests of foreign, unAmerican automakers at the expense of the jobs of American families' livelihoods. Case in point, these G.O.P. lawmakers want UAW to sell its members down the river, and agree to a substantial decrease in their salaries and benefits for their families, while they continue to reap the benefits of a $5,000.00 cost of living raise that these Senatorial "fat cats" voted for themselves to receive in this year's session. It clearly demonstrates a "Me First" over their National convention "Country First" marketing tool, with an underlying current of exclusivity with the American people being disregarded. Think about those Republican, Democratic, and Independent citizens who are experiencing job loss and economic difficulty, and remember your representative at the voting polls on next election.

This analysis of these politicians placing "Country Last" is but an example of what it will take to become competent citizens to the election process and employers of your leaders and representatives. However, if you are willing to conduct your research, discuss your findings with your fellow voters, and form a voting bloc which will hold them accountable with the consequences of losing their seats in the "Midterm elections," then we can create the country that most Americans and nations foreign and domestic are proud to be affiliated with. After all, "Sacrifices need to be made." I wonder where are these same supportive G.O.P. Senators who turned their backs on these three

American car companies, contributed to the mass unemployment of more Americans, now that their choice of Toyota has been driving people to their deaths. I tell you where they are. They are somewhere conspicuously absent from the debate.

CHAPTER FOUR

CLOSING REMARKS: WHAT WE MUST DO NOW

As we end this journey of enlightenment, it is my prayer that the reader has gained a clearer understanding of the magnitude of deception that the power structure will engage in, in an effort to maintain their monopoly on politics, power, communications, money, and government. Unless "We the People" stand up and take back our power in these areas, then our families will perish, our liberty will continue to be compromised, our cries for reform and change will remain essentially ignored, our nominated change agents will continue to prostitute themselves to the highest bidder at the people's expense, state and local government infrastructures will continue to collapse with the citizens suffering in the abyss of poverty, anger and division as a nation, with our leaders becoming wealthy and not caring about our demise. Because realistically, the bail-outs have been extended to every financial establishment except we the taxpayers, who are their employers; it is likened to our representatives entering our homes without our permission, and taking our wallets or purses from our homes and spending "our money" on everyone but the owners. That is the reason why the economy has been failing miserably, because no one is investing in the citizens of this country but are continuously investing in the Capitalist institutions of this country who are responsible for this countries' current state. Our current President Barack Obama promised to rule this country with integrity, compassion, and inclusion. However, his goals for bipartisan utopia may be short-lived as I consider the current climate of jealousy, hatred, greed, division, supremacy, and entitlement that is being displayed by the G.O.P., and the neocolonial marionettes of the right who are operating their media puppets for the sole purpose of undermining the agenda of Mr. President. Placed in proper context, these parties have indicated to We the People that they are not interested in honoring the mandate that we have given to our President to move the country in a fundamentally new direction. Their desire is to continue to filibuster, stonewall, distort the truth, and fight "tooth and nail" the agenda of We the People while undermining the Obama administration. It reminds me of Brutus who hid his intentions of destroying Julius Caesar until he was positioned by his colleagues to deliver the fatal wound. They feel that in their ability to prevent progress that this will allow them to raise the argument through the media outlets, that the Obama administration has failed to keep their word to the people but we are not naïve! On the contrary, we will understand what the game is, and consequently what we the people must do now to counteract this cowardly agenda by the right is the following:

1) Realize that Hate does not take a day off:

Ladies and Gentlemen! Make no mistake, the Honeymoon is over! I know that this is hard to realize in the midst of watching a nation transform itself to a mature entity, which chose the best candidate regardless of color, but everyone was not happy that President Barack Obama won the election. To that end, there has been an established mandate by the secret society of this nation to destroy the image of Mr. President in the eyes of the People, by transferring the blame for this nation's condition onto him and his administration, while calling into question his leadership capability, competence to serve, and overall lack of experience!

It is oftentimes difficult to identify because it is disguised under the cloak of "Political Commentary!" Systematically and on a daily basis, America will continue to witness racist media publications like the New York Post type of articles published by media outlets that will incite the assassination of our President unchallenged! You will also witness radio and television talk shows that will relentlessly and with an un-American disrespect for the "Presidential office," attack him and his entire family with racist rants, yet the true meaning of any such publications and diatribes will never be admitted to by the racist, bigoted, and cowardly authors and commentators of such works.

By now, many of you have heard the shameless display of "tabloid" journalism where there is no regard for telling the people the truth. For example, if one must argue about the experience of our current President, in all fairness there must be a discussion about our most recent past President and Vice President's experience. The experience of George W. Bush Jr. as a C student on a good day, and an oil man every day, became apparent when he invaded a sovereign nation (Iraq) and proceeded to use taxpayer's money to fund a war that collapsed our economy. His experience was also instrumental in creating crisis after crisis to justify high gas prices, new republican millionaires, and record quarterly billion dollar profits for his corporate friends. Now he is gone and the new administration has to rebuild a depleted financial infrastructure that we call America, and his co-conspirators of the GOP now are hypocritically calling on fiscal responsibility! The experience of Vice-President Cheney as the former chief of Halliburton became apparent, when he parlayed his newly vacated position into a check! A check in the amount of $16,000.00 per month in compensation for services rendered or not? Interestingly enough, Halliburton received multiple millions of dollars in "no bid" contracts from the federal government to rebuild Iraq and New Orleans after Katrina. We are talking about experience right? You may wonder why there is such an attempt to sabotage the rebuilding of America, you may even wonder why there is not a clear understanding by this "secret society," as to the extent of insolvency that the GOP's infamous tax cuts for the wealthy, unregulated financial markets, and incompetence left us in. Yet at every turn of the corner, there is resistance, noncooperation, counterproductive speeches, media attacks, racist cartoon ads, refusal to serve their country in cabinet positions, refusal to accept multi-millions of dollars from the federal government to help their citizens that they vowed to protect, and a basic unAmerican attitude towards an American President. Why? Because Hate does not take a day off, and it is so deeply entrenched in the hearts of these men, that they would rather support and embrace an ideology that would bring death and destruction to the citizens of their States and this great country, than to humble themselves and submit to the authority of a black man who wants to help the entire country to survive this economic crisis. Because of the disdain that the majority of the GOP and the 22% of citizens polled who are under the influence of a hate-filled stupor feels towards President Obama, he will need for every unselfish American who has moved towards change, to be diligent in conducting their own research, conducting their own fact checking, and testing the credibility of what is being reported to them. In short, learn to think for yourself!

2) Your Representative is just not that into you:

I have and always will argue that a "devoted" capitalist will never betray his/her ideology and help persons who are less fortunate than they are. Consider the current economic state that America is in, who it affects, and what is being done to address it in the "current stimulus plan" that is being proposed by our President. Picture if you will, a backdrop of extreme poverty that has invaded the United States to the point of having "soup lines" in most of our states. However, President Obama has in his right hand a copy of the mandate that the people gave him as their chosen leader, and in his other hand he has a copy of the stimulus package passed by the house and moving towards rescuing the working and middle class families in America. There is only one problem! Standing between the deliverer of the people, and deliverance of the people are the Republican Senators, Conservative Democrats, and Governors who have continuously argued that this is too much money for these groups of people, and that they believe that the economy would recover on its own and through tax cuts for the wealthy. In addition, they do not think that it is fair to punish the deceptive banks and brokers who deceived homebuyers, ignored bad credit, limited income to maintain payments on these teaser mortgage rates, yet signed many citizens into mortgage contracts just so they could earn millions of dollars in commissions. This logic of allowing the economy to fail, not holding their corporate friends accountable and bailing out their constituencies that lacked business acumen will cause its constituencies to lose everything due to their careless and bad decision-making is ludicrous! However, it is important to give the banks a second disbursement of stimulus money with no strings attached. Think about that my fellow Americans. Our economy is on "life support" and the Republicans want to disconnect the respirator by choosing not to accept the stimulus money for their states! Think about that for a minute. The Republican Governors have decided nation-wide to choose a selfish ideology, over representing the interest their people who are in distress and suffering needlessly, while they live in the lap of luxury. This does not sound like someone who is supposed to be representing the people's interest. Unfortunately, the time has come to admit to yourselves that your Representatives are just not that into you, but rather they serve their own selfish interests and always will, because money and greed controls a capitalist, not Service! The question is what will you do about it? Anytime you find a leader who is interested in serving all people, you may want to embrace that person and not reject them.

3) Demand a balance between entertainment and current events:

This area is one of the most important sections of this book, as it will determine the direction that your life will take you. What we should understand is that there is a plethora of misinformation that is being revealed to you by many media outlets. I am beginning to wonder who you can trust to reveal the most accurate information to you that affects your lives on a daily basis. I say that because I am mindful of the Economic Power and influence that the "secret society" wields in our nation and on our political landscape! Permit me to explain. When one examines Social Conflict theory and Social Reaction theory, one needs to understand that the two utilized in the same thought explains the relationship between influence, power, and control of the masses. First of all, through my relationship with you, I form the ability to either win your trust or develop mistrust. This is accomplished by my ability to have enough information concerning a particular person or subject matter in an effort to make an intelligent decision about it, and to utilize that information to formulate my beliefs about that particular subject. In other words, I need to be privy to all of the factors present if I am to make an intelligent decision about the matter, the candidate, or the legislation, and to be able to vote accordingly. To that end let us consider the media who is controlled by the power base of this secret society, its influential relationship to society, and the procedure that is followed to influence the masses that is well orchestrated. Because of the telecommunications act, the repeal of the fairness doctrine, and capitalism, a small group of billionaires were able to obtain special waivers and purchase the majority of the media outlets (newspaper, magazine, television, and radio), and then proceeded to silence any opposition to their agenda by terminating the services and voices of many liberal personalities on their stations. We as citizens who desire a balance of conservative and liberal viewpoints for educational value, but who have developed an understanding of what media personalities we can trust, must demand to receive our marching orders from our media generals. We must demand "equal exposure and airtime" for General(s) Winfrey, Boazman, Sharpton, Ballentine, Joyner, Madison, Baisden, O'Brien, Harvey, Lemmon, Madison, Martin, Jones, Scott, Maddow, Olbermann, Dr. J. White, Robinson, Ski, Smith, Ogletree, Dr. West, Jackson, Roker, Brown, Hughley, Roberts, King, etal who allows integrity and character to determine their reporting content. However, our Generals must strive to exhaust their searches of all persons who have the ability to contribute to revealing the truth to their listening audiences, invite them to their shows, and even assist them in hosting their own shows by sitting in for you in your absence. Our Generals must tell the people in their camps to make their contact information accessible to the public and gladly receive new books, leads, and information of those persons who have not been heard from before nationally or locally, and do not just assume that the audience will respond to "name recognition only." Stop making access to you equivalent to breaking into the Denver Mint or Fort Knox. After all, the common denominators of your success are your listeners and without them, you would not be on the air and growing in stature as you are currently doing. "United We Stand, but Divided We Fall." The counter-oppositional forces that divide this nation are well aware of this reality, and I can assure you that Fox News is bringing in "new and unknown talent" who are not celebrities, Juris Doctors, and Doctors of Philosophy on to their shows to engage in their discourses because it is about furthering their agenda which is not "star specific!" Hannity has a high school diploma, Rush and Beck flunked out of college but as long as these persons share in their common goal of division, misinformation, hatred, and racism that diverts America's attention from their ultimate goal of Capitalism and Imperialism then they are paid well and accepted by the mainstream media machine! Sometimes one must change their "thought patterns" and adopt those standards that have contributed to the continued successes of their competitors. Because unfortunately and in direct opposition to "fair and balanced reporting," is the conservative agenda to create a one dimensional thought process in the mainstream that will influence thought against any liberal way of thinking, and allow them to maintain their economic stranglehold on this country. In addition, this agenda continues to perpetuate a capitalistic class system in this country that systematically violates civil rights, employment laws, mis-education of generations of people, maintains poverty, and fuels racism and division. Unfortunately, the victims are the masses such as the besieged middle class and the working poor, with the winners being a capitalistic establishment who continues to amass their wealth.

To that end, I have clearly outlined the manner in which the one-dimensional message of the right has continued to flourish without opposition. But now, I am becoming increasingly concerned with the possibility of the otherwise trusted messages of some of the faithful few of our black talk radio personalities being deceived by the mainstream into giving subliminal messages of mistrust towards our current President, Barack Obama. I say that as I consider some of the shows' persons and contents that have aired on some of the Syndicated One radio stations and against the dissent of the hosts, irresponsibly argued that our President was committed to the black communities' demise, that he was not interested in addressing any of our race's concerns; concerns such as healthcare, poverty, employment, economic oppression, and blacks' overrepresentation in the criminal justice system. These subliminal messages made by charlatan prognosticators have drawn these conclusions before the first 100 days of his Presidency! In order to embrace such a premise, one would have to disregard the developmental process of our current President. Here I would argue that one would have to believe that this black male who fully grasps the history of oppression to a people, who has a life history of grassroots political action, who has endured racism as a black male and as a political candidate, who has fostered the trust of a nation of oppressed Americans, who loves and relies on God to utilize him to uplift people, who has lived transparent before the people, and who developed a grassroots political base that is unprecedented in the history of this country; would become President and then succumb to being a clandestine puppet for a neocolonial, class-based, racist, capitalist, oppressive system who vehemently opposed his democratic nomination as President; an establishment that supported a Clinton Presidency, and arguably would probably not even invite him to serve drinks as a waiter at their meetings. This group would now seek to formulate a relationship with him, and utilize him to undermine an entire nation of people who are depending on him for their very survival. A nation who decided one last time to trust in a process that has been systematically wrought with corruption, special interests, political sell-outs, and media messages fraught with misinformation and trickery. To think that this man, who is arguably the first to rise from the masses, and who was not born with a silver spoon in his mouth, would be this deceptive towards the people of this country is unfathomable! It totally defies logic and what we understand about this man. It now begs the question, who can you trust? After all, I know that I cannot trust the mainstream media stations that are committed to the fulfillment of the secret societies' agenda, but now we are challenged in our perceptions of the traditionally trusted media outlets of the masses! Why? Because it appears that some of them are unknowingly furthering the agenda of the secret society as well. Have you asked yourself why there has been so much opposition towards our new President? Have you asked yourself why there is such an onslaught of attempts to destroy the credibility of this man? But most of all, why is the target audience of their attacks the American people who support him? Because the only way for the secret society to reacquire their power and control over this country and its citizens, is for them to destroy our opinion and TRUST in our President to the point of us withdrawing our support of him at the polls.

The way this will be realized is through the message that is communicated to us. But this message will lose its effectiveness and control would be lost, if there was an equal and oppositional opinion that is communicated to the masses. Remember, there is a battle being waged for your opinion and support. That is why there is a systematic call for an agenda of the "secret society" that includes the emphasis of "entertainment" in the black community! Now before anyone asks the question what is wrong with entertainment, there is nothing wrong with it. Actually, it is a welcomed addition to our otherwise troubled society. I enjoy attending concerts, movies, sporting events, ballets, and other entertainment venues, but I am not a one-dimensional being. On the contrary, I am an intellectual, educated, inquisitive, and politically conscious student of life who thinks more than I dance. Therefore, I not only need to be entertained, but I even more so have a need for intellectual stimulation and enlightenment! To that end, the more compelling question is why the "secret society" would want you to be entertained and not informed about current events. Well consider the meaning of the word "entertain." The word "Entertain," as a noun is defined as a "diversion that holds the attention," and an "agreeable occupation for the mind." The thesaurus traces this word back to the word "beguilement," which means "entertainment that provokes pleased interest and distracts one from worries and vexations." My beliefs were further corroborated by the current resurgence of R&B and conservative talk radio stations that are replacing black talk radio in major metropolitan markets. A prime example is the cancellation of the Warren Ballentine show in the Atlanta market. When this decision was questioned, there was no comment. Now the major stations of 97.5 and 107.5 fm are now owned by Radio One Majik FM which purchased WAMJ-fm. These two media titans were carried in this market by Radio-One, but were cancelled and the two radio stations now simultaneously play the identical music on both stations. This begs the question as to why Radio-One cannot air talk radio on one station and R&B music on the other station. After all, Fox News has no problem airing on the radio airwaves the racist and conservative viewpoints of Bill O'Reilly, Sean Hannity, Laura Ingraham, Glen Beck, and Tammy Bruce to name a few. Has the owner of Radio-One made a commitment to further the agenda of the secret society by not providing the listeners with an opposing viewpoint to the neocolonial establishment on black talk radio? If that is the case, then the answer in who we can trust is "we only." Therefore, we must take some necessary steps to understand this agenda, that media is a business that is controlled by sponsorships of programs and not believe any of the one-sided rhetoric of the Right, and to do our own research once the information is conveyed to us.

4) We the People must save ourselves by divorcing our current abusive partner:

When one decides to divorce, hopefully after careful deliberation they have made a decision to "legally dissolve their marriage." Oftentimes the couple cites as their reasons, "irreconcilable differences" which means "one of two or more conflicting ideas or beliefs cannot be brought into harmony." Now if you have become "politically conscious" in this last election like I have, you believe that there is a fundamental responsibility for any government for the people, by the people, and of the people, to protect and support the interests of their electorate. In this past eight years, you also learned that when you elect shiftless, trifling, and selfish representatives who are not interested in serving the electorate collectively, but rather are inclined to serve the interests of the rich while accepting no responsibility for their oppressive economic philosophies, then the people will truly suffer. I realize there are philosophical differences concerning the responsibility that our government has to the people. Capitalists/GOP believes that "big government" should be eliminated, and that the people should pull themselves up by their bootstraps. However, the problem with that philosophy is that whenever taxpayers' money is involved, then one can logically infer that the needs of the "taxpayers" should be paramount, and the needs of any group or subculture who leeches off of the country, extend to themselves corporate welfare, and do not pay their fair share of taxes should have to fend for themselves. After all, taxpayers' money belongs to, "the taxpayers." On the other hand, my philosophy argues that those groups who have been spending taxpayers' money but not getting taxed fairly are technically stealing money from this country. Not to mention the offshore tax havens of the rich that is costing taxpayers billions of dollars. The time has now come for that 3% of the wealthiest Americans to pay back what they have taken from the economy and have not paid back through being taxed. In other words, no one is coming to save us, so the time has come for us to save ourselves through the implementation of new inclusive economic policies for this nation. Unfortunately, the culprits that initiated these oppressive, draconian, trickle down economic laws that the GOP, their millionaire friends, special interest groups, and capitalists alike benefitted from, are now waging war against our President and his administration. It begs the question as to why these media and political representatives do not want the taxpayers to be assisted in their time of need. I mean why is it that they do not want any of the people who contribute to the economy through paying taxes to be assisted in their time of need, and believe that those persons who have received tax cuts/exemptions for decades, have stockpiled their money, are entitled to any of the taxpayers' money? It is a completely ludicrous, incoherent argument and should not even warrant a discussion, but since we need to have this discourse, then let us begin by looking at the tax structure and the wealth distribution in the United States.

According to data from the IRS, the bottom 50 percent of income earners pay approximately 4 percent of income taxes. The top 25 percent of income earners pay nearly 83 percent of the income tax burden, and the top 10 percent pay 65 percent. The top 1 percent of income earners pay almost 35 percent of all income taxes. The top 400 richest Americans paid 1.58% of total income taxes in 2000.

The average tax rate paid by the richest 400 Americans fell by a third to 17.2 percent through the first six years of the Bush administration and their average income doubled to $263.3 million, new IRS data show. The 17.2 percent tax rate in 2006 was the lowest since the IRS began tracking the 400 largest taxpayers in 1992, although the richest 400 Americans paid more tax on an inflation-adjusted basis than any year since 2000. The drop from 2001's tax rate of 22.9 percent was due largely to ex-President George W. Bush's push to cut tax rates on most capital gains to 15 percent in 2003.

It seems that it is a good thing to be rich, because the richer you are the less taxes you pay, and these tax cuts, to the best of my knowledge, have not expired yet.

Not to mention the reality that corporations (insurance, pharmaceutical, healthcare, etc.) can continue to increase their prices for service, but the minimum wage cannot increase to a living wage nor can the taxpayers receive any cost of living raises, but can be furloughed in some states and lose more money.

The Wealth Distribution in the United States

In the United States, wealth is highly concentrated in a relatively few hands. As of 2007, the top 1% of households (the upper class) owned 34.6% of all privately held wealth, and the next 19% (the managerial, professional, and small business stratum) had 50.5%, which means that just 20% of the people owned a remarkable 85%, leaving only 15% of the wealth for the bottom 80% (wage and salary workers). In terms of financial wealth (total net worth minus the value of one's home), the top 1% of households had an even greater share: 42.7%.

Now in spite of the facts, whenever there is a conversation, it is usually a one-sided argument with the capitalist media's sole purpose being to divide public opinion and conquer the conversation with the facts of the argument being lost in translation. Now divider Rick Santorum of CNBC enters the conversation, who incidentally became wealthy with his close ended news reporting style, and in his ability to fully utilize the "fairness doctrine" to his advantage while he confuses the issues. He calls the bail-outs for the people who are struggling "irresponsible" and a burden on "the taxpayers!" However, the bail-outs of the financial institutions and the brokers who manipulated and circumvented the mortgage laws, while receiving outlandish commissions does not even deserve honorable mention! Therefore, he does not report both sides of the issue, and due to Santorum's "skewed journalism," the taxpayers of this country are demonstrating, picketing, and calling for a Boston tea party nation-wide in the midst of their poverty. Done by design? You bet it is! Because it has always been a conservative capitalist's goal to divert attention away from themselves, while they continue to exploit America and its citizens for profits. I wonder if Rick will write out any checks to save any of these demonstrators' mortgages. Of course he won't! Because Rick represents the manner in which issues are addressed; spin the issue, accept no responsibility for the problem, and utilize the public relations' experts in the media to change the subject with "weapons of mass distraction." That is why we will always have "irreconcilable differences" with this party because after careful deliberation, we must realize that one of two or more conflicting ideas or their beliefs cannot be brought into harmony, and we consequently need to divorce ourselves from our current obstructive representatives and their selfish and self-serving party.

5) Decide this day if you are really Committed to change:

As we approach the end of this journey of enlightenment, it is my hope that the reader understands the fierce urgency of now. By now, we understand that the sleeping giant that is America is slowly awakening from their government and media induced stupor, to realize that our country has a date with destiny. When we as citizens decided to forego and reject hate, division, hateful rhetoric, the politics of exclusion, and elect a man of integrity who believed in this country's promise of democracy, and who believes that all men are created equal, then what we decided on that date, was to commit to change in this country. However, what must be understood is that "change" defined and applied, calls for this country to undergo transformation, transition, and substitution! Transformation must be of the heart as we learn to love and care for those who are less fortunate than we are. For far too long, our leaders and politicians have convinced Americans that the poor and disenfranchised of this country were in a self-imposed state of helplessness! That it was their deliberate intent to live in squalor and hopelessness, as they look to their government to take care of them. That they want this country to give them handouts, and should be cut off, only to take the same money belonging to the taxpayers and give it to their corporate and wealthy friends in order to protect their "special interests." Is this no less of a handout? However, as I look and speak to this population of people, I realize that each one of them has the will to improve their lives, but are struggling to maintain their self-respect, all because they simply encountered "misfortune." Now the interesting thing about the concept of misfortune, is that it is race neutral and attacks all races of people, it is selfish and does not care what your pedigree or socioeconomic status is when it strikes, it is enlightening as it allows us to understand who our friends truly are, and it is educational as it assists us in gaining insight as to which public servants actually represent our interests, and which servants leave us to fend for ourselves, after they have manipulated our votes to retain their seats. Never has this type of behavior been more telling than with our former President who was "ride or die" with his friends, corporate buddies, fellow Republicans, and associates, as he made millionaires of them all while leaving America with a check that was returned to President Obama marked "insufficient funds." However, in spite of the obvious absence of the basic requirements of character, integrity, and love that a public servant must possess towards all races, colors, and creeds; our former President then, and the Republican Party now, remains committed in their refusal to pass legislation that will benefit the entire nation and restore the dignity back to its citizens. That is why it is now imperative that if we are committed to change, that we must move beyond the division, diversions, racial hatred, and the government imposed oppression in this country, and live in the 21st century! Live in the reality that simply because a person is the same color as you are, simply because they share your same political party affiliation, simply because they allegedly share your basic belief system, does not necessarily mean that they are "protecting your interests." Uh, Oh, I am in trouble now, and I even know that this is going to become a bitter pill to swallow for many Americans. Because coming to this realization is likened to a person who is in a bad marriage, "Neither one of us wants to be the first to say goodbye." But you remember at the beginning of this discourse I asked you a question. A question that will forever change the course of this country! "Are you really committed to change?" Do you want to continue to feel the "spiritual and emotional ecstasy" and forever enshrine in your memory, what America looks like when perfect love conquers fear and hate. Do you want to feel that you are indeed a part of America, democracy, freedom, justice, and Liberty, and not just an invisible concubine who is called upon when it is time to vote?

I can only assume that if you are still reading this book, that you are indeed committed to change and all that it entails. What must be realized is that not only does the question have to be answered concerning change, but there must a commitment to the final two elements of how to create the change that we can all believe in. Those final two elements are Transition and Substitution. Now that our minds have been transformed with the truth of our reality, then we must make the decision to transition or move beyond our painful past! A past that has been defined by broken dreams, empty promises, loved ones who walked out on us, governmental double-standards, lovers who disappeared, homes that were lost, cars that we walked away from, jobs that are gone, families that we witness suffering, and our representatives telling us that "we are on our own." We must understand that with our current President and his administration, we now have a choice to either become empowered to change our destinies, or remain paralyzed with anger, fear, cynicism, and excuses. Now don't get me wrong, I too understand that change is never easy. I also understand how difficult it is to move beyond your pain. No one knows better than I, how suffering can make you bitter and cynical. I indeed understand how you work hard to put yourself through college and try to hold your emotions in check while you have your mother and father die without notice, and you are looked upon to be strong. Then you look at God to keep you while you have preachers telling you to "hold on" a little while longer, because your suffering will one day "pay off." But your reality is that your family needs to eat now, your bills are due now, you live in a house where you can look in the front door and see the backyard, and your children needs clothes now, and are too young for you to explain to them that Santa Claus and Christmas are not coming this year. Can we be real? However, in the midst of my setbacks and disappointments, I also understand that I do not have the time to remain paralyzed, dwelling on my setbacks. Because the common denominator that ties all Americans together is the universal desire for us to simply be given "a fair opportunity to succeed." To live in a country that will provide an environment where our talents, experience, and education will afford us an "equal opportunity" to succeed in whatever discipline, service industry, political office, or job that we aspire to. To live in a country that will not politically block opportunities to succeed, and blame me for my failures. So as we transition beyond our pain, failures, setbacks, and excuses, and move towards transformational change, we must finally embrace the element of substitution. Substitution of the 22% of Americans, many of whom we have discussed, who utterly despise President Barack Hussein Obama, who relentlessly attack him and his family, and are determined to keep us imprisoned in our past. Now this atavistic subculture foolishly believe somehow that the "South will rise again" and they will somehow be empowered to live in a society that embraces "uni-racial utopia." Fortunately these opinions and beliefs consist in the minority of our society, but unfortunately these groups have been strategically implanted in our employment/recruitment offices, our courts, our governments, our corporations, our churches, our criminal justice systems, our healthcare industries, our schools, our colleges, our law school and medical school admission offices, and our media industries, and in many respects and consequently, we have embraced the philosophy that this minority group possesses all of the power in our nation! That due to the perceived power of this "secret society," we have come to believe that we can never change the course of our future as Americans. To you I say that if you are truly committed to change, you need to understand the place where true power dwells. True Power dwells in the hands of a "united people who vote intelligently and without emotion."

Not like the brazen giant of Greek fame, with conquering limbs astride from land to land; here at our sea-washed, sunset gates shall stand a mighty woman with a torch, whose flame Is the imprisoned lightning, and her name Mother of Exiles. From her beacon-hand Glows world-wide welcome; her mild eyes command the air-bridged harbor that twin cities frame. "Keep, ancient lands, your storied pomp!" cries she with silent lips. "Give me your tired, your poor, Your huddled masses yearning to breathe free. The wretched refuse of your teeming shore. Send these, the homeless, tempest-tost to me; I lift my lamp beside the golden door!" (Emma Lazarus, 1883)

That golden door that she, (the Statue of Liberty) lifts her lamp to is America, who welcomes the heavy-laden, the poor, the huddled masses seeking freedom, and gives them rest. She remembers what it took to become a great nation, she remembers the reasons why she became a country, she understands that Democracy is not about her only, but about men and women who love God, country, freedom, and all of its races of people for here lies the True Patriot. We Are The People and United We Will Stand and Overcome, but Divided, We Will Surely Fall.

America has demonstrated during this one last chance to redeem itself as the entire World watched and the election unfolded, that they can elect a candidate of character and integrity with an attitude of inclusivity. What America did and why they did it, revealed much about her character and determined how other nations perceived her and ultimately treated her and I was so proud of her. Nevertheless, as God and America watches as this new day unfolds, we realize that there is much work that needs to be done to restore the American Dream. What the American people do with that power will determine whether we live or die and whether we succeed or fail as a nation. God Bless the United States of America and God Bless Each and Every One of You.

Works Cited:

Acts of the 104th United States Congress, Public Law 104-104:
Telecommunications Act of 1996.

Alexander Zaitchik (September 21, 2009). "The making of Glenn Beck:
His roots, from the alleged suicide of his mom to Top 40 radio
to the birth of the morning zoo". Salon Magazine. Allport, G. W.
and B. M. Kramer (1946). "Some roots of prejudice." Journal of
Psychology 22: 9-39.

Beck, Glenn (November 2007). An Inconvenient Book. Simon &
Schuster.

Books by Glenn Beck, Amazon.com

Cogswell, Kelly, "Globalization: Viva La Fast Track!"

"Elder Statesman," interview in Reason Magazine, 1996.

Ellen Magazine, Report dated March 23, 2008.

Fremont-Brunswick, E. and R. N. Sanford (1938). "The Physiological
Basis of Aggression." Child Study 15: 1-8.

Frenkel-Brunswick, E. and R. N. Sanford. (1945). "Some personality
factors in anti-semitism." Journal of Psychology 20: 271-291.

George Gerbner, A First Look at Communication Theory, 3rd Edition,
McGraw-Hill, 1997.

Glenn Beck biography at Salon.com

Helan Page, White Supremacy in the 1990's: Racists learn to tap mainstream America, Albion

Monitor Commentary.

J. Hector St. John Crèvecoeur, Letters from an American Farmer. Edited by W. P. Trent and Ludwig Lewisohn. New York: Duffield, 1904.

Journal article, Conceptualizing Stigma by Bruce G. Link, Jo C. Phelan; Annual Review of Sociology, 2001.

Kevin Bales (ed.), Understanding Global Slavery Today. A Reader, University of California Press, 2005.

"Let's Rid Ourselves of Those Silly Race Boxes," commentary in The Abolitionist Examiner by Ward Connerly.

Larry J. Siegel (2007). Criminology: Theories, Patterns, and Typologies (Ninth Edition).

Thomson Wadsworth, Thomson Learning Inc.

Montagu, M. F. A. (1952). Man's Most Dangerous Myth. New York, Harper & Brothers.

National Vital Statistics report, Volume 56, Number 6.

"Neo-Nazi/White Supremacist Hal Turner confirms friendship and kinship with Sean Hannity." Article written in Ellen Magazine, March 23, 2008.

"Obstructionism: Senate Republicans Filibuster Their Own Bills," commentary in America Blog, 2007.

"Our Heritage of Unity and Fellowship: The Writings of Leroy Garrett and W. Carl

Ketcherside," ed. by Cecil Hook. New Braunfels, Texas : Cecil and Lea Hook, [1992].

Ralph Ellison, Invisible Man, Random House, 1982.

Roland Martin, March 21, 2008 Blog, Essence magazine.

www.ingramcontent.com/pod-product-compliance
Lightning Source LLC
Chambersburg PA
CBHW062118020426
42335CB00013B/1012

"Sean Hannity confronted over his relationship with Neo-Nazi Hal Turner," article in Huffington Post by Jason Linkins, March 23, 2008.

"Sold Out: How Wall Street and Washington Betrayed America," article in Wall Street Watch, March 4, 2009.

Stossel, John (2009-06-10). "Glenn Beck on Glenn Beck". 20/20 (ABC News). Retrieved 200907-31.

Sutherland, Cara A. (2003). The Statue of Liberty: The Museum of the City of New York. Barnes and Noble Publishing.

"The Fear in the U.S. Media," article in Today's Alternative News by Dr. Sam Hamod, May 30, 2005.

Theodore Allen, The Invention of the White Race, The New England Free Press, 2000.

Thomas M. Shapiro, Hidden Cost of being African American, Oxford University Press, 2005.

Tim Wise, This is your Nation on White Privilege, September 13, 2008.

"Who Benefits From Political Polling?" by Dr. James N. Herndon, September 6, 2007

"Who's Counting Bush's Mistakes?" article in News for Real by Stephen Pizzo, February 20, 2006.

William J. Bowen et al, The Shape of the River, Princeton University Press, 2000.